James Richard Joy

Twenty Centuries of English History

James Richard Joy

Twenty Centuries of English History

ISBN/EAN: 9783741186707

Manufactured in Europe, USA, Canada, Australia, Japa

Cover: Foto ©ninafisch / pixelio.de

Manufactured and distributed by brebook publishing software (www.brebook.com)

James Richard Joy

Twenty Centuries of English History

Chautauqua Reading Circle Literature

TWENTY CENTURIES

OF

ENGLISH HISTORY

BY

JAMES RICHARD JOY

MEADVILLE PENNA
FLOOD AND VINCENT
The Chautauqua-Century Press
NEW YORK: CINCINNATI: CHICAGO:
150 Fifth Avenue.   222 W. Fourth St.   57 Washington St.
1898

been made to supplementary reading in poetry. The ballad literature of England and Scotland might be further drawn upon with profit.

Should this work serve its chief purpose, by inspiring its readers with a desire to know more of English history, a few suggestions may be helpful. This book would best be followed by Gardiner's "Student's History of England," or, if one cares for more of the social life and less of drum and trumpet, by Green's "Short History of the English People." To cover the ground more thoroughly read Green's "Making of England," Freeman's "Norman Conquest," Froude's "History of [Tudor] England," Gardiner's still incomplete "History of England, 1603–1660," Macaulay's "History of England from the Accession of James II.," Lecky's "History of England in the Eighteenth Century," Stanhope's "History of England, 1701–83," Martineau's "History of England, 1800–1854," Walpole's "History of England from 1815," McCarthy's "History of Our Own Times." It should be remembered that most of these historians saw through Protestant spectacles. The Roman Catholic authority is Lingard, whose history is of great value.

Much of the early course of English history, especially during the period when England was a continental power, should be read atlas in hand. The best historical atlas for the purpose is Gardiner's.

In conclusion let me frankly acknowledge beforehand my debt to J. R. Green, whose writings have renewed the popularity of English history, and to H. D. Traill, whose valuable volumes on "Social England" have contributed much to the notes.

JAMES R. JOY.

Plainfield, N. J., June 1, 1898.

CONTENTS.

CHAPTER		PAGE
I.	The Home of the English	11
II.	England before the English, 55 B. C.–410 A. D.	28
III.	The English in Britain, 410 A. D.–837 A. D.—From the Roman Evacuation to the Rise of Wessex	38
IV.	The English and the Northmen, 837 A. D.–1066 A. D.—From the Supremacy of the West Saxons to the Norman Conquest	53
V.	The Norman Kings, 1066 A. D.–1135 A. D.—From the Accession of William I. to the Death of Henry I.	68
VI.	The Rise of the Barons, 1135 A. D.–1216 A. D.—From the Accession of Stephen to the Death of John	86
VII.	The Plantagenet Kings, 1216 A. D.–1327 A. D.—From the Accession of Henry III. to the Death of Edward II.	106
VIII.	England and France, 1327 A. D.–1422 A. D.—From the Accession of Edward III. to the Death of Henry V.	124
IX.	Lancaster and York, 1422 A. D.–1485 A. D.—From the Accession of Henry VI. to the Deposition of Richard III.	145

- X. THE TUDOR DESPOTISM, 1485 A. D.-1547 A. D.—HENRY VII. AND HENRY VIII. 161
- XI. THE LATER TUDORS, 1547 A. D.-1603 A. D.—FROM THE ACCESSION OF EDWARD VI. TO THE DEATH OF ELIZABETH 184
- XII. CAVALIER AND ROUNDHEAD, 1603 A.D.-1649 A. D. — FROM THE ACCESSION OF JAMES I. TO THE EXECUTION OF CHARLES I. 216
- XIII. THE COMMONWEALTH AND THE RESTORATION, 1649 A. D.-1685 A. D.—FROM THE EXECUTION OF CHARLES I. TO THE DEATH OF CHARLES II. . . 250
- XIV. THE ERA OF THE PROTESTANT REVOLUTION, 1685 A. D.-1714 A. D.—FROM THE ACCESSION OF JAMES II. TO THE DEATH OF ANNE 263
- XV. THE HANOVERIAN SOVEREIGNS, 1714 A. D.-1837 A. D.—FROM THE ACCESSION OF GEORGE I. TO THE DEATH OF WILLIAM IV. 278
- XVI. THE VICTORIAN ERA, 1837 A. D.-1897 A. D.—FROM THE ACCESSION OF QUEEN VICTORIA TO THE "DIAMOND JUBILEE" OF HER REIGN 295

ILLUSTRATIONS.

Map of England (full-page colored map), *First front lining page.*
English Empire in Tenth and Eleventh Centuries (full-page colored map) . . . . *Second front lining page.*
The Houses of Parliament . . . . *Frontispiece.*

	PAGE
Bust of Julius Cæsar	30
Stonehenge, on Salisbury Plain	33
Boat for Fourteen Pairs of Oars, found at Nydam, Jutland	39
Jutish or Danish Mail-coat in use before 450 A. D.	40
Old English Glass Vessels	44
Ships of the Northmen	54
St. Dunstan at the Feet of Christ	60
Canute and His Queen	62
William Sailing to England	66
The White Tower (Tower of London)	80
Great Seal of Henry I.	82
Dover Castle	88
The Standard, 1138	89
Canterbury Cathedral	92
A Crusader	99
Simon de Montfort	108
Dominican (Black) Friar	111
Oxford, from Magdalen Tower	113
The English Coronation Chair	116
View of Windsor Castle, showing the Great Round Tower	125
Cannon used at Crecy	127
William of Wykeham, Bishop of Winchester	132
John Wyclif	134
Joan of Arc	147
The Traitor's Gate, Tower of London	157
The Princes in the Tower	163
Henry VIII.	167
Cardinal Wolsey	168
Anne Boleyn	171
Sir Thomas More	173
Ruins of the Cistercian Abbey of Fountains	175

Illustrations.

Hampton Court Palace	178
Westminster Abbey	181
Mary Tudor	190
Queen Elizabeth	196
Bedroom of Queen Mary at Holyrood	200
Hatfield, an Elizabethan Manor	207
Ruins of Kenilworth Castle	210
James I.	217
Charles I.	226
John Hampden	227
William Laud, Archbishop of Canterbury	232
England and Wales, December 9, 1643	243
Oliver Cromwell	251
St. Paul's Cathedral	255
John Milton	259
James II.	264
Buckingham Palace	267
Windsor Castle, East Front	269
The Bank of England	271
Blenheim Castle	274
George I.	279
William Pitt	282
Lord Clive	283
The Throne Room, Windsor Castle	285
Nelson Column, Trafalgar Square	288
Arthur Wellesley, Duke of Wellington	291
Daniel O'Connell	292
Queen Victoria in Her Coronation Robes	296
John Stuart Mill	297
John Tyndall	299
Charles Darwin	301
Thomas H. Huxley	302
Ruins of Residency, Lucknow	303
William Ewart Gladstone	305
Henry M. Stanley	306
Whiffingham Church, Isle of Wight	307
Queen Victoria	309
Possessions of the British Empire (two-page colored map),	

End lining pages.

The required books of the C. L. S. C. are recommended by a Council of six. It must, however, be understood that recommendation does not involve an approval by the Council, or by any member of it, of every principle or doctrine contained in the book recommended.

C. L. S. C. MOTTOES.

We Study the Word and the Works of God.

Let us keep our Heavenly Father in the midst.

Never be Discouraged.

Look Up and Lift Up.

TWENTY CENTURIES OF ENGLISH HISTORY.

CHAPTER I.

THE HOME OF THE ENGLISH.

THE student of the marvelous history of England, her progress from weakness and poverty to surpassing wealth and dominion, must be impressed by the way in which the physical characteristics of his home land have molded the development of the nation. The most obvious of these influences has been the most effective, and England is now the ruler of continents because for centuries her domain was limited to a small island. There first she learned to rule herself. It was this insular position—distinct, though not distant, from Europe—that delayed and restricted the Roman Conquest; this it was which tempted the Anglo-Saxon invaders, and later left them free to consolidate the kingdom they had won; and not until the Norman-French conquerors had lost their continental dominions and become simply the lords of the island did England begin to take her rightful place as mistress of the seas and first in the roll of commercial empires. Sitting thus by herself, removed a step from her brawling neighbors, England has followed her own lines of development. A study of the chief events in the history of the English folk should be prefaced by some account of their beautiful island.

The British Isles, of whose area England comprises

Physical influences.

Independent development.

about one half, exceed five thousand in number, though many of them are but barren, rocky islets and only two, Great Britain and Ireland, are of considerable size and historical importance. On the westward the Atlantic Ocean, a thousand leagues wide and a thousand fathoms deep, separates them from the American continent and furnishes a roadway for the commerce of two worlds. The North Sea rolls its shallow waters on the east, inviting communication with the Baltic and the hundred harbors of Northern Europe. To the south the sea narrows to the Strait of Dover, where the French sentinel at Calais may descry the chalk cliffs of England across twenty miles of choppy waves. The strait relaxes again in the English Channel, which washes the southern shore of England and the northern coast of France. Again two channels—the North and St. George's—together with the Irish Sea, furnish a continuous waterway on the west between the two greater islands of the British group.

North of Great Britain are two rocky groups of islands, the Shetlands—famous for hardy ponies—and the Orkneys, weather-beaten, sea-bird-haunted cliffs. Westward, and not far from the Scottish coast, are the stormy Hebrides. Among these are Lewis, Skye, little Staffa, famed for Fingal's Cave, and Iona, the mission station of Celtic Christianity. Advancing southward past Islay and Arran, the voyager in the Irish Sea would reach the Isle of Man and Anglesey. West of Land's End, at the southwestern angle of England, are sprinkled the Scilly Islands, a welcome sight to the eastward-faring mariner, and nestling close under the southern coast is the fair Isle of Wight. Twenty leagues away to the southward are cattle-breeding Jersey, Guernsey, Alderney, Sark, and the other

The British Isles.

Surrounding seas.

Outlying islets.

Channel Islands,[1] appearing now like British outposts, but in reality the poor remnant of a once vast continental realm. On the east coast of Great Britain but one island need be named—the Holy Isle,[2] near the mouth of the Tweed. Channel Islands.

Great Britain itself comprises about two thirds of the British group. Its area is 84,000 square miles, with a maximum length of 600 miles, from Land's End to John O'Groat's House,[3] and a breadth varying from 33 to 367 miles. Although now under a single crown, it is divided into three sections anciently independent—Scotland, Wales, and England. Scotland has an area of 24,000 miles, a length of 286, and a breadth of from 33 to 160 miles. It is a land of rugged mountains, beautiful glens, and crystal lakes, but its soil, save in the southern Lowlands, is thin and its climate harsh, and neither in wealth nor population can it compare with England. Wales is rugged, and among its mountain-masses still survive the descendants of the ancient Celtic race. The principality covers 7,400 square miles, and until the dawn of the present era of metals and steam the Welsh people were as poor as they were scattered. Mining and quarrying for coal, iron, and slate have changed this for the better. Great Britain.
Scotland.
Wales.

East of Wales and south of Scotland, occupying two thirds of Great Britain, the choicest territory of the England.

---

[1] The Channel Islands have been under English rule since the reign of King John (1204). They are a fragment of old Normandy, and the language of the people is a modification of the old Norman French. English is now taught in the parish schools. Lying within ten miles of the French coast, their strategic importance is great and their fortifications are elaborate. The population of the entire group is less than 100,000.

[2] "The Holy Isle," or Lindisfarne, was the seat of an abbey founded in the seventh century by Aidan. St. Cuthbert's missionary labors made it famous. See description in Scott's "Marmion."

[3] "John O'Groat," according to the legend, was a Dutchman who lived at the northern extremity of Scotland about 1550. Having eight sons, he avoided disputes as to precedence among them by building an octagonal house with a front door on each side, and with an eight-sided table. This odd dwelling became a landmark.

Physical configuration.

island, lies England. It measures only 350 miles from north to south and nowhere more than 370 from east to west. Its area, stated roundly, is 50,000 miles. It will make matters clearer to survey its physical features, note where its mountains rise, where its great plains are spread out, and whence and whither its rivers run. The backbone of England is the Pennine chain, a line of mountains and high plains, or moors, extending southward from the Scottish border to the heart of the kingdom, where it ends in the Peak of Derbyshire. On the one side—west—of the Pennine range is a knot of lofty mountains, the Cumbrian Hills, among which rise

Mountains.

Scafell (3,162 feet), "the brow of mighty Helvellyn" (3,118 feet), and Skiddaw (3,054 feet). In the folds of these mountains are the lakes Windermere, Ullswater, Derwentwater, Thirlmere, Buttermere, Coniston Water, and others, which have made this picturesque "lake district" the favorite haunt of poets. East of the Pennines is the great plain of York. A range of uplands separates these levels from the fertile valley of the Thames, which stretches nearly across the kingdom, and from the Severn valley, which cuts off the Welsh highlands from the gentle levels of the East. Cornwall, the narrow southwestern prolongation of England, is mountainous, like Wales, but the greater part of Southern England is a rolling country traversed by four ranges of uplands or high plains. North of them, beyond the valleys of Thames and Severn, under a pall of smoke, lies the manufacturing center of the world, drawing its sustenance from the iron, coal, and lead of the Pennine chain, the wool from the northern and southern grazing lands, and the cotton of both hemispheres.[1]

[1] Industry and Commerce: The value of the metallic and mineral produce of the United Kingdom in 1891 was £100,524,000, of which about one third was coal and one tenth iron. In 1890 there were in the United Kingdom

Navigable seas surround the island, fine harbors indent its coasts, and numerous rivers water its plains and thread its valleys. Deep bays and prominent headlands give to England and Wales a coast-line of nearly 2,000 miles. The eastern shore is generally low and level. The rivers that enter the German Ocean are the Tyne, which flows through the northern coal-beds, the Tees, the Humber, which gathers to itself a sheaf of streams—the Trent and Ouse among them—the Wash, a shallow estuary, and the Thames, the main watercourse of Great Britain. The south coast runs through many variations of height, from the low chalk cliffs of Dover to the iron-bound promontories of Cornwall. Its rivers are unimportant, but the arms of the sea, which embrace the Isle of Wight, provide the splendid harbors of Portsmouth and Southampton, and farther toward the west is Plymouth Sound. Rounding Land's End and coasting northward, the sailor enters the broad waters of Bristol Channel, the estuary of the Severn. North of Wales the rivers Dee and Mersey discharge into the Irish Sea through broad mouths, the former now choked by "the sands o' Dee," the latter harboring the second seaport of the realm (Liverpool). The Ribble cuts another deep notch in Lancashire, a little south of the wide Bay of Morecambe, which receives the Lune and other southward-flowing waters from the Cumbrian Hills. The northerly meres and torrents find their way into Solway Firth by the Eden and Derwent.

Inland waters.

English rivers.

The climate of the British Isles is remarkable. The group lies between parallels 50° and 60° of north lati-

Warmth and humidity of the climate.

7,160 textile factories employing 1,081,631 persons. Cotton and woolen goods are the leading manufactures. The shipping of Great Britain exceeds that of all other nations combined. The mercantile marine in 1892 comprised 21,543 vessels of 8,279,297 tons, or, with the colonial marine, fully 10,000,000 tons. The value of imports, chiefly breadstuffs and raw materials, was (1892) £423,819,000; the value of exports, chiefly manufactured products, £227,060,000.

tude, as far north as Labrador or Central Russia, yet the temperature is mild throughout the year. It is their insular position, and especially the proximity of the warm ocean-river, the Gulf Stream, which sweeps past their western shores, which secures to these islands warmth and evenness of temperature and plentiful moisture. Ireland is as warm as Virginia, and the Isle of Wight basks in the sun and air of Italy. The extremes of temperature familiar to New Yorkers are unknown in London. Rains are frequent and copious. The prevailing west winds gather moisture from the Atlantic. Ireland receives the first downpour, and its emerald fields are watered by showers upon 208 days in the year. The mountains of Britain—Scottish, Welsh, and English—next intercept the heavy clouds. The rainfall upon their western slopes is enormous—seven feet every year in some districts. These waters reach the sea in short and rapid torrents. The eastern counties have but a moderate amount of rain, but nowhere is the land too dry for pasturage, and in general the humid atmosphere nourishes the lawns, fields, and hedge-rows, which give luxuriant verdure to the English landscape. This moisture, with the temperate climate, makes the soil productive of rich crops of cereals. Wheat thrives almost everywhere, and barley and oats in the North. Ireland's chief crop is potatoes, though flax is cultivated. Grazing is successful in all parts of the United Kingdom, and the best breeds of horned cattle and sheep bear the names of the English counties and islands where they were bred.

Verdant landscape.

Moor and fell, lake, stream, and chalk cliff remain much as they were when the first Greek or Roman discoverer set foot in Britain, but among these the modern traveler or student finds new names and places

Political subdivisions.

that mark the island as the habitation of man. England has a political geography no less interesting than its physical features. At the outset the student does well to fix in his mind its leading facts—the counties and towns of England, their names, positions, and characteristics.

With the help of a map we shall again commence at Berwick, on the river Tweed—the English Rubicon—and, moving southward, note them in rapid succession.

The first of the forty English shires, or counties,[1] is Northumberland, the old border-land where English Percy and Scottish Douglas met in frequent foray. The Tweed on the north and the Tyne on the south form outlets for the rich coal-measures which contribute to the prosperity of North Shields and Newcastle-on-Tyne, the latter city ranking after London and Liverpool in trade.

The shires of England.

Northumberland.

Durham, which lies next, between the Tyne and Tees, surpasses its northern neighbor in the variety of its industries. Its coal-beds are extensive; near them

Durham.

[1] The counties received their present names more than a thousand years ago. Their area and population (1891) are as follows:

Shire.	Area. Sq. M.	Population.	Shire.	Area. Sq. M.	Population.
Bedfordshire	461	160,729	Lincolnshire	2,762	472,778
Berkshire	722	238,446	Middlesex	283	3,251,703
Buckinghamshire	746	185,190	Monmouthshire	579	252,260
Cambridgeshire	820	188,862	Norfolk	2,119	456,474
Cheshire	1,027	730,052	Northamptonshire	984	302,184
Cornwall	1,350	322,589	Northumberland	2,016	506,096
Cumberland	1,515	266,550	Nottinghamshire	825	445,599
Derbyshire	1,029	527,886	Oxfordshire	756	185,938
Devonshire	2,586	631,767	Rutland	148	20,659
Dorsetshire	980	194,487	Shropshire	1,320	236,324
Durham	1,012	1,016,449	Somerset	1,640	484,326
Essex	1,542	785,399	Staffordshire	1,169	1,083,273
Gloucestershire	1,225	599,974	Suffolk	1,475	369,351
Hampshire	1,621	690,086	Surrey	758	1,730,871
Herefordshire	833	115,986	Sussex	1,458	550,442
Hertfordshire	633	220,125	Warwickshire	885	805,070
Huntingdonshire	359	57,772	Westmoreland	783	66,098
Kent	1,555	1,142,281	Wiltshire	1,354	264,969
Lancashire	1,888	3,926,798	Worcestershire	738	413,755
Leicestershire	800	373,693	Yorkshire	6,067	3,208,813

is iron ore, and its river valleys are checkered with fertile farms. The shire-town bearing the same name is a quiet little city on the river Wear, with a famous cathedral church—"half church of God, half castle 'gainst the Scot."[1] Sunderland and South Shields are the other cities.

Yorkshire. York, the largest of the shires, occupies the plain between the Tees and the Humber, drained by the dozen streams which swell the latter river through the channel of the Ouse. In the center of this rich farming district is the city of York, one of the oldest of English towns and prominent in the chronicles of war and peace, church and state. It has a splendid cathedral, the seat of one of the two Anglican archbishops. Moors and uplands rich in metals and coal skirt this river-basin, and at the southwestern angle among the Pennine foot-hills populous manufacturing cities have sprung up around the woolen-mills of Leeds, Bradford, Halifax, Huddersfield, and the edge-tool shops of Sheffield. Hull, on the Humber, is the port for much of the export trade in the products of these factories.

Lincolnshire. Lincolnshire lies between the Wash and the Humber. Its northern "wolds" are upland pastures. Its lowlands are the vast marshes called "the fens." This "hollow-land," or "Holland," has been diked and drained and is now rich grass-land, while myriads of water-fowl breed among its canals. The capital is the beautiful cathedral city of Lincoln, and the chief port is Boston—St. Botolph's town—both located on the river Witham and both bearing names dear to Americans.

[1] English Cathedrals: A cathedral church is the chief church of a diocese, in which the bishop has his official seat or throne (*cathedra*). There are cathedral churches at Canterbury, York, Durham, Winchester, Carlisle, Ely, Norwich, Rochester, Worcester, London, Chichester, Exeter, Hereford, Lichfield, Lincoln, Salisbury, Bath, Wells, Manchester, Ripon, Bristol, Gloucester, Chester, Newcastle, Oxford, Peterborough, Southwell, Truro, Wakefield, and St. Albans.

West of Lincolnshire the river Trent drains an inland region comprising the four Midland counties—Nottingham, Derby, Stafford, and Leicester. All except the last named border the Pennine chain and delve for its minerals. In Nottinghamshire was Sherwood Forest, the haunt of Robin Hood and his greenwood rangers. Nottingham city is famous for its laces, and there is no other large town, the farming people being dispersed among many market-towns and villages.[1] Northern Derbyshire contains the rugged region of the Peak (1,981 feet high) and its eastern section is rich in coal and iron. Derby is the thriving county seat. Rich Staffordshire lies next, on the southwest. Coal in the north and coal again in the south, alternating with rich beds of clay, have made the Staffordshire potteries the largest in England. Stafford, a "shoe-town," is the county seat, but Stoke-on-Trent is the center of the earthenware manufacture. In the south are Wolverhampton, with extensive iron furnaces, Burton-on-Trent, a brewers' city, and peaceful old Lichfield, with its stately cathedral. The least of the midland shires is Leicester. Its pleasant farms lie wholly south of the Trent, and are watered by the river Soar. Leicester, where court is held and wool is spun and woven, is the only large city among a score of rural towns.

The Midlands: Nottingham, Derby, Stafford, and Leicester.

The Peak.

With Lincoln, noticed above, five other shires—Rutland, Northampton, Huntingdon, Bedford, and Cambridge—are sometimes classed as counties of the Wash or the East Midlands. Rutland is the smallest shire in England; the court-house is at Oakham. The watershed of Central England extends through long and narrow Northamptonshire; numerous herds graze

The East Midlands: Rutland, Northampton, Huntingdon, Bedford, Cambridge.

[1] From Austerfield and Scrooby, two villages at the corner of the three shires of Nottingham, York, and Lincoln, began the Puritan exodus to New England.

upon these uplands, and rivers springing here find their diverse ways to the Wash, the Severn, and the Thames. Northampton, the capital, is the center of the shoe-trade, but Peterborough, with its towering cathedral, is far more interesting. About the farms of level Huntingdon lingers the memory of Oliver Cromwell, its most famous landholder; and Bedford, the county seat of the adjoining Bedfordshire, is better known for its dreaming tinker, John Bunyan, than for the numberless straw hats and bonnets plaited there and at Dunstable. The last of these six counties bears the renowned name of Cambridge, its county seat, where in simpler times the little river Cam was bridged, and where one of the two historic English universities has been for six centuries a center of learning. The northern section of the shire is fen-land, and from the marshes rises the Isle of Ely, a religious center from the earliest English times.

The Puritan country.

Between Cambridge and the east coast lie the two East Anglian[1] counties, Norfolk and Suffolk, the "north-folk" and "south-folk" of the Angles, who first conquered this district. Farms in the interior and fisheries on the seaboard give employment to the inhabitants. Norwich is the capital and Yarmouth—famed for its herrings—the seaport of the northern shire. Ipswich is both capital and port of Suffolk. In the interior is the historic Bury St. Edmunds.

East Anglia: Norfolk and Suffolk.

The Thames is the chief English river. It is two hundred and fifteen miles long, and eight counties lie within the region which it drains. Essex, Middlesex, Hertford, Buckingham, and Oxford lie on its left bank, opposed on the other shore by Berkshire, Surrey, and Kent. Essex got its name from its East Saxon conquer-

The valley of the Thames: Essex, Middlesex, Hertford, Buckingham, Oxford, Berkshire, Surrey, and Kent.

[1] The larger number of the early settlers of New England emigrated from the East Anglian counties. Two thirds is John Fiske's estimate of the proportion. See "Beginnings of New England," pp. 62-5.

ors. Where once stretched the royal hunting preserves of Epping and Hainault is now a land of farms and rural prosperity. At Shoeburyness, guarding the Thames-mouth, is the artillery school of the British army. The Middle Saxons gave their name to Middlesex, smallest but one and most populous of all the English shires. Its capital is Brentford. Westward, by a heath once infested by Sir John Falstaff and fiercer cut-purses, is Hounslow, and a few miles to the north is Harrow, the home of a famous public school.

But in comparison with its great city the towns of Middlesex sink out of sight; for within this county lies the greater portion of London, the greatest city that the world has known. The population of 4,000,000[1] souls gathered here overflows upon the Surrey side of the Thames, and the docks and warehouses of its abounding commerce line the river to its mouth. London is the seat of the English government and the capital of the world's trade. Hither run all the roads in England, and hither tend keels on every sea. Middlesex cuts off Hertford from direct contact with the Thames. St. Albans is a town of ancient note. In Buckinghamshire is the great public school of Eton. Agriculture is the prevailing industry, as it is in Oxfordshire, which adjoins the former on the west. Oxford, the county seat, has also a cathedral and a university seven centuries old. In the northwest are the Edge Hills, and in the center of the county is Woodstock, where the poet Chaucer lived and wrote "The Canterbury Tales."

London.

Oxford.

Crossing to the right bank of the Thames, and following it to the sea, we pass through Berkshire, an-

[1] Statistics of London: London occupies 75,442 acres and in 1891 contained 4,232,118 inhabitants. It was growing at the rate of one per cent a year. The population exceeds that of Scotland and approaches that of Ireland. The Thames is navigable up to the Tower of London, and the commerce of London exceeds that of any city in the world.

other land of farmers, having the royal castle of Windsor in its northeastern angle. The Hampshire Downs, a range of chalk hills which crosses Berkshire, also traverse the adjacent county of Surrey. Here the influence of London has turned the farming hamlets into thrifty suburban towns, and two populous divisions of the metropolis, Lambeth and Southwark, lie wholly on the Surrey side. Kent lies between Surrey and the Straits of Dover, confronting Europe. On this coast are Dover[1] and Folkestone, whence steamboats cross to Calais and Boulogne in France. Ramsgate and Margate are the popular seashore resorts of the London crowds. Canterbury's grand cathedral, the seat of the first Anglican archbishop, is perhaps the most venerated spot in the kingdom. Tunbridge Wells, on the southern border, was the fashionable watering-place two hundred years ago; at Rochester is an ancient cathedral, and near by at Chatham is the arsenal of the royal navy. Deptford, Greenwich, Woolwich, and Gravesend, which elbow each other for a water-front upon the Thames, present mile upon mile of docks, crowded with the shipping of the globe. Marking the mouth of the Thames is the North Foreland light.

Leaving the Thames counties, our traveling student of political geography may follow the Channel coast into Sussex, a name bringing memories of the South Saxons. The surface of this shire is broken by the South Downs, a range of crumbling chalk hills ending at the Channel shore in Beachy Head. Between these hills and the North Downs is the Weald, a plain of clay and sand,

Windsor.

Canterbury.

The Channel coast: Sussex.

---

[1] The Cinque Ports: The governor of Dover Castle is also "Lord Protector of the Cinque Ports." These Channel towns, originally five in number (Dover, Hastings, Romney, Hythe, and Sandwich), furnished most of the ships and sailors for the defense of the kingdom before the existence of a navy. For this they received a special charter granting them extraordinary political rights. See "The Cinque Ports" in Historic Towns Series.

which was until recently a tangled wilderness. Among the Sussex coast towns are Hastings, where William the Conqueror fought, and Brighton, the English "Coney Island." Chichester, now decayed, has the court-house and bishop's church.

The Hampshire Downs, of which the North and South Downs are the eastern branches, extend across northern Hampshire, rising in places to the height of about 1,000 feet. Between their wall and the Channel is a gently undulating and fertile region, of which the ancient royal and cathedral city of Winchester is the center. Two harbors, Portsmouth and Southampton, indent the southern coast, the former being a naval post, the latter the entry port of an active commerce with the Mediterranean, and the landing-place for lines of transatlantic steamers. Southampton Water, with its arms, the Solent and Spithead, divides the Isle of Wight from the Hampshire mainland. The climate of the island is charmingly mild and its scenery beautiful. West of Southampton Water is the wide tract of woodland called the New Forest, the game preserve of the Norman kings. *Hampshire. Southampton Water.*

Wiltshire, though wholly inland, is linked with this southern range of counties by its rivers, which flow into the English Channel, though parts of it are drained by affluents of the Thames and Severn. Much of its surface is high and barren—Salisbury Plain and Marlborough Downs. Salisbury is the capital and cathedral city; Wilton's carpets are unsurpassed; Stonehenge is a circle of massive stones marking, perhaps, the center of the idolatrous exercises of the druids. *Wiltshire.*

Dorset lies between Wilts and the Channel. Much of its surface is high, and clay for the Stafford potteries is almost its only mineral product. *Dorset.*

Somerset.

Devon.

Cornwall.

The wedge of Bristol Channel splits off a slender sliver of land, which is divided between the three counties of Somerset, Devon, and Cornwall. Somersetshire borders the Bristol Channel and is cut in two by the river Parret. East of this river are low hills and fertile valleys. There are cathedrals at Bath and Wells, and Glastonbury was early the site of the most extensive monastery in the island. West of the river masses of rocky mountains take the place of the ridges of chalk and lime which cross the eastern counties, and few villages are found in their isolated glens. The mountains of Devonshire rise higher, and are rich in metals. Exmoor is the name given to the highlands of North Devon, and Dartmoor to the more extensive southern plateau. Yes Tor, the Dartmoor summit, exceeds 2,000 feet in height. Mines of lead, iron, tin, copper, and quarries of valuable building stone enrich South Devonshire, and have built busy ports at the mouths of the rivers: Plymouth, Devonport, and Dartmouth. In the plain between these two strips of moorland are bred the Devon cattle, and here are the towns of Exeter, another cathedral city, and Honiton, famous for its lace. The point of this southwestern sliver of Britain is the county of Cornwall,[1] which is again riven at its western tip into the two headlands—Land's End and Lizard Point. Granite rocks and scanty soil form the forbidding surface of the shire, but the hard rocks of the utmost west are richly veined with lead, copper, and tin. The chief Cornish towns are Truro, Falmouth, and Penzance.

Turning northward from the mineral-bearing rocks of

---

[1] "The delectable duchy" of Cornwall is an appanage of the heir-apparent to the English crown. The inhabitants are of Celtic race, akin to the Welsh, though their language has been displaced by English. The tin mines have been worked from prehistoric times, and Cornishmen are found in all mining regions of the world.

The Home of the English.

Devon and Cornwall, we find a group of six West Midland counties lying in the valley of the Severn, between Wales and the already mentioned Midland shires. They are Gloucester, Worcester, Warwick, Monmouth, Hereford, and Salop, or Shropshire. The first named is an agricultural region, notable for the wool of its Cotswold flocks and for the commerce and manufactures of its city of Bristol, which trades extensively with Ireland and the West Indies. Tracing the course of the Severn northward, one enters Worcestershire, a land of fertile valleys, rich in farms and orchards. Worcester, its capital, has famous porcelain works, carpets are woven at Kidderminster, and iron and glass are manufactured in a busy district at the north. The river Avon, the main tributary of the Severn, flows midway through lovely Warwickshire. This is Shakespeare's county. Rugby, dear to many generations of English schoolboys, is in the Avon valley. So are Coventry, where the chaste Godiva rode at noonday, and the ruins of Kenilworth. Beyond the charming valley is the populous manufacturing city of Birmingham, ranking fourth in England. Across the Severn, from Gloucester, is Monmouthshire, taken from Wales by the eighth King Henry. The Welsh mountain spurs which enter the county from the west yield coal and iron, and the basin of the river Usk is fertile. The Wye, which here enters the Severn, has come down through the orchards and hop-gardens of Herefordshire. The sixth and largest of the West Midland counties is rural Shropshire.

The four remaining counties of England—Chester, Lancaster, Westmoreland, Cumberland—are washed by the Irish Sea and run back to the Pennine chain. The double advantage of mineral wealth and waterways

West Midlands: Gloucester, Worcester, Warwick, Monmouth, Hereford, Salop.

Shakespeare's county.

Chester.

has raised them in wealth and population. Cheshire has the Mersey, with the seaport of Birkenhead on its northern, and the sandy Dee, with Roman-walled Chester, on its southern boundary. Midway flows the river Weaver, through a valley whose salt springs were savory before the invasion of Cæsar. Copper and lead mines, coal-fields and stone-quarries, are worked in the eastern districts, which thus gain importance as a manufacturing center. But the county of Lancaster, or Lancashire, stands easily first in manufactures. Lancaster is a long and narrow county, comprising the isolated lakes and mountains of Furness, the thinly settled pasture-lands of North Lancashire, and, between the Ribble and Mersey, South Lancashire, a swarming hive of industry. The coal-fields of the Lancashire moorlands and the use of steam-power have changed this desolate country into a populous and wealthy section, until, as a recent writer says, "the whole county has now the appearance of one unbroken city of mills and factories, all busied in the same trade, the weaving, dyeing, and printing of cotton." Bolton, Oldham, Rochdale, and Manchester—the latter now linked with tide-water by a ship canal—are cities of spindles and looms, and Liverpool, on the Mersey, the second city of England and second seaport of the world, is the outlet and inlet for the materials and products of this enormous industry. Westmoreland, which only comes down to the sea at the head of Morecambe Bay, is the most mountainous and barren of the English counties. Yet the poets who have haunted its valleys and sung of the glories of Helvellyn and the beauty of Windermere have made this lake region forever charming. Cumberland, rich in mineral-bearing mountains, completes the tale of the shires. Gray old Carlisle is its county seat.

Margin notes: Lancaster. The cotton district. Westmoreland. Cumberland.

The reader turns now from this survey of crowded cities, bustling marts, great mills, and gray cathedrals. The beginnings of English history must be sought before the Englishmen landed in Britain, and when rude Celtic tribes tilled the plains and hunted through the forests of the island.

England's beginnings.

TOPICS FOR READING AND SPECIAL STUDY. WITH LIBRARY NOTES.

1. THE LOCATION AND PHYSICAL CHARACTERISTICS OF GREAT BRITAIN AS FACTORS IN THE DEVELOPMENT OF THE ENGLISH NATION.

    The Growth of the English Nation. K. Coman.

2. THE GEOGRAPHY OF THE BRITISH ISLES.

    A Short Geography of the British Isles. J. R. and A. S. Green.

3. THE CITY OF LONDON.

    London. W. J. Loftie. (Historic Towns Series.)
    London. W. Besant.
    London: Life and Labour of the People. C. Booth.

For a general description of England and its people read "A Trip to England," by Goldwin Smith, "Our Old Home" and "English Note-Books," by Nathaniel Hawthorne, "England Without and Within," by Richard Grant White, "Old England," by James M. Hoppin. Baedeker's "Great Britain," though designed as a traveler's guide, is an admirable handbook for the historical student. Gardiner's "Atlas of English History" is a desirable companion.

CHAPTER II.

ENGLAND BEFORE THE ENGLISH, 55 B. C.–410 A. D.

The predecessors of the English in Britain.

THE pagan English who landed in Britain in the fifth century after Christ found the island already occupied by the Britons, a Celtic people who had adopted the manners and religion of Christian Rome. The Roman pioneers who preceded the English by five centuries found a remnant of a still earlier people in the island. Of this swarthy, curly-haired race little is known. The Britons were akin to the Celtic Gauls of what is now France. The theory is now widely accepted that from some prehistoric mother-land successive waves of migration were sent forth to people the European continent. This family of nations is variously named Aryan, Indo-European, and Indo-Germanic.[1] To it belong most of the tribes which peopled Europe at the dawn of history, including the Hellenes, of the Greek countries, the Italians, from whom sprang the Romans, and the multitudinous races of Northern Europe—the "barbarians" —who were by turns the slaves, the soldiers, and the conquerors of Greece and Rome.

Britons.

Silures.

The Aryan migrations.

The Celts.

From evidences of location and speech it is concluded that the Celts were among the first Aryan families to seek new homes. Nearly four centuries before Christ they threatened the gates of Rome, and the dawn of

---

[1] Recent investigation locates its primitive home near the Baltic Sea, contrary to the earlier opinion that placed it in Western Asia. The eight main groups of languages from this stock are (1) Indo-Iranian, (2) Armenian, (3) Greek, (4) Italic, (5) Celtic, (6) Teutonic or Germanic, (7) Balto-Slavic, (8) Albanian.

history found them settled among the peninsulas and islands of the West.

The Celts of the British Islands are of two branches, the earlier Gaels—still represented by the Irish, the Manx, and the Scottish Highlanders—and the Cymri, who originally held most of Southern Britain, but who found refuge from the Romans and Germans in the mountains of Wales, where the language and national type survive.[1]

Gaels and Cymri.

It is believed that Phenician trading vessels visited Britain a thousand years before Christ in quest of metallic ores. Herodotus, "the Father of History" (450 B. C.), doubtless has Cornwall in mind when he writes of the "Tin Islands," and the oceanic isles Albin and Iverne of Aristotle cannot be other than white-cliffed Britain and Hibernia (Ireland).

Earliest notices of Britain.

A traveler, Pytheas, from Gaul visited Britain in the fourth century B. C. and wrote of its wide stretches of marsh and forest. He stated also that sheep and cattle grazed in the oak openings and on the upland pastures. Wheat he found growing near the coast, and he noticed also that barns must be built for storing the crop, the frequent rains forbidding the more careless husbandry of Gaul and sunny Sicily.

Pytheas of Marseilles.

About sixty years before the birth of Christ the Roman power first reached Britain. Julius Cæsar, commanding against the Gaulish tribes of France, learned that the enemy received succor from certain Britons

---

[1] The surviving representatives of the Celtic language in the British Isles are the Gaelic, still existing in modified forms as Irish, Highland Scotch, and Manx, and the Cymric or Welsh. The old Briton long lived in the recesses of Cornwall, but died out in the eighteenth century. For examples of Gaelic and Welsh see John iii. 16 in those languages:

Gaelic of Scotch Highlands.—Oir is ann mar sin a ghràdhaich Dia an saoghal, gu'n d'thug e 'aon-ghin Mhic féin, chum as ge b'e neach a chreideas ann, nach sgriosare, ach gu'm bi a'bheatha shiorruidh aige.

Welsh.—Canys felly y carodd Duw y byd, fel y rhoddodd efe ei uniganedig Fab, fel na choller pwy bynnag a gredo ynddo ef, ond caffael o hono fywyd tragy wyddol.

who inhabited a great island a few leagues west of the mainland. With two legions and a hundred small vessels he crossed the Straits of Dover (August, 55 B. C.). The watchers on the chalk cliffs gave the alarm and when the Romans attempted a landing (near Deal) the shore was lined with fiercely yelling Britons, horrible with war-paint and driving their heavy war-chariots up and down the beach. The ships had to anchor far down the sand, and the legionaries, cumbered with armor, must wade ashore through tumbling breakers, in the face of arrows and javelins.[1] Once landed, their victory was easy, and in obedience to Cæsar's iron discipline they fortified a camp and rested from battle and labor. Bad weather soon drove the invaders back to their winter quarters in Gaul.

The following July Cæsar returned with a powerful force. The painted Britons came crowding into Kent

BUST OF JULIUS CÆSAR

55 B. C.

Cæsar's first invasion.

Cæsar's second invasion.

---

[1] Cæsar narrates that while his soldiers hesitated to plunge in, the standard-bearer of the tenth legion, having prayed that his act might succeed, cried to his comrades: "Leap down, my men, unless you wish to betray your eagle to the enemy. I shall certainly have done my duty to my country and my general." Every man in his ship followed him over the side, and the conquerors of the world were soon on Britain's sod.

to expel the intruder. Tribal feuds were laid aside in
the face of the common peril, and one Cassivelaunus—
so Cæsar Latinized the Celtic name Caswallon—was Caswallon.
made leader of the horde. With the courage of numbers and a righteous cause the Celts engaged the legions
in repeated combats, hurling their chariots through the
Roman lines, the horsemen leaping to the ground and
engaging the infantry hand to hand. But the veterans
of five campaigns in Gaul were not to be stampeded by
undisciplined islanders, and it was not long before the
Britons, checked and disheartened, forsook their chief
and sought safety, tribe by tribe, in submission. Cæsar
pursued Caswallon northward across the Thames and
took his stronghold. In early autumn the Romans
withdrew across the Channel, leaving no garrison, but
taking many noble youths as hostages to secure peace
and the payment of tribute. How regularly the tribute
money was paid no records tell. Other events turned
Cæsar's face eastward, and he never revisited the island.

In his history, Cæsar wrote:

The interior of Britain is inhabited by a race said to be
aboriginal; the coast regions by invaders from Belgium, whom Cæsar's description of land and people.
war or foray has brought thither, and who have afterward
settled in the country. There is a large population, the buildings being numerous and closely resembling those of Gaul.
Cattle form their chief possession. For money they use
copper or iron in bars of fixed weight and value. Tin is found
in the interior, and iron sparingly near the coast. Whatever
copper they use is imported. They have the forest trees of
the mainland, except the beech and fir. It is forbidden by law
to eat the flesh of hare, goose, or chicken, and these creatures
are domesticated for mere amusement. The island has a
milder climate than that of Gaul.

Of all the tribes the Kentish men stand first in civilization. They dwell on the seaboard, and differ little in customs
from the neighboring Gauls. Farther back from the coast

many tribes sow no grains, subsisting chiefly upon the milk and flesh of their herds, whose skins form their clothing. Every Briton stains himself blue with the juice of the woad, giving him a horrible appearance in battle. The men shave their faces, excepting the head and the upper lip. Ten or a dozen men have wives in common.

War-paint.

Of their system of society, government, and religion Cæsar makes little note, but by likening their customs to those of Gaul he justifies us in quoting as true of the Britons what he says of their Gaulish cousins. He found, then, that there were practically two main bodies in the nation, the people and the privileged classes. The former were little better than slaves of their more fortunate masters. The latter class was made up of knights and druids. The knightly families were those who were distinguished for wealth or valor. Of the Gaulish druids Cæsar says:

Knights.

Druids.

The druids have charge of all matters of religion; they officiate at public and private sacrifices and interpret the omens. The people hold them in high honor, and many young men resort to them for education. They decide almost all lawsuits, judging and passing sentence in civil and criminal cases, murder, disputed wills, and boundaries. Any person or tribe that dissents from their decision is declared an outlaw. Over them all is an arch-druid, elected by his fellows for life. . . . The system is said to have originated in Britain, and thither go many Gauls to learn its principles. The druids are exempt from taxation and free from civil and military duties. These privileges attract many novitiates, and many others are sent to them by parents and kindred. They have to commit to memory a great number of verses, the full course of training sometimes running through twenty years. This knowledge of theirs is a sacred secret, and it is unlawful to write it down. I think they have two reasons for this: they do not want their system published to the outside world, and they hope thereby to cultivate the memory of their pupils. The chief doctrine of the druids is that the soul of man does

A guild of priests.

England before the English.

not perish, but has everlasting life, passing at the death of one body to renewed existence in the person of another. Thus they would incite courage by removing the fear of death. They have much lore concerning the stars and their motions, concerning the universe and the earth, concerning natural objects, and about the power and purposes of the immortal gods. Such things are the staple of their discussions, and it is learning of this kind that they hand down to their young disciples.

Cæsar found them worshiping many gods whom he identified with Mercury, Apollo, Mars, Jupiter, and Minerva, of the Romans. He describes their bloody sacrifices of human beings in their groves of sacred oaks. The oak, its leaves and acorns, were held in veneration, and it is said that the mistletoe, which grew upon its branches, was the sacred symbol of man, *Human sacrifice.*

STONEHENGE, ON SALISBURY PLAIN.

upheld and nourished by divine power. The island of Mona (the modern Anglesey) was a favorite school of the druids in Britain, and many hold that Stonehenge,[1] the circle of gigantic stones which has stood on Salis- *Stonehenge.*

[1] Stonehenge is one of the most impressive and mysterious relics of British antiquity. It is a series of circles and ovals of monoliths, connected with various earthworks. Authorities differ greatly as to its builders, its date, and its purpose, but the modern archaeologists think it was built by the druids and used as a temple before the birth of Christ. Human sacrifices probably took place here.

bury Plain from time immemorial, was the sanctuary of the arch-druid, the prehistoric cathedral—so to say—of Britain.

For a century after Cæsar's invasion Rome had enough to do without extending her conquests in the West. To the Latin poets of that time the Briton, remote and unsubdued, served as the type of perfect freedom. But in 43 A. D. the Emperor Claudius resumed the conquest of "the isle beyond the world," and gained sufficient glory to receive a formal triumph and the title "Britannicus." Vespasian followed him, and brought to Rome the British chieftain Caradoc (Caractacus) as a trophy. On viewing the splendor of the world's capital the noble barbarian exclaimed, "Strange that the owners of all this should envy us our miserable huts!"

Cymbeline and Caradoc.

In Nero's reign the strong arm of Suetonius Paulinus cleansed the druid-nest on Mona's isle, which had been the center of British resistance in the West, and then visited a terrible punishment upon the eastern Britons, who under the warrior queen Boadicea[1] had burned Londinium (London) and massacred thousands of the subjects of Rome. After this chastisement Britain accepted its destiny and became a province of the world-empire of the Cæsars.

The massacre of Mona.

Boadicea.

A Roman province.

Agricola, who was sent to govern the province in the year 78, added Wales to the Roman domain, and as a barrier to the savage Caledonians built a line of forts across the island from Forth to Clyde, reënforcing this by a second line of forts from Solway to the Tyne. To

Agricola.

---

[1] Boadicea had been scourged, her daughters outraged, her people oppressed and plundered by the Romans. Her forces against Suetonius are said to have numbered 120,000. A Roman historian describes her as a gigantic Amazon, with flowing red hair, stern features, and a voice like a trumpet-call. She wore a gay tartan and a military cloak, and brandished a heavy spear. The queen is said to have poisoned herself after the rout of her army.

the southern Britons the rule of Agricola was a period of peace. They now began to adopt the Roman ways of life. Fortified towns sprang up at the mouths of the rivers; trade began to divide with agriculture and grazing the attention of the people; the mines were worked to advantage, and the clothing and domestic arrangements of Rome were gradually adopted by the children of the woad-stained warriors who had confronted Cæsar and followed Boadicea and Caradoc to battle.

As the peace and prosperity of the province increased, its northern marches were the more threatened by the untamed Caledonians. Hadrian, Rome's vigorous monarch, the memorials of whose travels were set up in nearly every province, visited the island (120 A. D.) and gave orders for strengthening Agricola's southern line of forts. The barrier was afterward improved and many times repaired. There are evidences that it was eighty years in building; and after fifteen hundred years of decay, destruction, and neglect this relic of old Rome may still be traced throughout its seventy-three miles of windings from Wall's End to Bowness.[1] {Hadrian's visit.} {The Roman Wall.}

Of the internal condition of the people during the centuries of Roman decay very little is known. The South enjoyed peace, and the northern walls afforded some protection against the assaults of the Picts and Scots—the latter a fierce tribe which had come from Ireland to fix its name upon North Britain. The plowman, the grave-digger, and the delving builder of our own time contribute whatever information we have of {Relics of Roman civilization.}

[1] The works consisted of a trench on the north side, averaging thirty-six feet wide by nine feet deep; a wall of stone eight feet high and eighteen feet thick; fortified encampments at frequent intervals for troops, with strong watch-towers a fourth of a mile apart; earthen ramparts and a trench; and a system of fine military roads for facilitating the movement of troops to threatened points. It is said that it must have required a garrison of 10,000 men. Other walls were built by later emperors.

the social condition of the British people under the Romans. Plowshare and spade have turned up bronze helmets and battle-axes of Roman workmanship, funereal urns and baser pots and kettles for household use, and many coins bearing the effigies of Roman emperors. Remnants of porticoes and inlaid floors in Roman style have been laid bare, testifying to the magnificence of the villas which once dotted the pleasant country. Remnants of old Roman city walls may yet be seen at Chester. The straight lines of old Roman roads strike across moor and plain. In the geographical names ending in -cola (Latin *colonia*, "colony") and -chester (Latin *castra*, "camp") is revealed the hand of Rome.¹

Although the Roman civilization prevailed and Latin was the language of court and church—for Christian missionaries had established the new faith in the island—nevertheless the Roman blood and tongue show themselves but slightly in the nation we now call English. On the Continent—in Italy, in France, in Spain—Rome made conquests which influenced permanently the national character and language. Their people, inextricably mingled now with the conquering tribes which swept down from the North to the south of the Roman Empire, are still the "Latin races"; their languages, modified as they have been by the clumsy organs of Lombard and Frank and Goth, are still the "Romance" (*i.e.*, "Romanish") languages, and are closely akin to the speech of Cicero. England stands apart from these nations. Like them, she was for centuries a

---

¹ Roman Remains in Britain. Of Roman buildings in Britain have gone to ruin. Not a single Roman column is now standing in its own place anywhere to be seen. At London is some arch of a Roman gateway. At Dover Castle the remains of an old Roman Roman building are traceable and at Colchester, Winchester, St. Albans, Bath, Silchester, Aldborough, and elsewhere fragments of porticoes, houses, baths, etc., have been unearthed. Roman keys, coins, and bits of glass, arms, pottery, armor, brooches and marbles are found here and there in sufficient quantities and these still prove the presence of Rome in Britain of the past.

portion of the Roman realm, and, like them, she was overrun by tribes of heathen Germans, yet out of the long welter she emerges with not a trace of Roman manners and with scarcely a Latin syllable upon her lips.

TOPICS FOR READING AND SPECIAL STUDY,
WITH LIBRARY NOTES.

1. THE EARLY BRITONS.
    Life in Early Britain. A. C. Windle.
    The Story of Early Britain. A. J. Church.
    Early England. F. Y. Powell.
    Social England. Vol.I. H. D. Traill.
2. THE RELIGION AND LANGUAGE OF THE CELTS
    Celtic Literature. W. K. Sullivan. Art. in Ency. Brit., Ninth Ed.)
3. VESTIGES OF ROMAN CIVILIZATION IN GREAT BRITAIN.
    Romano-British Remains. G. L. Gomme.

FICTION, ETC.

The Count of the Saxon Shore. A. J. Church.
Daybreak in Britain. A. L. O. E.
Edol the Druid. W. H. G. Kingston.
Celtic Fairy Tales. Joseph Jacobs.

CHAPTER III.

The English in Britain, 410 A. D. to 837 A. D.—From the Roman Evacuation to the Rise of Wessex.

The advance of the German "barbarians."

THROUGHOUT the fourth century there had been a mysterious drift of barbarian tribes across Northern Europe. It was perhaps another pulse-beat of the Aryan heart which in prehistoric times had brought the Greeks, the Latins, and the Celts into the lands in which the dawn of history found them.

Withdrawal of Roman garrisons.

The vastly extended frontier of Rome was exposed to the attacks of these rough pagans, who were tempted by the wealth and weakness of the empire. To defend Italy and the Eternal City itself the outlying provinces were left bare. In 410 A. D. the Emperor Honorius recalled the legions which had manned the northern ramparts of Britain and guarded the Channel ports from the Saxon sea-wolves. Rome was past saving: while the fairest provinces of Italy, France, and Spain were overwhelmed by the barbarians, other Germanic tribes conquered Roman Britain and began the making of the English nation.

The invaders of Britain.

It was in 449 A. D., according to the chronicles, that the Teutonic invaders first set permanent foot on British soil. They were Jutes, from the southern part of the peninsula now occupied by Denmark, although still retaining the name of Jutland. South of them and along the coast dwelt two nearly related peoples, the Saxons and the Angles. The success of the first comers soon tempted these to similar migrations, which ended in Anglo-Saxon sovereignty, spreading over the island their English language and finally giving to it the name of Angle-land, or England.

Vortigern,[1] British king of Kent, is charged with first admitting the Jutes into the island. The Picts harassed him, Rome could not protect him, and the German pirates plundered his seaboard. He conceived the plan

The Jutes in Kent.

BOAT FOR FOURTEEN PAIRS OF OARS, FOUND AT NYDAM, JUTLAND.

of playing off pirate against Pict, in the hope of destroying both. Two Jutish chiefs, Hengist and Horsa, accepted his terms, drove out the Picts (449 A. D.), but instead of retiring with their reward turned their swords upon the men of Kent. Horsa perished in the war, but Hengist lived long enough to establish a strong Jutish kingdom of Kent.

Hengist and Horsa.

Before the spirit of Hengist, the Jute, took its flight to Valhalla, reports of his rich prize had crossed the sea, and Ella, the Saxon, with three sons and three ship-loads of buccaneers, had set sail for this land of

Ella and the South Saxon kingdom.

[1] The legend is that Vortigern promised Hengist the kingdom of Kent for his daughter's hand. The Kentish nobles protested, and Vortigern assembled three hundred of them in council. For each British noble present there was a Saxon chief, and at a word from Hengist each Saxon plunged his dagger into a British breast. So the kingdom passed to Hengist.

promise, no longer guarded by the Roman buckler. Landing on the southern coast, they carved out a place for their kingdom of Sussex (South Saxony). Such terror of the Saxon name was burned into the Celtic mind that the English traveler still finds himself called a "Saxon" in Celtic Wales or in Celtic Scotland. As the British Celts called all these Teutonic invaders "Saxons," so the invaders had but one contemptuous term for all the islanders; they were "Welsh" (*i. e.*, foreigners or outlanders) to them, and Welsh we call their descendants to this day.

Welsh or outlanders.

JUTISH OR DANISH MAIL-COAT IN USE BEFORE 450 A. D.

Cerdic founds the West Saxon monarchy.

The third English kingdom was destined to become the greatest. In 495 the Saxon Cerdic came coasting down the Channel and fought the Britons near Southampton Water. Though twice repulsed he gained ground at last and founded the kingdom of Wessex. To this day the blood of Cerdic, mingled with Northman, Plantagenet, Tudor, Stuart, and Brunswick, flows in the veins of the sovereigns of England. It was this chief who in one of his campaigns was repulsed by a British chieftain, Arthur,[1] whose name is interwoven

King Arthur.

---

[1] This famous British victory was at Badon Hill, near Bath. Arthur became the transfigured hero of a multitude of romantic legends and ballads, preserved by the Welsh and other Celtic peoples. (Another theory makes the historic Arthur a chief of the northern Britons at about the same period.) The legendary Arthur sleeps mysteriously beside his magic sword Excalibur until the Celtic power shall rise again.

with the legends of that time, and has gained new luster in the poetry of our own.

About London the Middle Saxons located (Middlesex), and Essex, farther east, betrays the location of a fourth Saxon state. Middlesex and Essex.

The Angles, who were to bequeath their name to the whole land, settled in the valley of the Trent. Between the Thames and the Wash lay their kingdom of East Anglia, divided between the "north folk" and the "south folk" (now Norfolk and Suffolk). North of the Humber, and extending beyond the present limits of England, was Northumbria, at times a united and complete kingdom of the Angles, at another period under divided sway—Deira in the south and Bernicia in the north. In mid-Britain was the latest of these heathen states—Mercia, the border or marchland. The seven leading states, Kent, Sussex, Wessex, Essex, East Anglia, Northumbria, and Mercia, have been grouped under the name of the Saxon Heptarchy (seven-fold state). They were in no sense a confederacy. No sooner had they subdued the Britons than they began to fight each other, and the story of their interminable brawlings is a tangled and profitless tale. From time to time some powerful king made himself overlord (Bretwalda).[1]

East Anglia.

The Saxon Heptarchy.

"Bretwalda."

The seventh century dawned upon a Britain one third of which was British, two thirds English. The Celts had retired into the hill country of the West, leaving the eastern plains and river-basins to the invaders. The Celtic lands were West Wales (now Cornwall), North Wales (the Wales of later times), *Celtic frontier.*

---

[1] The seven Bretwaldas named by the early historian Bede are: Elle of Sussex; Ceawlin of Wessex; Ethelbert of Kent, the fortunate husband of a Christian queen, and the first English monarch to be baptized; Redwald of East Anglia; Edwin of Northumbria, founder of Edinburgh, and his sons Oswald and Oswy.

Cumbria (Lancashire and the "lake country"), and Strathclyde, lying on both sides of the Scottish border.

It is time to inquire what manner of men were these early English who had now superseded the Romans as masters of Britain.

Celt and Teuton.

The German invaders brought with them the religion, government, and social system under which they had lived in the older Angle-land beyond the North Sea.[1] Their religion was that of all the North German and Scandinavian tribes—a belief in many divinities, male and female. Woden, or Odin, the war-god, the ancestor of their royal family; Thunor, the thunder-wielder; Frea, giver of peace and plenty; Sætere, little known to us, and Tiw, an avenging deity—all these names we, the children of the North, unconsciously commemorate in the Tiw's-day, Woden's-day, Thor's-day, Frea's-day, and Sætere's-day of our calendar. Eostre, the English goddess of the dawn, strangely gives name to the Christian Easter. Nicor, a mischievous spirit, is the "Old Nick" of our colloquial speech. But beyond these names and certain local superstitions lingering obscurely among English peasants, the old religion has perished utterly.

German religion.

The early English system of government has proved more enduring; the revolutions and changes of a thousand years have obscured but not quite effaced the principles which the English brought with them to their new abode. The German people were clannish. Those of the same name and family connection dwelt together, forming village commonwealths. The freemen of the

German political institutions.

Village communities.

---

[1] Sir Walter Besant puts this description of the English invaders into the mouth of a London Briton of the fifth century: "These devils, who had fair hair and blue eyes and were of greater stature than our people, carried swords a yard long, and round wooden shields faced with leather. Some of them also had girdle daggers and long spears. They were extremely valiant and, rushing upon their foes with shouts, generally bore them down and made them run."

village, the lesser "churls," and the more wealthy and influential "earls" met in town-moot or meeting to consider questions of public concern, and to try criminals and award justice in disputes between freeman and freeman.[1] Besides these freemen there were many serfs and slaves—the former personally free but without political rights, the latter captives in war or churls whom desperate poverty had forced to sell themselves.

Town-meetings.

The tribe, which was made up of a number of these village communities, had its ealdorman (alderman), and in their English conquests several tribes united under a king. The crown was partly hereditary, partly elective. It remained in one family, but did not pass by law from father to son. The elders, or wise men (witan), in their moot or meeting (witenagemot), selected from the men of royal blood the one best fitted to lead them in war and guide them in peace. This council of the elders met frequently, and besides electing the monarch gave him advice in times of need. The king led the armed freemen to battle, and decided their most serious lawsuits in time of peace. He owned land like a common freeman, but he had likewise the management of the public land, or folk-land. This he granted to his followers in return for service done—to his best lieutenants in war and to the trusted body-servants who formed his household, or court, and superintended the details of his business. These thanes, or servants of the king, acquired such wealth and influence that they soon outranked the older aristocracy (the

King and council.

Witenagemot.

---

[1] For example, Irvington is the "ton" or village of the Irvings. The men of several villages held hundred-moots and the men of an entire tribe met twice a year in a folk-moot, for the settlement of important questions. "An ealdorman presided, the elders' spoke and the warriors listened and signified their opinion by shouting 'Aye' or 'Nay,' and rattling their weapons." John Fiske points to these moots as the lineal ancestor of the New England town-meeting.—" Beginnings of New England."

earls of the village commonwealths), and thane became a coveted title of nobility.

Early English manners and customs.

From the architecture and domestic arrangements of the Romans to the homely dwellings of the English was a long step downward. The newcomers were agriculturists and fighting men—not traders or city dwellers[1]—and active commercial intercourse between England and the Continent was interrupted for years. The farmers bred swine and horned cattle, and sowed wheat and barley in the better soils. They lived in rough huts and halls of wood or stone, with no glazed windows, a hole

 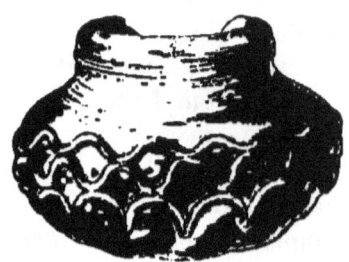

OLD ENGLISH GLASS VESSELS.

in the roof for a smoke-flue, beaten earth or flagstones for floor, with rushes strewn upon it for carpets. They sat at meat, instead of reclining in the Roman fashion, and they ate with knives of steel and spoons of iron or horn. They were none too nice in table manners, and the need of forks was yet to be felt. Beef and pork formed their principal food, washed down with copious draughts of ale and mead. They were hard drinkers and hard fighters, these early English, and their wild lives were usually cut short by battle or pestilence.

[1] Their rude outdoor life seemed to have given them a distrust of civilized dwellings. They were superstitious about living in houses built for other people. When they captured the British towns they desolated them. Even London (Augusta), a city of some 50,000 people, is thought to have been abandoned by its inhabitants and left in ruins for a generation. See Besant's "London."

Their tankards and drinking horns show few traces of artistic ornament; and of the literature of this heathen time only two rude songs survive.

The English differed in one important particular from the kindred nations which wrested France, Italy, and Spain from Rome. Those conquering races adopted the religion as well as the language, and to some extent the laws, of the conquered. Scarcely a British word survives in the English language, scarcely a Celtic line in the English countenance and character, and it was no British mission, but one straight from Rome, which first won the English pagans from their idols to the living God. The feeling between the two races was too bitter to encourage the British Christians to mission-work among the Saxons. The English invaders came slaughtering and burning, and the horrified Britons who escaped their axes and arrows fled westward, cursing the barbarous intruder. The British priest Gildas speaks with utter loathing of these blonde butchers, "hateful not only to man, but to God himself." Their souls were scarcely worth the saving. Four generations were born and buried before this horror died away, and intercourse between the peoples gradually obliterated differences of race.

Yet the Christian remnant of the Britons sent out one famous missionary, St. Patrick, who led in the conversion of the wild Irish Celts in the fifth century. From Ireland, which became the seat of an active Christian Church, missionaries lifted the Celtic cross in the heart of Europe, on the seacoast of Holland, and among those Picts who had once been the terror of the British Isles. St. Columba, the apostle of the Picts, founded a school and monastery on the Isle of Iona, which became a center of Christianity in North Britain.

The tradition is that a young priest was attracted by the faces of some fair-haired youths in the motley stock of the Roman slave market. "Who are these?" he asked of the dealer. "These are English—Angles," said the man. "What sweet faces! Surely not Angles, but angels!" (*non Angli, sed angeli*), exclaimed the pitying priest. "Whence come they?" "From Deira." "*De ira!*" was Gregory's Latin comment. "'From God's ire' verily they are snatched, and they shall come to know the mercy of Christ! Who rules in that land?" "Ælla." The young man passed on musing, and straightway vowed that "Alleluia" should be sung in Ælla's realm. Years after, when the young priest became Pope Gregory the Great, he kept his vow.

Kent was the threshold of Britain, and Ethelbert, its pagan king, had married a Christian princess, Bertha, daughter of a king of the Franks. She was permitted to worship the Christian's God in the royal town of Canterbury.[1] To her Pope Gregory commended his missionary Augustine (597 A. D.). Suspecting sorcery Ethelbert received the monks under the open sky. He accepted their doctrines and many of his court were baptized. Augustine was made archbishop of Canterbury and pushed the work with all zeal. Essex turned from Woden to Christ. Bishops were appointed for London and Rochester.

Edwin, king of Northumbria, was the next point of attack. He is the fifth Bretwalda of the old historians, though in his feeble boyhood it had seemed unlikely

---

[1] Augustine and his associates advanced in solemn procession to the momentous interview. A silver cross was carried before them; a richly adorned picture of Christ was borne after it; the monks followed, chanting a prayer. St. Martin's Church, Canterbury, known as "the Mother Church of England," still exists, though many times rebuilt. Here Queen Bertha worshiped; here Augustine was allowed to hold service; and in the old font the king himself was baptized.

that he would ever rule even the kingdom to which his birth entitled him.[1] Edinburgh, on the Forth, was "Edwin's burg," or fortress, in the North. His queen, Ethelburga, was the daughter of Ethelbert, Augustine's royal convert, and she, like Bertha, was allowed to worship her mother's God in this heathen court. Paulinus, the queen's chaplain, preached Christ to the king in his witenagemot, before his priests and lords. Said a noble[2]: *Paulinus.*

> So seems the life of man, O king: as a sparrow's flight through the hall when you are sitting at meat in winter-tide, with the warm fire lighted on the hearth, but the icy rainstorm without. The sparrow flies in at one door, and tarries for a moment in the light and heat of the hearth-fire, and then flying forth from the other vanishes into the winter darkness whence it came. So tarries for a moment the life of man in our sight, but what is before it, what after it, we know not. If this new teaching tells us aught certainly of these, let us follow it.

King and witan were won over to the Christian side, and the aged high-priest Coifi led the band which desecrated the heathen temple. Thus began the conversion of the Northumbrians. *Coifi.*

Mercia became the rallying ground of the adherents of the old faith, and King Penda its defender. With the aid of Cadwallon of Wales he made a fierce onslaught on the Christian states about him. Cadwallon was stopped by Oswald of Northumbria in the battle of *Penda leads the pagan reaction.*

---

[1] In his years of exile Prince Edwin, says the legend, was one day accosted by a stranger, who asked, "What reward will you give to him who shall deliver you from your troubles?" "He shall have my heartfelt gratitude," said the royal exile. "And what if he shall promise you power beyond that of any English king?" "I will give myself to him." "And if he tell of new doctrines of salvation will you give ear?" "I will," said Edwin. The stranger laid his hand on the prince's head and departed. Years after, when he had triumphed over his foes, the monk Paulinus, for he was the mysterious stranger, claimed the fulfilment of the pledge, and the king consented to give the Gospel a hearing.

[2] Green's "Short History of the English People."

"Heaven's field." The cross on Oswald's standard owed its origin to the Celtic monks of Iona. Oswald[1] owed his conversion to them and opened his kingdom to their missionary preachers, making Aidan its bishop, with his seat at Lindisfarne (the Holy Isle), near the mouth of the Tweed. Wherever Oswald carried his conquests he set up the cross. Wessex, already the preaching-ground of Gaulish monks, owned his overlordship, and its king accepted his Christ. In 655 the Mercians were conquered and the last hold of paganism fell.

The cross of Iona.

Lindisfarne.

Oswy and Penda.

From the landing of St. Augustine to the defeat and death of the pagan champion was scarcely sixty years. It was only in courts and towns and upon the cultivated few that the early preachers made their impression. The farmer on the moorland, the peasant in his hut, the miner, the shepherd, and the fisherman long lived in utter darkness until the self-sacrificing zeal of the monks brought the Gospel to their humble doors. The Abbey of Lindisfarne was the great northern school which trained many missionaries. Ceadda, or St. Chad (whose memory is still revered at Lichfield), was the evangel of middle England. St. Cuthbert[2] is the patron saint of the north countrymen. Melrose Abbey, in the Scottish Lowlands, was his mission station, whither he returned after long tours among the villagers. Himself a North-

St. Chad.

St. Cuthbert.

[1] "One day King Oswald was dining when word was brought that a throng of poor people was seeking alms at his gate. He commanded the viands to be taken untasted from the table and distributed to them, and breaking in pieces his great silver bowl he gave the fragments to the beggars. The monk Aidan, who sat near, seized the king's right hand and blessed it, saying, 'May the hand that has wrought this deed never decay!' When the limbs of Oswald, slain in battle, were impaled on stakes and exposed, this blessed hand, says the beautiful legend, was found uncorrupted."—*A. J. Church.*

[2] The cathedral church of Lichfield is dedicated to St. Chad. St. Cuthbert was one of Aidan's disciples, and, judging from the scant accounts of his life, another Wesley for his eagerness to instruct the common people in the truths of the Gospel. His remains were removed from Lindisfarne during the Danish raids and buried in the cathedral church of Durham, whose most precious relic they remain.

umbrian shepherd boy, he was nearer to the hearts and lives of his people than were Augustine's Romans or even the Irish monks of Iona and Lindisfarne, and his broadcast sowing brought a rich harvest.

The English Christians of the seventh century were not united. Each kingdom had its independent bishop and clergy. While the southeastern churches looked up to the Roman pope, as they had been taught by Augustine and his Canterbury monks, the North, into which had shined the clear light from Lindisfarne, acknowledged the supremacy of the Celtic Church, which St. Patrick had nurtured in Ireland and St. Columba had revived in Britain. The protracted isolation of the Irish and Roman branches had given rise to bitter differences. The controversy concerned only such slight matters as the date of Easter, form of tonsure,[1] and minor ceremonials, but while it lasted it was an evil, and King Oswy of Northumbria did well to bring it to an end. In 664 he summoned representatives from Iona and Canterbury to the monastery of Whitby, and bade each party to set forth its case. His decision for the Roman usages cleared the way for the unification of the English Church. Theodore, a Greek whom the pope consecrated archbishop of Canterbury (668), brought order and system into the religious establishment. His far-seeing eye laid off the English kingdoms into dioceses, each in charge of a bishop, each bishop subject to the primate or archbishop of Canterbury. (It was not until after Theodore's death that the northern dioceses were gathered into a second province under the primacy of the archbishop of York.) The wandering preachers gave place to local parish priests,

The Synod of Whitby.

Theodore of Tarsus, "Founder of the Church of England."

[1] The Roman tonsure (the mark of a priest) was a shaven circle on the crown of the head. The Celtic priests were required to shave all the hair in front of a line drawn over the top of the head from ear to ear.

and churches and chapels, monasteries and schools were multiplied. For eight hundred years the Church of England, the center of its education and literature, acknowledged the pope of Rome as its earthly ruler. The result was twofold: England was again linked to the Continent, whose nations were now all Catholic Christians, and the unification of the English Church prefigured and expedited the unification of the English kingdoms.

<small>Far-reaching results.</small>

The English conquests at Britain began in the middle of the fifth century (449 A. D.); they were substantially completed by the middle of the sixth, when three fifths of England was divided among seven superior and a half-dozen lesser Anglo-Saxon kingdoms. Then followed the successive rise of separate states to temporary preëminence. Oswy extended the supremacy of Northumbria over Cumbria (now Lancashire and Westmoreland), and then (685), in battle with the Picts, lost his life and his country's position. Although Northumbria was no longer chief among English states it was a leader in religious and literary development. Here was Lindisfarne, ever reappearing in early history; Whitby, the home of the poor cowherd Cædmon, the Anglo-Saxon poet, whose "Song of the Creation" is among the earliest trophies of English literature; Wearmouth, whence apostles of the Gospel did foreign mission work in Europe; and Jarrow, a sacred house famous for its monk Beda, "the Venerable Bede."[1] He was the most

<small>Northumbria.</small>

<small>Cædmon.</small>

<small>"The Venerable Bede."</small>

---

[1] Beda (Bede or Bæda), deservedly called "the Father of English History," was born about 673 at Monkwearmouth and spent his studious life in the monasteries there and at Jarrow, hard by. His marvelous industry mastered all the learning of his time, and the titles of his forty written works form a veritable encyclopedia. His "Ecclesiastical History" is the most valuable of his extant writings. He translated portions of the Bible out of priestly Latin into the language of the common people, and on his death-bed dictated an Anglo-Saxon version of St. John's Gospel. His remains once rested in Durham Cathedral, where his tombstone is still shown with the now lying inscription: *Hac sunt in fossa Bedæ venerabilis ossa.*

learned man of his time, versed in Greek, Latin, Hebrew, and his mother tongue, the Low German dialect of the Angles. The fruits of his study were many books, the most valuable to us being a Latin history of the English Church, the most dear to him and his countrymen being, doubtless, the Anglo-Saxon version of the Gospels, which employed his last hours.

Mercia, in the Midlands, awakened from heathenism to new life, and, still ruled by a prince of Penda's Woden-descended line, aimed to reach the high place from which Northumbria fell. Wessex, on the south coast, the kingdom which Cerdic founded, became the chief rival of Mercia. The lesser kingdoms bowed now to Mercian, now to West Saxon, overlordship. The former reached its culmination under King Offa (755–794). His weak successors were overmatched by King Egbert, the great West Saxon. In his youth Prince Egbert had been a fugitive from his native land and had sojourned for a time on the Continent at the court of the Frankish Karl (Charlemagne), whose power was reviving memories of imperial Rome. That splendid court, thronged with statesmen, warriors, and scholars, afforded brilliant training to the exile. In 802 Egbert won back his kingdom. By masterly ability he strengthened Wessex and subjected the adjoining states. The old title of Bretwalda was revived and bestowed upon him, but he was more powerful than any of his Mercian or Northumbrian predecessors, and fairly merits the title of "First King of the English." He was not the only king in England; the old Saxon kingdoms retained their petty monarchs—some were merely tributary to Egbert of Wessex, some were under his personal government; but now for the first time since Hengist and Horsa plunged through the surf to the beach at

Mercia and Wessex.

Egbert.

"First King of the English," 802–837.

Ebbsfleet all England was in some degree answerable to a single ruler.

TOPICS FOR READING AND SPECIAL STUDY.
WITH LIBRARY NOTES.

1. THE ENGLISH IN THEIR CONTINENTAL HOME.
    The Making of England. J. R. Green.
    Lectures to American Audiences. E. A. Freeman.
    Germanic Origins. F. B. Gummere.
2. THE MYTHOLOGY OF THE GERMANS.
    The Vikings in Western Europe. C. F. Keary.
    Teutonic Mythology. Rydberg.
3. LEGENDS OF KING ARTHUR.
    Le Morte D'Arthur. Sir Thomas Malory.
    Idylls of the King. Tennyson.
4. ANGLO-SAXON LANGUAGE AND CUSTOMS.
    History of Early English Literature. Stopford Brooke.
    Anglo-Saxon Britain. Grant Allen.
5. THE CONVERSION OF THE ENGLISH.
    Fathers of the English Church. Frances Phillips.

FICTION, ETC.

Imogen. Emily S. Holt.
The Early Dawn. Mrs. Charles.

CHAPTER IV.

The English and the Northmen, 837 A. D.–1066 A. D. — From the Supremacy of the West Saxons to the Norman Conquest.

Before the close of the eighth century the wild rovers from the forests and fiords of Northern Europe renewed their raids upon the nations of the South. The history of the ninth, tenth, and eleventh centuries runs strangely parallel with that of the third, fourth, and fifth. In the earlier period the Roman Empire was overrun by German barbarians; in the later era these German settlers, now civilized and Christianized, had in their turn to meet the heathen hordes from Scandinavia. The Englishmen who had mastered Roman Britain now met, and after a stout and protracted resistance yielded to the Danes. *Fresh advance of Northmen.*

It was in 787 A. D., according to the ancient chronicle, that the Northmen first landed in the island.[1] At first they seemed bent on plunder only, and the English treated them as pirates. These "vikings" (men of the *viks* or bays) came in long ships driven by oar and sail, and more skilfully handled than any vessels of the *Vikings.*

---

[1] The entry in the Saxon Chronicle under 787 is: "In these days there came for the first time three ships of the Northmen to the land of the Herethi [Dorsetshire?]. The king's lieutenant rode thither and would have made them come to the king's house, for he knew not who they were. But there was he slain. These were the first ships of the Danes that came into England." Several viking ships have been unearthed in modern times. One found in a mound at Gokstad, South Norway, in 1880 was seventy-eight feet long, pointed at both ends, had a mast and sixteen pairs of oars, and was ornamented with shields placed along the gunwale, thirty-two on each side. The owner had been buried in his vessel, and with him lay his weapons and the remains of twelve horses, six dogs, and a peacock.

South. Single chiefs at the head of swift squadrons swooped down upon unguarded harbors of Western Europe and escaped with their booty. Although the earlier Danes made no attempt at a conquest of England they soon seized upon outlying portions of the British Isles. The Orkneys, Shetlands, and Hebrides, with portions of the Scottish Highlands and a large part of Ireland, were made tributary to Danish princes, and the early glory of Ireland—her church and civilization—

Danish conquest of Ireland.

SHIPS OF THE NORTHMEN. From the Bayeux tapestry.

was lost in the confusion of wars with the heathen Northmen. At times the Danes allied themselves with the Welsh for a combined assault upon the English, and it was such a mixed force that Egbert, the great West Saxon, defeated in his famous fight at Hengesterdun (835) in Cornwall.

Hengesterdun.

The successors of Egbert could not maintain his grip upon the English kingdoms, and some of them had much ado to hold their own realm of Wessex against the downpour of Northmen. Their ships came almost yearly, and they were only beaten off with heavy loss. In 851 an armada of three hundred and fifty Danish vessels entered the Thames and burned the great

From foray to settlement.

trading town of London and the sacred city of Canterbury before King Ethelwolf could hurl them back to their ships. The monasteries of the North were favorite prey of these pagan pirates. The abbeys of Wearmouth and Lincoln, Ely, Peterborough, and Croyland were plundered and burned, and their pious inmates ruthlessly massacred. Soon the buccaneers changed their tactics and came with their wives and children to conquer and dwell in English lands. Their *sagas*, or traditions, preserved in Icelandic literature, are fanciful tales of these Norse heroes. In 866 they mastered the kingdoms of Northumbria and Mercia. To Edmund, the last king of East Anglia, they offered his freedom if he would bow the knee to Woden. He defied them, and was put to death by torture. His constancy won the admiration of his subjects, and in the lapse of years, when the pagans had given up their gods for the Gospel, a splendid abbey was built above the grave of "Saint" Edmund, the martyr king.[1] Elated with their triumphs, the lords of half Britain rushed upon Wessex. But they found their match at Ashdune (871), where King Ethelred, with his young brother, Alfred, beat them with great slaughter. The death of Ethelred in this same year brought Alfred, the last of Ethelwolf's sons, to the throne.

Plunder of the abbeys.

St. Edmund.

King Alfred, "the Great," was twenty-one years old when he faced the responsibility of defending and ruling his kingdom. There still exists a life of this English king, written by one who knew and loved him well. His grace and beauty made him the favorite in the

King Alfred.

---

[1] Edmund, having been defeated in battle, was pulled out of his hiding-place under a bridge. When he refused to abjure his Christianity the sea-wolves bound him to a tree and made him a target for their arrows before cutting off his head. The shrine erected over his remains at St. Edmundsbury two hundred years later by King Canute became one of the chief holy places of medieval England and the resort of many pilgrims.

group of young princes, and his father had further distinguished him by sending him to Rome, at five years of age, where Pope Leo IV. consecrated his flaxen head for the crown it should one day wear. The prince had a busy brain, a strong arm, a marvelous memory, and loved books as he did the chase. In the first year of his reign he fought one doubtful battle with his ever-returning enemies, and then enjoyed a few years of respite while they were strengthening their hold upon the northern kingdoms. In 876, however, the Danes beset Wessex in great force, and could neither be bribed nor expelled. Alfred, hard pressed, fled from his palace.[1] The freemen of the South rallied to the standard of the good king at Athelney, where he raised a fort among the marshes, and whence he sallied forth in the spring of 878 to successful battle. Guthrum, the Danish king, agreed to the peace of Wedmore and was baptized into the Christian faith. The peace saved Wessex, but recognized the Danish sovereignty of almost the whole of England north of the Thames valley, the territory called the Dane-law.

Peace of Wedmore.

The Dane-law.

The history of most of the early kings is either blank or crowded with battles. Alfred was as great in peace as in war, and greater in nothing than in the moral purpose which pervaded all his activity. "To live worthily" was his motto. He devised a more effective

The glory of Alfred.

[1] While a fugitive in the wilds of Somersetshire he entered the hut of a cowherd and sat by the hearth making ready his bow and arrows, heedless that the housewife's cakes were burning under his very nose. His neglect got him the famous scolding, "Why dost thou tarry to turn the cakes which thou seest burning, seeing how glad thou art to eat them when they are baked?" A priceless treasure of Oxford University is a golden bracelet curiously wrought, which may have belonged to the king. It bears the Anglo-Saxon legend, *Ælfred mek het gewircan* ("Alfred had me wrought"). Near Uffington in Berkshire is White Horse Hill, so called from a huge figure of a horse 370 feet long cut in the chalk-down. It is said to commemorate Alfred's victory over the Danes at Ashdune. It is graphically described in "Tom Brown's Schooldays," and Goldwin Smith says of it: "The most important monument of the Anglo-Saxons is really the White Horse. This is the trophy of a great victory gained by the Saxon over the Dane, by Christianity over heathendom. . . . It deserves homage more than any Arc de Triomphe."

military and naval system. From the law-codes of the several English kingdoms he selected the best laws for his own people. To the administration of justice in the law-courts he gave personal attention, reviewing the decisions of the aldermen and thanes who sat as judges, and enforcing their awards and penalties upon the more powerful offenders. The king took note of all the activities of his people; he invented a clock for marking time by the burning of candles; he improved their methods of building, and suggested new and better processes in the handicrafts. The ignorance that had drifted in upon the island with the coming of the Danes vexed him sorely, and he labored like a monk to shed abroad a little of learning's light.[1] The king himself translated into the Wessex dialect the histories and religious books of the venerable Bede, and Latin histories of Europe and works on natural history and travel. Scholars came from the Continent at his invitation to revive a taste for learning among the English, and the sons of his nobles were carefully educated under the royal eye. By him, or by his direction, the invaluable "English Chronicle," a yearly record of events on the island, was compiled from existing annals. Kind of heart, simple in tastes and manner, strong of will, was this first English hero, who died in the first year of the tenth century, and at the threshold of the twentieth it must be confessed that no English monarch has since surpassed him in his fitness to rule.

A promoter of learning.

The "English Chronicle."

Of Alfred's five children, only one, Edward the Elder, wore a crown; one daughter, Ethelfled, married Ethelred, alderman of Mercia, and another daughter became

Edward the Elder.

---

[1] Alfred says that when he came to the throne there was not a man in England south of the Thames who could translate from Latin into English. Among Alfred's translations into the vernacular were books on the duties of a Christian minister, a history of the world, Bede's church history, and Boethius's "Consolations of Philosophy."

Countess of Flanders and grandmother of Matilda, the wife of William the Conqueror. Edward ruled twenty-four years (901-925), and reaped the fruits of Wedmore peace. That treaty had saved Wessex from the Danes, and Alfred's military and administrative reforms had laid the foundations of a stronger government than any yet known in the island. Edward took the offensive, and with the aid of his sister Ethelfled, the "Lady of the Mercians," won back the greater part of the Dane-law. The Danes of this region had settled down beside the English, adopting their religion and fitting themselves easily to the English ways of life. The two races were of kindred ancestry and spoke closely related languages; neither had been influenced by contact with Roman civilization. The lasting hatred which kept Briton from Englishman was unknown between Saxons and Danes, whose Christian children, dwelling peaceably on adjacent farmsteads, forgot the burnings and massacres of their heathen fathers. Over this mixed people of the North Edward gained lordship. All Britain—English, Danish, Welsh, Scotch—was subject either to him or to sub-kings who acknowledged his superiority.

Ethelfled.

Edward's flaxen-haired son, Athelstan (925-940), worsted the Danish viking Anlaf in the battle of Brunanburgh,[1] the hardest yet fought on English

Athelstan

Brunanburgh.

[1] Anlaf's allies were Danes from Ireland (with six hundred ships), Constantine of Scotland, Owen of Cumberland, and other Celtic chieftains. The Saxon minstrels long celebrated the deeds of that day in such rugged lines as these:

"This year King Athelstan, the Lord of Earls,
Ring-giver to the warriors, Edmund too,
His brother, won in fight with edge of swords,
Life-long renown at Brunanburgh. The sons
Of Edward clave with the forged steel the wall
Of linden shields. The spirit of their sires
Made them defenders of the land, its wealth;
Its homes, in many a fight with many a foe,
Low lay the Scottish foes and death doomed lay
The shipmen; the field streamed with warrior's blood," etc.

ground. His notable reign helped to make the English kingdoms feel their community of interest, while it brought the royal family into new relations with the outer world. Hugh Capet, the founder of a long line of French kings, was his nephew, and Otto the Great, the German emperor, was his brother-in-law. To show his own independence of the empire, which then claimed sovereignty over Western Europe, the Saxon king called himself emperor (*imperator*) of Britain. This "emperor" had been Alfred's favorite grandchild, and in him was some of his grandsire's wisdom. He made it easier for the yeoman to obtain justice in the law-courts, and made provision to relieve the wants of the poor.

Links with continental dynasties.

An English emperor.

Athelstan's brothers, first Edmund and afterward Edred, succeeded him. The latter reduced the once powerful Danish kingdom of Northumbria to a subject earldom and called himself "King of the Anglo-Saxons and Emperor of Britain." He was guided in his policy of empire by Dunstan, a monk of Glastonbury, who was, so to speak, the first prime minister of England. By his counsel, doubtless, was arranged the impressive coronation scene when the two archbishops, representing the United Church of England, jointly placed the crown on Edred's head, while representatives of all the island races, British, Danes, and English, shouted approval. In the next reign the great abbot was in disgrace, but the revolution which brought Edgar to the throne (959) placed Dunstan again at the head of the council board. As archbishop of Canterbury he was the actual ruler. The conquered Danes were treated like Englishmen, and their best men held high rank in church and state, however much the Saxons growled at the primate's "preference for upstart aliens." A royal

Edmund and Edred.

Dunstan.

Edgar.

Foreign trade.

navy, manned by the descendants of the vikings, guarded the English coasts and protected English commerce in the Channel; for a lively trade had sprung up between London and the French and Flemish cities, the English metals and farm products finding ready exchange for their fine cloths and manufactures.

The monastic establishments.

ST. DUNSTAN AT THE FEET OF CHRIST.
From a drawing by Dunstan's own hand, in the Bodleian Library.

This intercourse with Europe bore fruit in the church also, and Benedictine monasteries, patterned upon those abroad, were founded in England. Monks, cut off from the world by their vows of poverty, chastity, and benevolence, devoted themselves to the works of the church. The monasteries acquired great tracts of land, whose tillage brought vast wealth. The monks were the only scholars, and their libraries and schools were the only sources of learning. Quarrels between the favored monks, of whom Dunstan was the champion, and the slighted parish priests alone ruffled the peace of the kingdom. The Welshmen paid yearly tribute of three hundred wolf scalps, so says an old story, until the supply failed. A crew of vassal kings, says another boasting Saxon, manned the barge

Edgar's crew of kings.

which King Edgar steered from his palace at Chester, on the river Dee, to the Church of St. John. The death of this "British Cæsar," in 975, plunged the prosperous realm into a wretched strife over a disputed succession.[1] Ethelred, a wavering lad nicknamed "the Unready,"[2] was eventually placed on the tottering throne.

Since Brunanburgh the Northmen had left troubling England and had built up in the mainland their three kingdoms of Norway, Sweden, and Denmark; but toward the close of the tenth century their fleets again crossed the shallow German Ocean, bent on adding England to their Scandinavian empire. The "redeless" Ethelred, lacking the spirit of his ancestors who had vanquished the same foes, levied a tax, the hated *Danegelt* (Dane money), upon his people to buy immunity. This tempted fresh incursions. Though the cowardly king declined to take the field, brave Englishmen, aldermen, and commoners, even bishops, fought in defense of their own homes. Lack of union made the resistance futile. The more the king paid for peace the more peace he had to buy. Thirteen times in eighteen years parties of Northmen ravaged the distracted island. On the thirteenth of November, 1002, the weak and rash king gave the signal for the massacre of all the Danes in England. Among the victims was a sister of Sweyn (Svend "Fork-Beard"), king of Denmark and Norway.

Burning for revenge, the powerful Dane gathered all

Ethelred the Unready.

Danegelt.

The massacre of St. Brice's Day.

---

[1] King Edgar left two sons, Edward, aged thirteen, and Ethelred, aged seven. Dunstan had the elder lad crowned, but after a few years the queen-mother Elgiva procured his assassination to make way for her little son Ethelred. Dunstan is said to have made this direful prophecy at the latter's coronation: "The sin of thy mother and of the men that conspired with her in her wicked deed shall not be washed out but with the blood of many; and there shall come upon the English people such evils as it has not suffered from the day that it came hither until now."

[2] *Redeless*, without *rede* or counsel.

62 *Twenty Centuries of English History.*

Conquest of England by Sweyn and Canute.

his resources for the chastisement of the English. The island was burned and harried as never before, the agony lasted for a dozen years, but by neither bribes nor alliance with the Norman-French duke, his most powerful neighbor, could Ethelred avert the doom he had precipitated. His son and successor, Edmund

Edmund "Ironside."

"Ironside" (1016), made a brief but valiant stand, but his death left the field to the Danes. Sweyn seems not to have been crowned, but his worthy son Canute[1]

CANUTE AND HIS QUEEN.

(Cnut), was recognized as the king of England, as well as of Denmark, Norway, and part of Sweden. He strove to be an English king. No distinction was made between the Dane and English in the land. He enriched and strengthened

Canute's reforms.

the church, although it had been the center of the national resistance, and he honored Edmund, the martyr-

[1] THE DANISH KINGS OF ENGLAND.

SWEYN (Svend "Fork-Beard"),
d. 1014.
|
CANUTE (Cnut) — Emma of Normandy,
r. 1017–1035. | widow of Ethelred.
|

| Sweyn. | HAROLD I., r. 1035–1040. | HARDICANUTE, r. 1040–1042. |

king, by dedicating to his memory the shrine of St. Edmundsbury. "The laws of Edgar," as the people called the system of government which Dunstan had established in the reign of that good king, were restored.¹ For better government, he divided the English realm into four powerful earldoms: Wessex, Mercia,² East Anglia, and Northumberland.

<small>Four English earldoms.</small>

After Canute's death (1035) the great earls took advantage of the quarrels of his sons to increase their power. Godwin, Earl of Wessex, who became the principal man of the kingdom, eventually raised to the throne Edward, the weak son of Ethelred. This prince had been reared among the Normans, and he surrounded himself with foreign courtiers.

<small>An English king out of Normandy.</small>

---

¹ After Canute's pilgrimage to Rome in 1027 he addressed a pious letter to the English bishops, nobles, and nation, in which he declared his vow "to God himself to reform my life in all things, and justly and piously to govern, . . . determined through God's assistance to set right anything hitherto unjustly done," etc. The fruits of this "conversion" were seen in legislation, (1) reforming the administration of justice, (2) prohibiting the sale of Christians into slavery abroad, (3) forbidding paganism, and aiming to suppress its relics of superstition and witchcraft, (4) ameliorating the tax-levies and game-laws. For an interesting description of his religious foundation in honor of St. Edmund see Carlyle's "Past and Present."

The well-known story of Canute and the ocean was first told by Henry of Huntingdon, from whom A. J. Church makes this version: "In the very height of his power, he bade set his chair on the shore of the sea, when the tide was flowing, and to the tide he said, 'Thou art my subject, and the land on which I sit is mine, nor hath there ever been one that resisted my bidding, and suffered not. I command thee therefore that thou come not up on my land nor presume to wet the garments and limbs of thy lord.' But the sea, rising after its wont, wetted without respect the feet and legs of the king. Therefore leaping back he said, 'Let all dwellers on the earth know that the power of kings is a vain and foolish thing, and that no one is worthy to bear the name of king save only Him whose bidding the heavens and the earth and the sea obey.' Nor ever thereafter did King Canute set his crown of gold upon his head, but put it forever on the image of our Lord, which was nailed to the cross."

² Of Godiva (Godgifu), wife of Earl Leofric of Mercia, the tale is told that when she begged her husband to remit an oppressive tax he made the condition that she should ride naked through the town of Coventry at noon. She complied, taking care to have all doors and windows closed, and all citizens indoors.

"And one low churl compact of thankless earth
The fatal byword of all years to come,
Boring a little auger-hole, in fear
Peeped—but his eyes, before they had their will,
Were shrivell'd into darkness in his head,
And dropt before him. So the Powers who wait
On noble deeds cancell'd a sense misused,
And she, that knew not, passed."
— *Tennyson's Godiva.*

Earl Godwin: "England for the English!"

Earl Godwin became the leader of a strong party whose rallying cry was "England for the English!" He exercised great influence at court, married his daughter to the king, and secured earldoms for his nearest of kin. Once his Norman rivals supplanted him in the king's favor, but he lived to see their expulsion and his own son Harold directing the affairs of the realms.

Earl Harold of Wessex.

Earl Harold, Godwin's son, combined the statesmanship of his father with a military talent of his own. While Edward was busy with his chaplains founding churches and monasteries—the Abbey of Westminster[1] among them—Harold fortified his own position by giving earldoms to his brothers and leading the English armies. That he was the actual ruler of England did not escape the ambitious Duke William of Normandy, who kept keen watch from his neighboring duchy. In 1064 Earl Harold, with his vessel, was cast by mischance upon the French coast and became William's enforced guest. William afterward declared that Harold had then sworn to support his claim to the English crown at Edward's death. It is said that the duke outwitted the earl by smuggling sacred relics under the table on which the oath was taken, so as to increase the sanctity of the agreement.

Harold's promise to William.

Edward died in 1066. The priests, his friends—and biographers—mindful of his benefactions, have called him "St. Edward" and "The Confessor." He left no son. Of the direct line of Cerdic only Edgar, a stripling, and Margaret, a girl, survived. William of

---

[1] The abbey church was built in the Norman style on the site of a humble Saxon church which had suffered at the hands of the Danes. It was completed about 1065, and with few exceptions the English sovereigns since Edward have been crowned within its walls. It has been several times rebuilt, but parts of the original fabric remain in the pyx-house, the substructure of the dormitory, and "the Dark Cloister," so called. See Stanley's "Historical Memorials of Westminster Abbey."

The English and the Northmen.

Normandy claimed the crown by right of his mother's blood, Edward's pretended promise, and Harold's extorted oath. Harold had the advantage of being on the scene. The dying king seemed to designate him for the throne, though predicting for him a brief and doleful reign. The council recognized in him a strong man who might cope with the difficulties of the realm. So Earl Harold, "the last of the Saxons," was chosen king of England, and crowned in the new abbey church of Westminster.

Harold's reign fulfilled St. Edward's direst prophecies. Two mighty foes gathered to crush him. His own brother, Tostig, leagued with the king of Norway, the adventurous Harold Hardrada,[1] for the reconquest of England. The Norse fleet with the Scotch and Irish allies entered the Humber, to be routed at Stamford Bridge in Yorkshire by the English Harold.

Harold, king of the English.

The Northmen defeated at Stamford Bridge.

The most stubborn foe was yet to face. William the Norman, claiming the throne by right of inheritance and pledge, branding Harold as perjurer and usurper, spurring the Normans to avenge Godwin's insults, and possessing Pope Alexander's blessing as a missionary to the corrupted English Church—uniting conflicting parties by these specious claims—had gathered an army and crossed to Pevensey on the south coast.[2] King Harold returned in haste from Stamford to meet him. William's motley array of fortune-seekers picked up

The Norman invasion.

[1] Harold Hardrada ("stern in counsel") was one of the greatest of Norse kings. A seeker of adventure from early youth, he had lived at the Russian court, had commanded the viking life-guards of the eastern emperor at Constantinople, had visited Jerusalem and the Mediterranean countries, and after a most romantic history had come to the throne of his ancestors, the kings of Norway. He was a giant in stature, and the English Harold is said to have replied to his demand for the surrender of England that "he might have of English soil six feet—yea, seven—for a grave." He was killed at Stamford Bridge, with the greater part of his men.

[2] William's fleet consisted of single-masted, undecked vessels, of about thirty tons burden. His own ship, the *Mora*, had for a figure-head a golden boy, his right index-finger pointing toward England, his left hand pressing a horn to his lips.

The battle of Hastings (Senlac).

from all France and half Europe attacked the English position on Senlac Hill, near Hastings, on October 14, 1066. Much was against the Normans. Their leader had encouraged them with the pope's blessing, but on landing he had stumbled and fallen on his face. Rising, his hands full of sand, he cried to his horrified attendants, "See! by the splendor of God, the English soil is already in my grasp." In the desperate charges upon the English yeomen his courage, audacity, and constancy were everywhere apparent. "The duke is dead," cried a hard-pressed battalion. "I live!"

WILLIAM SAILING TO ENGLAND. From the Bayeux tapestry.

William the Conqueror.

cried William, lifting the visor of his helmet, "and by God's help I will conquer." Conquer he did. Harold and his body-guard stood by the golden dragon banner of Wessex all day long, until near sunset a shaft from a Frenchman's bow pierced the king's eye and he fell.[1] His English died around him, and that night William, the Norman duke, who ate and drank and slept on the

---

[1] The beach where the Conqueror landed is now a cultivated field. "The castle on the cliff at Hastings marks the spot where he first planted his standard. The ruins of Battle Abbey, the religious trophy of the Conqueror, are still seen and the site of the high altar exactly marks the spot where the fatal arrow entering Harold's brain slew not only a king, but a kingdom, and marred the destiny of a race."—*Goldwin Smith.* Legends say that Harold's body was found on the field by "Edith of the Swan-neck," a former favorite. It was first buried under a cairn on the cliff at Hastings, and afterward removed to a tomb in the Abbey of Waltham, which he had built.

field among the slain, was the real master of England.

The witan named as Harold's successor a young son of Edmund Ironside, but there was no iron in his composition, and he and his English adherents soon begged the duke to take the crown, as Harold's rightful successor. On Christmas Day, 1066, the archbishop of Canterbury set the crown upon the head of William the Conqueror. *William crowned.*

TOPICS FOR READING AND SPECIAL STUDY, WITH LIBRARY NOTES.

1. THE VIKINGS.
    The Viking Age. Paul du Chaillu.
    Norway. H. H. Boyesen. (Story of the Nations Series.)
    The Making of England. J. R. Green.
    The Vikings in Western Christendom. C. F. Keary.
2. ALFRED THE GREAT AND HIS TIMES.
    Alfred the Great. Thomas Hughes.
    Early Britain. A. J. Church. (Story of the Nations Series.)
    Social England. Part I. H. D. Traill.
3. THE LAST OF THE EARLY ENGLISH KINGS.
    The Norman Conquest. E. A. Freeman.
4. THE BATTLE OF HASTINGS.
    The Fifteen Decisive Battles of the World. Creasy.
    The Normans. S. O. Jewett. (Story of the Nations Series.)

FICTION, ETC.
Harold. Tennyson. (Drama.)
Harold. Bulwer. (Novel.)

CHAPTER V.

THE NORMAN KINGS, 1066 A. D.–1135 A. D.—FROM THE ACCESSION OF WILLIAM I. TO THE DEATH OF HENRY I.

The founding of the Norman duchy.

THE conqueror and his followers were themselves of northern blood, only a few generations removed from paganism. The viking Rollo had ravaged the banks of the Seine until Charles the Simple, king of the French, had been forced to grant to him the lands about the mouth of that river (912). In return for this territory Rollo gave up his wild life, acknowledged the sovereignty of Charles, wedded a princess, and settled down to enlarge the province he had secured. These Northmen, or "Normans," soon adopted the religion, manners, and language of the country. Under Rollo's descendants Normandy became one of the most powerful of the several dukedoms which made up the French kingdom.

William of Normandy.

William,[1] who succeeded to the ducal coronet in 1035, was the seventh ruler in direct line from the viking Rollo. A boy with a manful spirit, he had hewn his way through appalling obstacles to the chief place among the nobles of France. As an iron duke he had hammered his own turbulent barons into a sem-

---

[1] William's mother was a tanner's daughter. When he was seven years old (1035) his father, Duke Robert, setting out on a pilgrimage to the Holy Sepulcher, compelled his nobles to recognize the boy as his heir. During his minority they murdered his guardians, attempted his life, fortified their castles, and tried to establish their independence. At twenty, with the help of the king of France, he waged war on them and made himself their master. After a stormy courtship he married (1051) Matilda of Flanders, a descendant of Alfred the Great of England.

blance of order. Indomitable will and great political sagacity fitted this man above all others to undertake with a few raw troops the conquest and government of England.

The battle of Hastings did not complete the conquest, neither did the surrender of Edgar, the English prince, and the coronation of William firmly establish the Norman system. Yet the king dared to leave his new-won kingdom and hasten over to Normandy, where the Duchess Matilda ruled the barons as regent. To his brother Odo, bishop of Bayeux,[1] and his friend, William Fitz Osborn, he entrusted England in his absence. The king's policy was to treat the English as his legal subjects, not as a conquered people. By his own assertion he was the true successor of Edward. By the same reasoning Harold's followers were traitors to their rightful king, and their possessions were forfeited. These lands and houses William granted to the Normans, "who had come in with the Conqueror." His brother Odo and Fitz Osborn lacked the breadth of their master's views, and no sooner was his back turned than they began to persecute the unhappy English for their own advantage. Money, lands, and houses were wrung from the wealthy without distinction of guilt or innocence. Such tyranny aroused the slumbering spirit of resistance. Only a fragment of England had followed Harold at Hastings. The people of the northern earldoms cared little if a Norman should take from the Earl of Wessex the crown which his ambition had usurped. There was no such national feeling for Godwin's son as still survived for Ethelred's children, Edgar and the

The Conqueror's national policy.

Odo and Fitz Osborn.

---
[1] In the town-house of Bayeux in Normandy is preserved a strip of linen two hundred feet long by twenty inches wide, on which are worked in colored worsteds fifty-eight scenes from the life of William the Conqueror, including the voyage to England and the victory. This celebrated "Bayeux tapestry" is said to have been wrought by the Duchess Matilda herself.

Princess Margaret, now the wife of Malcolm, king of Scots. But these new tyrannies touched the life of the people. Every Englishman of wealth was liable to suffer at the hands of the Normans. The signal of revolt went through the island. The earls of the North rose, relying upon the promised aid of a Danish fleet. Malcolm of Scotland added his support. The western rebels found allies in the Welsh. In the eastern fenlands, upon the borders of the Norman territory, the outlaw Hereward, "the last of the English," held the isle of Ely with desperate valor. William returned to face the tempest. The Danes, the mainstay of the insurrection, he bribed into inaction. He succeeded in isolating the other centers of rebellion and crushing them severally. The king of the Scots was forced to admit William as his overlord, and Northumbria was reduced to a desert.

Rising of the English.

Hereward.

The Conqueror, having broken the spirit of the English, next applied himself to the government of his new realm. Local self-government was the basal principle of the political system which he found in England. The free people of a village met together to settle for themselves all minor political matters and to decide suits at law. The same system was applied to groups or "hundreds" of these villages; and a number of "hundreds" formed the shire or county, with its shire-moot, or court, where representatives of the "hundreds" met to hear appeals from the lower courts. The officers of this shire-court were the alderman, bishop, and "shire-reeve," or sheriff. The alderman was the representative of the nation, a sort of lord-lieutenant; the reeve was the king's personal officer, and the bishop attended to points of church law. The judges, or rather the jurymen, were the freemen assembled in the court.

The English political system.

Town-meetings.

If a convicted man appealed from the judgment of the hundred-court to the men of the shire he might take the "ordeal," or judgment of God, proving his innocence by walking unshod over hot iron or eating of poisoned cakes.[1] In general the accused brought "compurgators," men who swore to his innocence and general character for good. The "compurgators," or oaths-men, of the plaintiff swore to the contrary, and the assembly of freemen compared the weight, not of evidence, but of the two parties of compurgators. In early times "an earl's word balanced six common churls [freemen] and one alderman's testimony outweighed a township's oath." Punishment was commonly by fines, paid not to the state, but to the injured party. Above the shires of England was the king, and to him in his council of great men—the witenagemot—the man might appeal from the judgment of the lower court. The royal power was, however, ill-defined. Through many changes it had grown to its full proportions under such ambitious rulers as Canute and Harold. These later sovereigns were kings of England as well as chieftains of its people. The public land—once the common possession of the whole folk—had come to be considered the private property of the monarch, and he might dispose of it at will, the witan assenting. Those who received land from him, and many who received none, became his thanes or vassals, owing him service. The greater thanes he summoned to his witenagemot with the abbots and bishops. With this body he made laws, laid taxes, deliberated on peace and war, and appointed

Ordeals.

Judicial matters.

The royal power.

Thanes.

---

[1] Queen Emma, the mother of Edward the Confessor, having been accused of a crime, purged herself of the guilt by treading barefoot and unhurt upon nine glowing plowshares. In memory of the deliverance she bestowed nine manors upon a church. The theory of the ordeal was that God would perform a miracle to save the innocent from harm. It existed in many forms among Teutonic people, and is still practiced by barbarous African tribes as a test of witchcraft.

the officers of state. The system of thaneship extended throughout society, the smaller landowners and even landless freemen agreeing to do service to an overlord or thane in return for his protection. Some of these thanes seem to have acquired authority as magistrates to try lawsuits between their dependents or in the towns ("burgs" or "boroughs") which sprang up on their lands. Again, certain towns had purchased from their overlord, or from the king, the privilege of holding their own courts, subordinate to the shire-moot, but of equal authority with the assembly of the hundred. To this brief statement it should be added that the English shires were allotted among four earldoms—the four powerful earls being chosen by king and council from among the royal thanes.

The feudal system.

In Normandy the feudal system was carried to its full extent. The king of France was, in theory at least, lord of all the land, and every man who held a foot of soil rendered military service for his fief as vassal to some overlord. The dukes held their duchies directly from the king, and so long as they paid the stipulated services they were supreme in their own dominions. These domains were similarly subdivided. The duke—himself a tenant of the king—granted his lands to barons, or lesser vassals, on similar terms of faithful service.

Landlord and tenant.

The tenants of the barons also did service for the estates they held. In each case, from duke to smallest farmer, the same ceremonies and terms prevailed. The land held was the "feudum," or "fief"; the vassal, or "man," swore fealty (fidelity) and did homage, placing his bare head in his lord's hands, and on bended knee vowing to become "his man" through all perils. This was "feudal tenure," and property thus held passed, with the attendant obligations and privileges, from father to son.

In France this land and social system was also a means of government. For with the land the king granted jurisdiction over its inhabitants, and duke and baron each held his own manorial court, in which the lawsuits of his dependents were tried. Each tenant of the king was bound to contribute a certain number of armed men to the royal army; and these soldiers of the dukes and barons were frequently employed in private wars, one baron against another. The whole system imperiled national unity, for the king himself, when standing alone, had less power than any one of a half-dozen of his proudest vassals. It was by feudal tenure that Duke William held Normandy from the king of France, and by the same system his quarrelsome barons held of him. We shall see how he and his successors combined the old Saxon system with French feudalism. *Manorial courts.*

When the English landowners who fought for Harold were declared guilty of treason their lands reverted to the crown. The rebellions against the Conqueror resulted in the confiscation of nearly all the remaining English estates. With these William founded his feudal system—granting them on feudal terms to the Normans of his train. For a hundred years not an English name appears in the list of barons. He did not transfer the continental system to the island unchanged. The semi-independence of the four great English earldoms which he had encountered warned him against granting too extensive fiefs. Instead of four earldoms he created nearly forty—an earl to a shire—and where he would show especial honor by granting him extraordinary possessions he took care that the lands of any one man should be well distributed over England. Warned likewise by the continual wars of his own barons in Normandy, he exacted from all freemen, at a meeting at *William combines the Norman and English feudalism.*

Salisbury (1086), the oath of allegiance to himself as sovereign, thus making it treason for any to obey his lord contrary to the king. William thus became the real head of the English people, not simply the feudal sovereign of a few great barons—his "tenants-in-chief." He further laid his hand upon the acts of the people by defining the sheriff's duties, and making him the officer who attended to the king's fees and revenues in the county courts. While he gave to the barons jurisdiction over their tenants, it was provided that appeal should run from the baron to the hundred-court and to the king. The old village courts were left intact, trial by battle[1] for Norman offenders being added to the usual ordeals. In place of the Saxon assembly of wise men (witenagemot) William gathered about him a great council of his feudal barons, who now superseded the English thanes. In this also sat the high officials of the church, and a committee of this body, called the *curia regis* (court or senate of the king), acted as a high court of appeals. The Anglo-Norman system, therefore, was feudal in its tenure of land, but English in its recognition of local self-government. Through it all stretched the strong arm of the king, exacting taxes from noble and commoner alike—all classes alike doing him homage and owing him service.

Socially the Conquest transformed England. At the head of society stood the king and his Norman barons—proud of their possessions on both sides of the Channel, despising as barbarous the common Englishmen and their Anglo-Saxon tongue. French was the spoken

---

[1] This was in fact a legal duel in which the innocence or guilt of the accused person was "proven" by a free and fair combat. An accused lord often sent one of his men to fight in his stead, and "priests and women were ordinarily represented by champions." This method of trial was invoked as late as 1818 to save a murderer's life. The other ordeals were abolished by law in the reign of Henry III.

language of the conquerors, though the lawyers and priests wrote a degenerate Latin. The English thanes disappeared after the early rebellions, being deprived of their lands, and so pressed down into a lower social grade. The middle-class Englishmen, dwellers in towns and coming into frequent contact with the foreigners, soon met them on equal terms in trade and society. The lowest class, the serfs and slaves, suffered little from the change of masters, and clung persistently to the language and manners of the Anglo-Saxons.

The Conquest gave new political power to the church. The Conqueror entrusted the primacy to Lanfranc,[1] the most learned abbot of Normandy. The reigning pope, Gregory VII., the celebrated Hildebrand, was bent on compelling all Christian monarchs to acknowledge the headship of the papacy in things temporal as well as spiritual. This William swore he would not do. "Peter's Pence" he would faithfully pay, but homage for England's crown he owed no man. He willingly forbade the priests to marry, and allowed Lanfranc to engraft the strict rules of the continental monasteries upon the lax religious establishments of the island. Bishops' courts were set up in each shire to decide offenses against morals or religion. But he ordered that without his royal leave no pope should be acknowledged in England, no papal bull be read, no bishop appeal to Rome, and no royal tenant be excommuni-

Lanfranc.

Pope and Conqueror.

---

[1] Lanfranc was a Lombard, born and educated in Northern Italy. He settled in Normandy as a schoolmaster and was nearly forty years of age before he became a monk. His talents soon made him prior of the monastery of Bec, where his school numbered some of the most celebrated men of the age. For opposing the duke's purpose he was ordered to quit the duchy, but on the road he fell in with William himself, and got into his good graces. He was the Conqueror's chief adviser in all matters relating to the reorganization of the English Church. A fragment of the Canterbury Cathedral, as rebuilt by him, is still visible.

cated. Thus William thwarted Hildebrand's[1] scheme of including England in his universal empire, and thus the trenches were dug for the foundations of an English national church free from papal domination.

Hildebrand baffled.

Not all of these changes were completed in William's reign, but the beginnings of most of them are found there, though their course of development runs through more than a century. In his own lifetime the king's hands were full. The barons of England were galled by his yoke. In Normandy they had been almost independent of their duke, but the modified feudalism of England placed them directly under the sovereign's control. He had hardly checked their revolt when a fresh trouble summoned him across the Channel. His paternal duchy he had promised to his son Robert in case the attempt on England proved successful. But the king repudiated the promises of the duke. "I shall not strip till I go to bed!" was the answer he flung at his reproachful son. The breach of faith cost him a long war with Robert's partisans.

The Barons' Revolt.

Robert's insurrection.

It was in these years that a great assembly on Salisbury Plain ordered every free man to swear direct and immediate allegiance to the king as his own sovereign. The "Domesday Book" dates from this period. It was compiled "(1) to give a basis for taxation; (2) to serve as an authority by which all disputed land-titles might be settled; and (3) to be a census and muster-roll of the nation." At the royal command census-takers went to the head men in every shire, borough,

"Domesday Book."

---

[1] Hildebrand (Gregory VII.), the greatest of the popes (1073-1085), made the holy see independent of emperors and kings, and made all ecclesiastics, from the humblest parish priests to the proudest archbishops, accept the supremacy of Rome. Before his time the popes had been dependent upon the German emperor, and the patronage of the church in every country had been in the hands of the temporal ruler. His plan, which he failed to realize to its fullest extent, would have made the Roman pontiff the supreme ruler of Christendom, temporal as well as spiritual.

parish, and manor and asked these questions: "What is the name of your township? Who was lord thereof, bishop, or abbot in the reign of Good King Edward? How many thanes, how many freemen, and how many serfs are there? How many acres and what were they worth in the Confessor's days? What property has each freeman?" etc. The answers were collected by the royal clerks and written down in the book called "Domesday,"[1] which still exists, an invaluable exhibit of the condition of the kingdom of England in the year of our Lord 1086.

The Conqueror's end was at hand. While besieging a French town in 1087 a fire-brand from a blazing building caused William's horse to swerve, throwing his corpulent rider heavily upon the pommel of his saddle. At Rouen the Conqueror breathed his last. Many prayers and much confession came from his thick lips in the closing hours. His eldest son Robert was assuredly to have the Norman inheritance; England he had wrongfully conquered he confessed, but he hoped God would permit his second son William to rule there; for Henry, the scholarly son, there was a certain treasure of five thousand silver pounds; the remainder of his goods the priests and monks should have for the poor and the church. So he died, deploring his wicked deeds and boasting of his benefactions. His sons hastened from his bedside to secure their inheritance, and the monarch's remains were thrust

Death of William.

---

[1] "Domesday," or "Domesday Book," is the popular name for several volumes containing the record. "The first volume is a large folio written in double columns on 382 double pages of vellum in a small, clear character. The second volume is in quarto on 450 double pages of vellum, single column, in a large, fair hand. The survey was so minute, says a contemporary, 'that there was not a single hide or yardland, not an ox, cow, or hog that was not set down.'" The accuracy of the record made the book the test of all disputed land-titles. In popular phrase, its sentence was as authoritative as the day of judgment (doomsday), hence its famous name. The original manuscript is preserved in good condition in the Public Record Office in London.

into a humble grave in the Norman church of Caen.
William Rufus (the Red) made straight for England.
Lanfranc pronounced for him and the assembly of
nobles was prevailed upon to name him as king. The
barons who held estates on both sides of the Channel
were restless under a divided sovereignty. In Normandy they did as they pleased with the visionary Robert, but in England they had to deal with a choleric and
tyrannical master. The Red King was bold, prompt,
and fearless. He lacked his father's self-control, and
for the Conqueror's moderation exchanged a reckless
extravagance and profligacy.

William Rufus, 1087-1100.

His ambitious uncle Odo, whom the Conqueror had
imprisoned, now conspired with the barons to place
Robert in the Red King's seat. William rallied the
old English element against this project, and with an
English army he quelled the earlier outbreak and a later
plot which sought to crown his cousin Stephen.

Three parties divided the England of those days—the
king, a foreigner; his barons, rich and powerful, but
rebellious against the overshadowing authority of their
sovereign; and the mass of the common people. The
impact of these forces struck out the spark of English
liberty. A king hard-pressed by his barons would yield
concessions to his people in return for their assistance,
and the barons, tyrannized by the king, would unite
with the people to force the king to terms. By such
indirect means the cause of English freedom was advanced.

Three parties.

The king's wild way of life soon dissipated the treasure in the Conqueror's coffers, and his ministers were
required to swell the revenue. They had recourse to a
new form of tyranny. The English Church owned a
large share—some say one fifth—of all the landed prop-

erty in England. Bishops and abbots were feudal princes like the secular barons, and did military service for their lands. As they were unmarried monks their estates were not hereditary, and vacancies caused by death or removal were filled by the king. Prompted by Bishop Ranulf of Durham, he now allowed vacant abbacies and bishoprics to go unfilled for years together, their revenues meanwhile being converted to his own purse. In this way the highest offices in the church lay vacant. Even the see of Canterbury had no head for four years after Lanfranc's decease. But an illness, which dragged William to death's door in 1093, seemed to his superstitious mind a judgment for his wickedness, and he compelled Anselm,[1] abbot of Bec, in Normandy, to become archbishop. This Anselm was a worthy successor of his friend Lanfranc. But their ways were not the same. Both were high-minded men, profoundly learned, and devoted to the Christian Church; but Lanfranc was a man of the world as well as of the cloister, and could lead and control the rough, unlearned Norman nobles as well as gentle scholars. Anselm's world was one of books and meditation, and lay far from that of the headstrong William, whose recovered strength was put to its first use in a close-locked struggle with the quiet but unflinching monk. The question at issue was the supremacy of king or pope, and Anselm ranked the pope's authority above the monarch's. After four years of obstinate debate the archbishop withdrew to Rome and William greedily pounced upon the rich revenues of Canterbury. Neither side gained a victory, but the noble example of a single freeman resisting the

Plundering the church.

Anselm.

Church against crown.

[1] St. Anselm (he was canonized about 1494) was an Italian who had drifted into Normandy, and coming within Lanfranc's influence had become a monk. He was one of the earliest and ablest philosophers and theologians of the Middle Ages, and a gentle, kindly, high-minded churchman.

encroachments of a king was not lost upon the nation, which had some questions of the same kind accumulating for settlement at no distant day.

Duke Robert mortgages Normandy.

William Rufus had agreed with his brother Robert that on the death of either the dominions of both should be united under the survivor. In 1096, however, the duke joined in the first crusade. To equip his quota for the expedition to Palestine he borrowed £6,666 of his brother William's ill-gotten gains, pledging his duchy of Normandy in payment of the loan. While the duke was absent the king made friends of the Norman nobles, and secured a firm hold upon the duchy.

THE WHITE TOWER (TOWER OF LONDON).

At home the king's acts of oppression multiplied. "Never day dawned," says one gloomy historian, "but he rose a worse man than he had lain down; never sun set but he lay down a worse man than he had risen." Yet William the Red was no savage. The castles and churches that he built are noble structures, as he may testify who has looked upon the ancient portions of the Tower of London and Westminster Hall.[1]

The Tower of London.

[1] In every large town the Normans built castles to overawe the inhabitants. The Tower of London was such a fortress, built by Gundulf, bishop of Rochester, for the Conqueror himself, and remains a splendid example of Norman military architecture. Westminster Hall, "the great hall of William Rufus," as Macaulay terms it, was rebuilt three centuries after the death of the Red King. It now forms an entrance hall to the Houses of Parliament.

The Conqueror "did heartily love the tall deer," said a writer of his time. The chase was his chief sport, and in Hampshire he cleared the tenants from a vast range of farm-lands and woodlands to make the deer park, which still retains its first name, "the New Forest."¹ *The accursed forest.*

The evicted English cursed the king for his cruelty in taking their lands, as well as for the cruel forest laws, by which he kept the game for his private pleasure, and they predicted that the New Forest would be fatal to his line. But William Rufus feared nothing. He was a mighty hunter, and often rode with his bowmen after the deer-hounds. One day, when he had ridden afield flushed with wine, the forest curse fell upon him. His huntsmen found him dead under a tree with an arrow in his breast. No one knows whose bowstring drove the arrow to its mark. Dying unshriven, he was buried without Christian services at Winchester, the old West Saxon capital, and even after his dishonored body rested in the earth the tower of the abbey church above it fell in ruins, betokening, so wagged the English tongues, God's righteous wrath. *Death of the Red King.*

Prince Henry himself was of that merry hunting party, and when they told him of his childless brother's death he spurred his horse to Winchester, seized the royal treasure, and demanded the crown. By the old agreement his elder brother Robert was the rightful successor, but Robert was far away. Promptness gained the day, and in the words of his proclamation, "by God's mercy and the common counsel of the barons of *Henry I., 1100-1135.*

---

¹ The ancient chronicle says of "New Forest" and the Conqueror's passion for the chase: "He planted a great preserve for deer, and he laid down laws therewith, that whosoever should slay hart or hind should be blinded. As greatly did he love the tall deer as if he were their father. His great men bewailed it, and the poor men murmured thereat; but he was so obdurate that he recked not of the hatred of them all, but they must wholly follow the king's will, if they would live or have land or property, or even his peace." The New Forest, which was made at the cost of so much hardship, still covers a tract of over one hundred square miles near Southampton.

Charter.

the whole realm of England," he was crowned king. The Red King's rule had been so hateful and his own title was so doubtful that the new king was forced to bid high for popularity. A paper, or "charter," was granted by the monarch to the nation. He pacified the barons by releasing them from many of the feudal assessments on their manors; better laws —those of the venerated Edward the Confessor — were provided for the common people, and the church was promised immunity from the depredations of the preceding reign. As an earnest of good intentions, the king

GREAT SEAL OF HENRY I.

recalled Archbishop Anselm from Rome, and, himself a native of England, he took to wife the Saxon princess Edith, henceforth called Matilda, the daughter of the king of Scots and great-grandchild of Edmund Ironside. His partiality for the islanders was such that the Normans, taunting him with "Anglomania," nicknamed the royal pair "Goodrich and Godiva." Henry I.'s surname, "Beauclerc" (the Scholar), was not won by any marvelous achievements in learning, but by the contrast between his tastes and those of his father. Until his coronation Henry had lived a life of pleasure on his estates in Normandy; but throughout his reign he exhibited the force and wisdom of his race. Order was his first law, and he cared less for fresh conquests than for the submission of his father's subjects to his own undisputed will.

Beauclerc."

The Norman Kings.

In 1101 Duke Robert invaded the island, claiming his inheritance, and many barons did him homage and led their retainers to his camp; but Henry, supported as William had been by an English army, and wielding a powerful weapon in Anselm's threat of excommunication against the rebels, bought peace. Robert gave up England, and kept Normandy, receiving a yearly payment from the king. The peace was brief. Henry's vengeance pursued the rebel barons across the Channel and took his brother captive, making himself master of all the Conqueror's dominions.

England and Normandy united under one crown.

If the union of England and Normandy was the event of Henry's reign, the quarrel with Anselm and the quest for an heir were its absorbing political questions. The ecclesiastical struggle was not unlike that of Rufus's reign. Both pope and king claimed the right of "investiture" (the ceremony of presenting to the newly elected abbot or bishop the staff and ring which betokened admission to the temporal possessions—authorities, lands, and revenues—belonging to the office). For the king to surrender this right to any foreign power, even to the pope himself, meant the introduction of a dangerous element into the state. Anselm went into exile rather than yield, but Henry recalled him and the dispute was compromised, each side retaining a check on the action of the other.

Investiture.

Henry's hopes for a successor were bound up in the person of his beloved boy William, "the Atheling," as the English called this son of the Saxon princess, and from the day when the *White Ship* bearing the prince went down (1120) in the Channel the monarch was never seen to smile. No woman had yet ruled in England, yet the king compelled his barons to swear allegiance to his daughter Matilda, the widowed empress

The loss of the White Ship.

of Germany. To save her Norman dominions from the neighboring counts of Anjou, he wedded her again (1128) to the count's son, Geoffrey the Handsome, a gay Frenchman, from whose habit of decking his cap with a sprig of common broom (*planta genista*) sprang the family name "Plantagenet." The fruit of the union was a son, and before his death (1135) the king had the satisfaction of seeing his nobles repeat their oath of fealty to Matilda and his grandson Henry, a babe in arms.

Plantagenet.

The miseries of the next generation caused the people to look back with regret to the "good old times" when Henry I. was king. Yet he had been at heart a despot. The reforms which he had promised and the smaller number which he had executed were made in the interest of better order and increased revenue for his own comfort and enrichment. He had little respect for the lives and fortunes of his subjects. Yet it so happened that his selfish policy produced internal peace and really improved the system of justice. The next reign was anarchy, but the little Plantagenet whose birth we have just recorded was destined finally to come to the throne, and in a long and useful reign to develop the crude forms of his grandfather's time into the well-regulated government of Henry II. the statesman.

TOPICS FOR READING AND SPECIAL STUDY, WITH LIBRARY NOTES.

1. THE NORMAN CONQUEST.
    William the Conqueror. E. A. Freeman.
    The Normans. Sarah Orne Jewett.
    William Rufus. E. A. Freeman.
    The Conquest of England. J. R. Green.

2. THE NORMAN BUILDERS. CASTLES AND CATHEDRALS.
  History of Architecture. James Fergusson.
  English Cathedrals. M. G. Van Rensselaer.
3. THE CHURCH UNDER HILDEBRAND.
  Hildebrand and His Times. W. R. W. Stephens.
  Holy Roman Empire. J. Bryce.
4. THE NORMANS IN WESTERN EUROPE.
  The Normans in Europe. A. H. Johnson.

FICTION, ETC.

Hereward the Wake. Charles Kingsley.
A Camp of Refuge. Charles MacFarlane.

CHAPTER VI.

THE RISE OF THE BARONS, 1135 A. D.–1216 A. D.—FROM THE ACCESSION OF STEPHEN TO THE DEATH OF JOHN.

IN the story of the twenty years that followed the death of Henry I. it is easy to find justification for the iron rule of the Norman kings. The moment the scepter fell from Henry's grasp hopeless anarchy seized upon the realm.

Stephen of Blois, 1135-1154. Among the Norman-English barons who swore fealty to the "Empress Matilda" and little Henry Plantagenet was the Conqueror's grandson, Stephen[1] of Blois.

---

[1] THE CONQUEROR'S CHILDREN.
(Showing descent of Matilda and Stephen and the Plantagenets.)

WILLIAM I.,
"THE CONQUEROR,"
reigned 1066-1087.

Duke Robert, d. 1134.	WILLIAM II., "RUFUS," r. 1087-1100.	HENRY I., r. 1100-1135, m. Edith (Matilda) of Scotland.	Adela, m. Stephen, *Count of Blois and Chartres.*
		Matilda, "THE EMPRESS," m. (2) Geoffrey, "PLANTAGENET," *Count of Anjou.*	STEPHEN, *Count of Blois,* King of England, r. 1135-1154.

HENRY II.,
r. 1154-1189,
King of England,
m. Eleanor of Aquitaine.

| Henry, "THE YOUNG KING," d. 1183. | RICHARD I., "CŒUR DE LION," r. 1189-1199. | Geoffrey, father of Prince Arthur, d. 1186. | JOHN, r. 1199-1216. |

He was a Frenchman, gay, gallant, hearty, ready with sword or song. Matilda and her foreign husband were distasteful to the great feudal lords of England. Stephen offered himself promptly as a candidate, and having the support of the Londoners was accepted. He was crowned at Westminster, and, having secured the royal hoard, hired an army to defend his claims. Like his predecessor, he dazzled the nation with empty promises of reform. The barons cared little for the rights of either claimant. They were quick to recognize that the accession of either a woman or an easy-going courtier was their opportunity. The administration of the law grew lax. Bad barons built strong castles on their lands, whence they might sally to rob the traveler, or wage war upon the neighboring earl or abbot; even the good nobles—if such there were—must needs fortify their houses to protect themselves from the outlaws and robbers. Thus the land was dotted with private fortresses.[1]

The barons' opportunity.

Castle building.

Foreign invasion and civil war were added to the terror. David, king of Scots, espoused his niece Matilda's cause, and hacked and burned his way into Yorkshire, until checked at Cowton Moor, August 22, 1138, in the battle of the Standard, in which archbishops, barons, and people united. The discomfiture of the Scots was complete, the English conquering under a standard which upheld a sacred wafer in a silver box. With the next year came Matilda herself and the

The Scots' invasion.

The "Standard."

---

[1] The contemporary writer says: "They filled the land full of castles. They cruelly oppressed the wretched men of the land with castle-works. When the castles were made they filled them with devils and evil men. Then took they those men that they imagined had any property, . . . peasant men and women, and put them in prison for their gold and their silver, and tortured them with unutterable torture. . . . When the wretched men had no more to give they burned all the towns, so that thou mightest well go all a day's journey and thou shouldst never find a man sitting in a town or the land tilled." "In olden days," wrote another, "there was no king in Israel, and every one did that which was right in his own eyes; but in England now it was worse; for there was a king, but impotent, and every man did what was wrong in his own eyes."

outbreak of civil war. The cruel Robert, Earl of Gloucester, was her chief partisan. Neighbors took sides and fought each other. The war was made an excuse for pillage, and the common people suffered, whichever party gained the advantage. Their law-courts were

The anarchy.

DOVER CASTLE.

closed, their property seized, their lives unsafe. The church did nothing to help them, and, hopeless in their misery, they said, "Christ and his saints are asleep." The misfortune of the war was universal, and its fortune wavered between Stephen and Matilda. The king was captured (1141), but was released the same year and besieged the empress in Oxford Castle, whence she escaped by stealth.

The church, Archbishop Theobald at its head, finally delivered England. Its interference, in 1153, when young Henry Plantagenet had landed in England to enforce his demand for his mother's rights and his own, secured the treaty of Wallingford. Stephen was left to rule in England, pledging that Henry should succeed

The Rise of the Barons.

him at his death. That event befell in 1154, and Henry II., the first of the Plantagenets, was crowned king of England. Henry was already feudal lord of half of France. As the descendant of their dukes, he held Normandy and Brittany; from Geoffrey, his father, he inherited the counties of Anjou and Maine; Gascony, Poitou, and Guyenne were the dowry of Eleanor, his wife. For these continental fiefs he did homage to the French king, but of England he was absolute lord.

Death of Stephen, 1154

Henry II., 1154-1189.

A thorough business man was this first of the Plantagenets. The blood of Norman and Saxon mingled in his veins, and in his reign the marked distinction between the two races began to disappear. French—and rather bad French at that—was the language of court and town. But French and English burghers and courtiers met on equal footing. The king chose his attendants and the officers of his government irrespective of race, and much work he found for them to do. For himself, he was never idle. "The hardest worker in the realm," men called him, as he turned from treasury accounts to diplomacy, from diplomacy to war, from war to statesmanship.

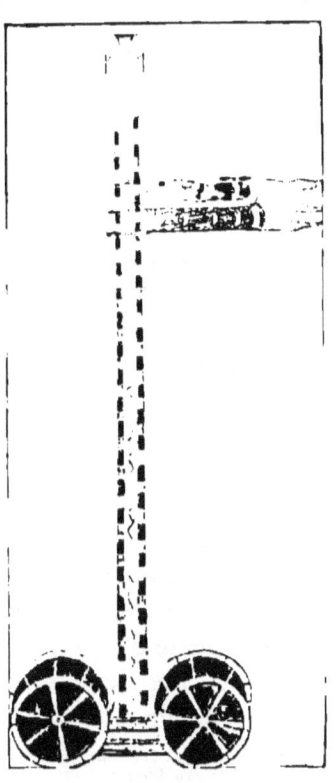

THE STANDARD, 1138.

A crowned statesman.

There was need for such a hard-headed, practical man. Order must be brought out of the anarchy of Stephen's reign. The barons had stripped the monarch of most of the power which the Norman kings had reserved to the crown. To reduce them to their subordinate condition, the king ordered them to pull down the castles which they had built since Beauclerc's time. Then he took from the barons the right to try law-cases, which they had seized when the local and hundred-courts were closed by civil disorders, and neither the king nor his traveling deputies came to hear appeals. Not satisfied with restoring the government, he sought to reduce all the business of the state to one system of which he should be the mainspring and center-point.

Bridling the barons.

Among the trusted clerks of the train of Archbishop Theobald—the peace-maker—was one Thomas à Becket, the son of a rich Londoner of Norman blood. The king discovered in him the stuff for a firm friendship. He rapidly advanced Thomas to the chancellorship, the highest civil office. The two young men together worked upon Henry's plans of reform, and on occasion the chancellor fought beside his master in the field. When the death of the old archbishop left the see of Canterbury vacant the king secured the election of Thomas.[1]

Thomas à Becket.

A sarcastic old prelate who had opposed the election of a courtier to this sacred office said Henry had worked a miracle that day in turning a layman into an

---

[1] A companion of Thomas wrote of the early friendship of king and chancellor: "When business was over they would play together like boys of an age; in hall, in church they sat together. . . . Sometimes the king rode on horseback into the hall where the chancellor sat at meat, . . . jumping over the table he would sit down and eat with him. Never in Christian times were there two men more of a mind or better friends." The pomp of the chancellor's retinue was royal. When he went on an embassy to the French court people marveled, "How wonderful must be the king whose chancellor travels in such state!" As soon as he was elected archbishop he gave up his civil office, turned away his retinue, wore haircloth, ate and drank the meanest fare, and daily washed the feet of thirteen beggars. He accepted the pope as his master, and undertook to establish the supremacy of the church above the crown.

archbishop, a soldier into a saint. The fact was that he had turned his ablest friend into his most determined foe.

Henry's policy required a friend at the head of the church, for he proposed to subject the ecclesiastical courts to himself. Since the Conqueror's time two systems of law and two judicial bodies had existed side by side in England; the king's courts—from merest townmoot to the shire-court and the royal council—and the bishop's court, which not only tried men accused of offenses against the church or canon law, but which had jurisdiction over every person who had taken the tonsure. The penalties in the bishop's courts were comparatively slight, and many a thief escaped hanging by claiming "benefit of clergy" (pleading some connection with the church), and so bringing his case before the bishop. The king wished to restrict the ecclesiastical courts to the trial of causes in which the church was properly concerned. At a great assembly of barons, abbots, and bishops held at Clarendon in 1164, the famous Constitutions of Clarendon were framed to cover this reform. They declared the king's supremacy in the English Church, and they furthermore established the king's right to decide in which court suits should be brought, to be represented by an officer at all ecclesiastical proceedings, and to hear and decide appeals from the bishop's decision. The man whom the king had made archbishop proved more loyal to church than to king. Becket denounced the Constitutions and fled from the presence of the angry monarch. After six years of exile the pope's threats forced the king to recall the primate. The two men acted a hollow reconciliation. But Henry would be rid of the rebel priest, and four knights who heard his ravings attacked the arch-

King's law and canon law.

Constitutions of Clarendon, 1164.

bishop in the Cathedral of Canterbury and slew him on the altar-steps on the fourth day after Christmas, in the year of grace 1170. The church paid high honor to his memory, and in later days pilgrims came in crowds to the shrine of St. Thomas, that "holy blissful martyr for to seek."[1]

Assassination of the archbishop, 1170.

If the independence of the church was to be feared, the arrogance of the barons was still more menacing to the crown. The foresight of William I. had cut into their feudal state by requiring all freemen to swear allegiance directly to the king, instead of the Norman usage of swearing to a lord who, in turn, vowed fidelity to a duke, the latter doing homage to the king. Henry II. applied William's principle to military service. All tenants owed this, but the king allowed them exemption by paying him a tax called *scutage*. With the proceeds he employed mercenary troops for his wars abroad. Thus the barons lost the private armies which in every feudal country had been a menace rather than a support to the throne. By the "Assize of Arms" (1181) all freemen were obliged to muster armed at summons from the king.

"Assize of Arms," 1181.

Of more importance to England than the reforms in church and army were those which were gradually engrafted upon the law. These are embodied in several "assizes." That of Clarendon revived and extended the "frank-pledge," a police system by which small clubs of freemen were formed for mutual security. It provided, moreover, a grand jury which indicted re-

Judicial changes.

---

[1] "Of the cowards that eat my bread is there not one who will rid me of this turbulent priest!" were the words which started the four knights on their sacrilegious errand. The populace (English) had taken sides with him in the struggle, and after he was made a saint (1172) his shrine became the goal of popular pilgrimage which lasted four hundred years. At the Reformation Henry VIII. destroyed the shrine, struck the name of St. Thomas from the calendar, and gave his ashes to the winds, in token of his abhorrence of the papal pretensions which Becket had championed.

puted criminals and presented them for trial by ordeal, by which "judgment of God" the old system of trial by "compurgators" was superseded. In 1216 an order of the church abolished the ordeal, leaving the word to

CANTERBURY CATHEDRAL.

our vocabulary, but replacing the judicial test by a petty jury, such as still remains the basis of English law.

The "Assize of Northampton" (1176) gave currency and system to Henry I.'s haphazard plan of sending deputy justices throughout the island to preside at courts in the king's name. Henry II. divided the kingdom into six such judicial circuits, and regularly heard appeals from their courts to himself in the council of his barons. From the committees of this council, appointed for especial branches of the law, arose the modern courts of King's Bench, Exchequer,[1] and Common Pleas.

The germ of the English judiciary.

[1] Exchequer: A playful name for the royal treasury, said to have been suggested by the parti-colored covering of some early treasurer's table, like a checker-board.

Henry in Ireland.

The king was as active among his generals as he was among his clerks and justices. He was engaged in three indecisive wars with the Welsh. After Becket's murder he went to Ireland, which now makes its first important entry upon the stage of English history. The island had been the scene of the utmost disorder for centuries. Once the abode of learning and piety, the ravages of the Danes had plunged it into a pit of ignorance and superstition. One Dermod MacMurrough, a fugitive king of Leinster, came to Henry and swore fealty to him in return for aid in regaining his throne. In 1170 Richard of Clare, called "Strongbow," an English noble of ruined fortune, led an irregular expedition to Ireland and conquered the southeastern districts. To him went Henry himself in 1172, perhaps to avoid the papal legates who came to curse him for the archbishop's murder. The next year he returned in time to meet the new legates, who brought absolution. Ireland, though now nominally an English fief,

"Strongbow." remained unconquered, save where "Strongbow" and his knights lorded it over the wretched Irish.[1]

Henry managed the affairs of his kingdom better than those of his own household. His unfaithfulness toward his wife Eleanor gave material for many stories, among which that of "Fair Rosamond" is most notorious. His sons, Henry, Geoffrey, Richard, and John, were the heaviness of their father. The principle of heredity was not yet fully admitted, and the king was anxious about the succession. To secure the crown to his eldest son, Prince Henry, he had his barons swear allegiance

---

[1] Hadrian IV. (whose original name was Nicholas Breakspeare, and who was the only Englishman who ever filled the papal chair) granted all Ireland to King Henry in 1155 by a bull in which he said, "There is no doubt, and your nobility acknowledges, that Ireland and all islands on which Christ the Sun of Righteousness has shone, and which have received the teachings of the Christian faith, rightfully belong to the blessed Peter and the most Holy Roman Church."

to him, and in 1170 had him formally crowned. From this time "the Young King" was a source of continual strife. He demanded that a part of the inheritance, either Normandy or England, should be given to him forthwith. The king had already made his will, but refused to be his own executor. At his death Henry was to have Normandy and England and Anjou; Richard's share was his mother's dowry, Aquitaine and Poitou, and Geoffrey should be Duke of Brittany. *"The Young King," 1170.* *The king's will*

John, the youngest son, was omitted in the distribution, and the people—perhaps his brothers began it—dubbed him John "Lackland." Little John was the king's favorite, and he tried to save a portion for him by persuading the elder brothers to cede him certain of their own castles and manors. The surly Henry rudely objected, and leagued with the king of Scotland and a number of French and English barons to wrest the sovereignty from his father. But the old lion scattered the French armies like a whirlwind, capturing the rebels. Meanwhile his lieutenants in England had found once more that the king's strength lay in the confidence of the English commons. The nobles were in revolt, but the royal army defeated the earls (1173) and captured William the Lion, king of the Scots. The victory was announced almost immediately after the king had made a humiliating pilgrimage to the shrine of St. Thomas at Canterbury. Little blood was shed in punishment for this rebellion; but more proud castles had to come down and more baronial power had to be yielded to the king. The king of Scots was not liberated until (1175) he swore on bended knee to hold his realm as a fief of the English crown. *John "Lackland." Scotland humbled, 1175.*

For the rest of his life Henry lived chiefly on the Continent. The richest of his possessions were there; and there, too, he might watch the course of his rival, the king of France, and keep an eye on his unfilial sons. England was ruled meanwhile by the king's justiciar, Ranulf Glanville.

Glanville.

In vain the king besought his sons to join hands for their common safety. Young Henry, who was eventually to reign, urged the brothers to swear fealty to himself. Richard reluctantly obeyed, but a bloody quarrel followed the act. The old king and Richard took arms to oppose the attacks of Geoffrey and "the Young King." The latter's death (1183) ended his career of mischief. Three years later Geoffrey died also—his widow soon after bearing an ill-starred son, Arthur of Brittany. Richard and the landless John survived. The experiment with one "young king" warned Henry of the imprudence of crowning another. But Richard made an alliance with Philip, king of France, and together they attacked the king, now broken in spirit by disappointment and by the conduct of his heartless sons. In 1189 he left England for the last time, as it proved. In July the sick and despairing monarch acknowledged Richard's claim to the crown of England. The list of conspirators was placed in his hands, that he might forgive them. At its head was John, the child of his heart, and when he saw that name he turned his face to the wall, lamenting, "No more, no more! Let all things go their way!" Two days later he died at Chinon. The garrulous courtiers said that when Prince Richard passed the royal bier accusing blood gushed from the nostrils of the dead king.

Death of "the Young King," 1183.

Death of Henry II., 1189.

Personal bravery was the most conspicuous trait of Richard of Poitou,[1] who as the "Lion-heart" (Cœur

---

[1] The crusading fervor of the time found vent against the innocent Jews of England. They were unpopular, as the only non-Christians in the realm, and as the only money-lenders—the creditor class. They prepared a rich coro-

de Lion) became the ideal of knightly honor. He was
a burly, red-faced man, more French than English,
unduly fond of rich armor and gay trappings. His
mother's French duchy was his real home. England
never knew him well, and some doubt his ability to
speak or write a single sentence in English; but the
fame of his exploits against the Saracen filled all Christendom, and long after his death Richard of England
was a name to terrify the Turk. The romance of his
life has caught the fancy of the world, and his extravagance and licentiousness are forgotten.

Queen Eleanor held England for her chivalrous son
until he came from France. His title to the throne was
unclouded, and he flung himself at once into preparations for the crusading enterprise which lay so near
his heart. The emperor of Germany and the king of
Sicily were already off for the East, and both Richard
of England and Philip of France had taken the cross
and were eager to join them in Palestine.[1]

Money was the king's pressing need, and he obtained
it by selling privileges. Scotland bought back its independence, bishops paid roundly for their temporalities,
earls for their earldoms, barons for their manors. The
offices of justice and sheriff were made to yield their
quota, also, to the enormous crusading fund. Before
quitting the island he endeavored to insure its peace
and good government. To John, his brother, he gave

Richard Cœur de Lio 1189-1199.

Money for the crusade.

nation gift for Richard, but were barred out of Westminster and a mob looted
their shops and dwellings in London. The monks, who had inflamed the populace by preaching up the crusade, encouraged the attacks upon the Jews.
At York fully five hundred were besieged in the castle, where they took their
own lives rather than fall into the hands of the mob.

[1] In October, 1187, the city of Jerusalem, which had been in Christian hands
since the first crusade, was captured by the Sultan Saladin. Christendom
was stirred to its foundations by the news that the Holy Sepulcher was in the
grasp of the infidel. The pope summoned chivalry to the third crusade, and
Richard the Lion-hearted, then Count of Poitou, was the first to take the cross.
The "Saladin tax," one tenth of his possessions, was laid upon every Englishman.

six English counties, so that he lacked land no more, but he gave him no voice in the government. The administration was left to the chancellor, William Longchamp, and to the bishop of Durham, whom he made justiciar, and who, as legate, also wielded the authority of the pope. Fearing trouble, he bound John and his half-brother, Geoffrey (not the father of pitiful Prince Arthur), to remain outside the kingdom for three years.

Longchamp.

Philip and Richard, progressing slowly and quarreling on the way, reached Acre in Syria in 1191, where a Christian army held a force of Saracens beleaguered. The English king performed astounding feats of valor in the remaining days of the siege, which soon ended in the surrender of the city. Philip got his fill of crusading and sailed for France. Richard pushed on toward Jerusalem, then in possession of Saladin, the most renowned and chivalrous of Mohammedan sultans. Having signed a truce with him, the English sovereign set out for home, where, as he had good reason to believe, his presence was urgently demanded.

Richard in Palestine.

John's term of absence was expiring, and Philip of France was now Richard's foe. While on his homeward journey the English king fell into the hands of the German emperor, who, to do France a favor, thrust him into an obscure prison. There he remained for thirteen months, while his minstrel Blondel, so the pretty legend runs, wandered through Europe singing the king's favorite air under many a dungeon wall, until at last Richard's own voice took up the strain and his place of confinement was disclosed.

Blondel.

The king was indeed wanted in England. William Longchamp had assumed full control, and his arrogance had inflamed both nobles and commoners against him. The better to curb the former, he deprived them of their

William Longchamp.

castles. Prince John seized the opportunity to return to England, where he made himself regent, and plotted with the French king to prevent Richard's return.

The English people were proud of their lion-hearted king, and left no stone unturned in their efforts for his release. His captor placed an enormous ransom upon him, and Philip and the false John put every obstacle in the way of raising it. But Queen Eleanor, the new justiciar, and Hubert Walter, archbishop of Canterbury, put themselves at the head of the enthusiastic nation, and the sum was made up. The rich gave liberally, and the common people contributed one fourth of their movable goods. In a twelvemonth the money was paid over.[1] The emperor kept his word, and Richard was set free. King Philip's messenger posted to John with the words, "Beware! the devil is loose."

A king's ransom.

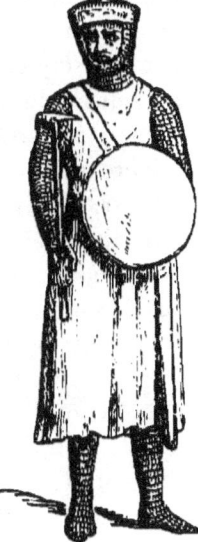

A CRUSADER.

King Richard arrived in England in March, 1194, just in time to witness John's surrender to Archbishop Hubert and to pardon his brother and Geoffrey. He spent but sixty days in the island in this, the last visit of his life, and he applied the time to the restoration of order and the levying of a tax to defray the expense of the war which he was about to carry on with France. In May he sailed for the Continent, leaving Hubert Walter to govern the realm and raise funds to meet the heavy drafts of the campaign. The archbishop was

War with France.

[1] The fact that such a sum, 150,000 marks ($3,500,000), could be raised in such a time shows that England was already outstripping in wealth all European states except Italy.

a well-trained politician, a prudent ruler, and a statesman. But not even he could continue uninterruptedly to exact money from the English to support an unpopular foreign war. In 1198 a great council of notables met his request for an extraordinary contribution with flat refusal, and he was glad to lay down his dignities in favor of a sterner man, Geoffrey Fitz-Peter.

The money wrenched from Englishmen went partly for war, partly for fortresses, and partly to buy alliances with the enemies of France. Had Richard been able to unite his French dominions with his English heritage for a common and hearty attack upon Philip of France he might have won, but his continental duchies and counties cared far less for him than did his English subjects, who in turn felt no interest in the war. To protect Rouen, his Norman capital, he built that splendid *Château Gaillard* (the "saucy castle") which Philip swore to take "were the walls iron," and Cœur de Lion vowed to defend "were its bulwarks built of butter." To crush the French monarch he and his stanch friend Longchamp intrigued with the courts of Western Europe. When the plot was nearly ready for execution death foiled it. In a private feud with the Count of Limoges, over a treasure-trove claimed by the count's master, the king received his mortal hurt from an arrow shot from the castle wall (1199). So died Richard I. of England, forgiving, in his chivalrous fashion, the bowman whose shaft had struck him down.

In the list of English kings since the Conquest many names are repeated: four Williams, eight Henrys, six Edwards, four Georges, and two each named James and Charles, but John has had no namesake; no English queen has dared to christen a son by that hated name. Of John Lackland, the prince, the reader knows some-

Château Gaillard.

Death of Richard I., 1199.

A name of ill omen.

thing—how his rebellion broke the heart of a kind father, and his treachery stole the kingdom from a brother in distress. This talented and fascinating monarch was foul in his life, and false to all men and women with whom he had to do.

King Richard died childless. By the Norman rules of inheritance his next of kin was not his younger brother John, but Prince Arthur of Brittany, son of his deceased elder brother Geoffrey. Yet John claimed the crown of England, as the ablest and most worthy male of the house of Plantagenet, and Hubert Walter secured his election and coronation. From his father, Geoffrey, young Arthur inherited Anjou and other French provinces, and the prince after receiving their allegiance lived at King Philip's court. John claimed these provinces for himself, and, with the advice and able assistance of his queen-mother Eleanor, used force to compel their submission; Philip left Arthur to shift for himself, and the prince, now fifteen years of age, fell into John's hands. A mystery shrouds Arthur's death, but his uncle's character makes plausible the story that he was murdered at Rouen either by John or by his direct command. Philip at least credited the report and ordered John, as his vassal, to appear in person and clear himself. The sentence of the court was forfeiture. The decree was enforced by arms, and not only Normandy but the entire English continental domain, save a small district in the south of France and the Channel Islands, was seized by the French.

The death of Archbishop Hubert Walter precipitated King John's disastrous conflict with the church. There were several candidates for the primacy. The Canterbury monks had one, John named another, and the bishops nominated a third. Innocent III., one of the greatest

King John, 1199-1216.

Prince Arthur.

John loses his French domains.

Conflict with the church.

of the popes, threw out all three, and gave the place to his former fellow-student and friend, Stephen Langton (1207). The enraged king swore that the pope's man should never set foot in the kingdom. For six years he kept his defiant word in the face of the most awful power in Christendom. Innocent launched his three thunderbolts successively against him. First an interdict was placed upon the kingdom. *The pope's bulls.* All public religious services were forbidden. Churches were closed and all church ceremonies save baptism ceased. The king retaliated by plundering the prelates who obeyed the pope, and by persecuting the Italian priests. Innocent then declared the king excommunicate, and his people were ordered to have no dealings with him. Still John was obdurate. Innocent's final act was the Bull of Deposition. The king was now a spiritual outlaw, and his vassals were released from their allegiance. To Philip of France the pope entrusted the execution of his decree against England. John would still have stood firm had he not discovered that his English barons were deserting him. By a sudden change of front he yielded all to Rome. On May 15, 1213, King John disgracefully surrendered his kingdom to the pope's commissioner, Pandulf, receiving it again as tributary vassal of Innocent III.[1]

John submits to Rome, 1213.

At his coronation, and twice or thrice thereafter when hard pressed, John had sworn to rule justly, after the laws of the best of his predecessors; but his promises were made only to be broken, and the oppressed barons secretly concerted measures for holding him to their

[1] The superstitious monarch never went on a journey without hanging a sacred relic at his neck. He had defied the pope, but when it was prophesied that he should lose his crown before Ascension Day, 1213, he flung himself into the arms of the church. He knelt before the legate, placed his head between Pandulf's hands, and formally gave up the kingdom, receiving it back by the favor of the pope and promising to defend it as a part of the patrimony of St. Peter.

performance. Archbishop Langton, of honored memory, added the influence of the church to the strength of the nobility, and the common people, finding their natural leaders united and their sovereign faithless, joined with them against the king. Langton found among the rolls a copy of the charter of rights which Henry I. had granted. This forgotten document he read to the barons assembled at St. Paul's Church in London, in October, 1213, proposing it as a basis for a new charter which should place definite bounds upon the power of the king.

Archbishop Langton.

Henry's charter.

John turned and twisted to free himself from the coil of difficulties gathering about him. To dissolve the union of the nobility, to win over the clergy, to secure the interference of the pope, taxed every device of the king's remarkably fertile brain; but Stephen and the men who believed in the righteousness of their cause and knew John's worthlessness would not be put off or gainsaid. They marched upon London and extorted terms from the isolated king. On the 15th of June, in the year 1215, on an island near Runnymede, in the Thames, between Staines and Windsor, he met the barons and signed with them the treaty which we reverence as Magna Charta, the Great Charter of the English nation.

Runnymede.

The Great Charter was a plain statement of the several rights and privileges which former kings had granted to the church, nobility, towns, and common people of England. It contained little or nothing that was new, but it expressed in definite shape the accepted principles of good government and provided means for applying them. It declared, "No freeman shall be seized, or imprisoned, or dispossessed, or outlawed, or in any way brought to ruin, save by the legal judgment

Magna Charta, 1215.

of his equals or by the law of the land." "To no man will we sell, or deny, or delay, right or justice." No tax could be levied save by the authority of the great council—this accords with that maxim of liberty, "No taxation without representation." All privileges granted by the king to his tenants-in-chief were to be granted in like manner by these barons to their under-tenantry. Trade was relieved from excessive duties, the rights which the city and town corporations had acquired were to be respected. These and many other provisions make up Magna Charta. The novel feature of the paper was the appointment of a committee of twenty-five barons to insure its execution.[1]

The pope against the people.

John did not dream of keeping faith. He was the pope's man now, and the weapons which had been fleshed upon him were at his disposal against his enemies. At his suit the pope annulled the charter and absolved the king from his share in its enactment. The barons rebelled, and the pope struck at them blow after blow. Excommunication was followed by interdict, and the king hired an army of continental ruffians to chastise them until they cried for mercy. Pandulf declared Archbishop Langton suspended from his episcopal authority. The barons mustered such forces as they could, and begged Louis, son of Philip of France, to rid their island of its monstrous monarch. The French landed in May, 1216. John was in the North, fighting the king of Scots. He turned southward to meet

---

[1] The original parchment signed by King John at Runnymede is still preserved in the British Museum, though time and fire and dampness have destroyed its legibility. Copies were written at the time for distribution throughout the realm, and the usual engravings called "facsimiles" are made from one of these. The king's rage at what he had been compelled to do was terrible. He threw himself on the floor, and snapped at sticks and straw like a mad dog. The king who had ignominiously given up his kingdom to the pope was infuriated by the appointment of the twenty-five barons to see that the provisions of the charter were observed. "They have given me twenty-five over-kings," he declared.

the new foe, but in crossing the sands of the Wash in Lincolnshire a high tide swallowed his treasure and left him weakened in the presence of his enemies. Death was more speedy than the dauphin's army. Fever—some whisper poison—ended his wretched life at Newark, October 19, 1216.

Death of John, 1216.

TOPICS FOR READING AND SPECIAL STUDY, WITH LIBRARY NOTES.

1. THE STATESMANSHIP OF HENRY II.
    Henry II. J. R. Green.
    The Early Plantagenets. W. Stubbs.
2. RICHARD I. AND ENGLAND'S SHARE IN THE CRUSADES.
    The Crusades. G. W. Cox.
    The Story of the Crusades. Archer and Kingsford.
3. THE GREAT CHARTER (*Magna Charta*).
    Constitutional History. W. Stubbs.
    English Constitutional History. T. P. Taswell-Langmead.
4. THE CUSTOMS OF CHIVALRY.
    Chivalry. L. Gautier (trans. by H. Frith).

FICTION, ETC.

Ivanhoe. Scott.
Becket. Tennyson.
The Talisman. Scott.
King John. Shakespeare.

CHAPTER VII.

THE PLANTAGENET KINGS, 1216 A. D.–1327 A. D.
—FROM THE ACCESSION OF HENRY III. TO THE DEATH OF EDWARD II.

Henry III., 1216-1272.

THE affairs of England were in woful case when the death of King John left his nine-year-old son, Henry of Winchester, to face the exasperated nobles and the ambitious dauphin. The tyrant's death removed the most serious grievance of the rebels. Patriotism detached some English nobles from the French prince; the prospect of more independence during the boy king's minority doubtless caused more to fall away. The barons were fighting to compel the king to observe his pledge of good government; opportunity now offered for the patriots and nobles to rally around an infant, and in his name to set up the system which his false father had spurned.

William Marshall, regent, 1216-1219.

A band of John's friends, chief among them William Marshall, Earl of Pembroke, Peter des Roches, bishop of Winchester, and the papal legate, had the little prince crowned king at Gloucester. In his name they reissued Magna Charta. William Marshall assumed the regency as "governor of the king and kingdom." He beat the French and their English allies at Lincoln, and cleared Louis out of the island.[1] Henry was

---

[1] Hubert de Burgh's victory over the French fleet in Dover Strait affords a glimpse of thirteenth century naval methods: The English came into close quarters, rammed and then grappled the enemy's vessels, pouring in a "fire" from bows, crossbows, slings, and unslaked lime. The boarding parties used swords, axes, and lances. The English were already recognized as skilful seamen, and the mariner's compass was just coming into use.

accepted as king by the remnant of the rebels, and in his name the regent reaffirmed the Charter, from which the pope had withdrawn his condemnation. In 1219 Earl William died, having saved the country from France and civil war. Peter des Roches, Pandulf, the papal legate, and the justiciar, Hubert de Burgh, jointly assumed the regency, and Henry was crowned again at Westminster by Archbishop Langton, whose share in the events at Runnymede was now forgiven and even applauded. *Hubert de Burgh.*

Hubert was the great man of the triumvirate, Bishop Peter was one of the many Frenchmen whom John had enriched, and Pandulf was the agent of the Roman pontiff. The justiciar succeeded in driving the French "carpet-baggers" out of the island, and upon the return of Langton the legate Pandulf was superseded, and England's church was left under the control of the archbishop of Canterbury. These were genuine triumphs for Hubert. In 1225, when the justiciar desired a grant of money to meet the expenses of a new war with Louis, now king of France, King Henry again, "by his spontaneous will," solemnly promised to respect the charter which his father had signed perforcedly. *Court parties.*

In 1227 Henry became of age and at once began to demonstrate his unfitness to rule. During the forty-five years of his active reign he lost no opportunity to rid himself of constitutional trammels and to show his disregard of the English nation and his subservience to the pope. By playing off one party against another he succeeded in freeing himself from the domination of Hubert[1] and the great nobles of the regency and filled their places with mere clerks. The authority of the

[1] Hubert de Burgh was a popular hero, and when he fell from power it is said that a blacksmith refused to forge irons for the man who had saved England.

Concentration of power.

great officers—justiciar, chancellor, treasurer—the king reserved to himself. With stubborn disregard of the demands of his subjects, he laid upon them repeated taxes to support his petty wars with Scotland, Wales, and France, and to lavish upon the gorgeous tourneys and feasts with which he celebrated the marriages of his family. To these expenses were added the great sums which he pledged to the pope.

"Parliament."

The bishops and barons debated each fresh tax-levy in a great council—now first called "Parliament." So far as they dared they resisted. The king generally gained their consent by promising to redress their wrongs. They were long in learning the vanity of his pledges. They lacked a leader until in Simon de Montfort, Earl of Leicester, they found the will and the courage to grapple with the king.

SIMON DE MONTFORT.

Simon de Montfort.

The great earl was a Frenchman who had won the king's favor and had married his sister, the Princess Eleanor, though he soon ranged himself among the barons who were bent on curbing Henry's tyranny. It may have been from motives of prudence that Henry kept this dangerous vassal constantly employed in foreign service. For a number of years he governed with rigorous hand the king's subjects in Southern France. In 1253 he returned to become the champion of English freedom.

The royal tyranny grew worse every year. In 1257 the king demanded of Parliament a grant of money to enable his son to become king of Sicily. The barons cut the appropriation down. The next year came a fresh demand. He had pledged his realm to the pope for a certain sum, thrice the annual revenue of the state; if the Parliament would grant it he would govern henceforth in accordance with their wishes. The " Provisions of Oxford," drawn up in June of that year, expressed the desires of the barons. They went beyond the terms of the Great Charter. The foreign favorites were to be expelled; the great offices, whose functions the king had monopolized, were to be revived, the liberal financial and judicial arrangements of Henry II. were to be restored. Twenty-four men, twelve by royal appointment, twelve chosen by the earls and barons, were to carry out the reforms. A select council of fifteen was to meet thrice a year to advise the king. Two other commissions represented the barons and the church. To all these acts Henry plighted his sacred word.

England had now fixed limits to its monarchy and outlined a constitution. But the king was as false as the traitor John, and the barons and earls were jealous and discordant. The Provisions had been in force only two years when Henry, taking advantage of the disunion of his enemies, renounced his oath, the pope granting him absolution for his perfidy. But the irrepressible conflict was not to be lightly avoided. Earl Simon took arms against the faithless monarch

Exactions.

" Provisions of Oxford," 1258.

The Barons' War.

and in a battle at Lewes (1264) made him a captive.[1]

Simon de Montfort's Parliament, 1265.

A new Parliament, in which four knights from each shire sat with the barons and bishops, drew up a new constitution, limiting the royal prerogatives still more strictly than the Oxford Provisions. Three counselors, of whom Earl Simon was one, were clothed with extraordinary power. By their advice the body known in history as "Simon de Montfort's Parliament" was summoned to meet in January, 1265. Here, for the first time in English history, the towns were represented by commoners, members who sat alongside the earls, barons, and bishops, who represented the feudal organization of the realm. This was a significant step in the direction of government by the people.

The germ of a House of Commons.

A quarrel between the earls reopened the civil war. Simon fell in battle at Evesham, and his party lingered, only to be beaten piecemeal. The king, though victorious, dared not revive the tyrannies of his early reign, but he summoned no commons to his Parliament and allowed no committee of barons to rule his actions. Prince Edward went crusading to the Holy Land, and in his absence (1272) his father died, after the longest and one of the most oppressive of English reigns.

The reign of Henry III. covers more than half of the thirteenth century, one of the most brilliant epochs in the history of the world. A revival of religion in the Christian Church sent forth two orders of preaching friars. The Dominicans, or Black Friars, and the Franciscans, or Grey Friars, were men who took the vow of poverty and consecrated themselves to preach-

The friars.

---

[1] At Lewes the church, the Londoners, and the common people fought the nobility. The Prince of Wales (afterward Edward I.), commanding one division of the Royalists, was victorious, but pursued his flying foe so far that the remnant of the royal army, with the king himself, fell into De Montfort's hands.

ing the Gospel to the common people.[1] Having no churches or monasteries, they preached in the streets and at the roadside crosses, living on the scanty alms of their hearers. These simple preachers did much to purify the life of the townspeople, and the more learned of their order were among the noted lecturers in the new universities. For it was during Henry's reign that Oxford[2] began to be known in England, Scotland, Wales, and Western Europe as a center of learning. A few students, assembled in the previous century to listen to lectures on divinity and Roman law, formed the nucleus of this university, whither

DOMINICAN (BLACK) FRIAR.
Thirteenth century.

The universities.

[1] The Dominicans followed the zealous Spanish priest St. Dominic (1170–1221), who was the father of the "Holy Inquisition," and who organized them to go through Christendom condemning heresy and worldliness. St. Francis of Assisi (1182–1226), "the most blameless and gentle of all saints," intended his order to exemplify the poverty and devotion of the first apostles. Both these mendicant orders furnished a marked contrast to the luxury and pride of the Benedictine monks. "The enthusiasm and success of the early friars have been compared with those of the English Methodists in the days of Wesley and Whitefield." The common people heard these street preachers so gladly that it is said the churches were deserted. The early friars were angels of mercy to the leper colonies of the Middle Ages, and their lodges or "friaries" were usually located in the most densely populated parts of the towns, where they were nearest to human need and suffering.

[2] In 1183 one Robert Pullen, a theologian who had studied at Paris, lectured on the Bible to a few eager pupils in an abandoned nunnery at Oxford. Before the end of the century the town had gained note as a resort of students. In 1257 it stood second only to Paris among the great schools of the church, and then numbered about 3,000 students. The beginnings of the sister university of Cambridge belong to the same period. The collegiate system was initiated when Walter of Merton endowed Merton College at Oxford, in which a number of students were to dwell together in conventual buildings under certain rules.

flocked young men from every nation, and where the friar Roger Bacon (1214-1292), "the first name in the roll of modern science," taught and wrote.

Edward I., "Longshanks," 1272-1307.

After two centuries of French Williams and Henrys the Saxon name of Edward reappears in the list of English kings, and—irrespective of the earlier bearers of the name—this Plantagenet is known as Edward "the First," or, in the familiar speech of his camps, as Edward "Longshanks." His boyhood witnessed the efforts of the barons to compel his father to respect the Charter; in his earlier manhood he learned patriotism and military skill from his famous uncle, Simon de Montfort, whose views he favored until he had reason to fear for his own succession. His strategy and valor ended the war at Evesham, and his wisdom then took him to distant Palestine, to allow time for the hot tempers of the kingdom to cool. The news of his father's death brought him home. He was then thirty-three years of age, vigorous in body and mind. On his homeward journey he paid his respects to the pope and knelt in homage to King Philip III. of France, as overlord of Gascony. It was 1274 when he set foot in England and the crown of his Plantagenet fathers was placed upon his worthy head.

A glorious reign.

Edward I. reigned gloriously for thirty-five years, extending the boundaries of England, exerting her influence over Wales and Scotland, and inspiring within the nation itself a pride and patriotism it had never known before.

The Welsh war was already forward when Edward returned from Palestine. Wales was peopled by a remnant of the Celtic race which Cæsar had found in Southern Britain, and which the Anglo-Saxon invasion had driven into the mountain fastnesses of the West.

OXFORD, FROM MAGDALEN TOWER.

Cornwall and the lesser Celtic states of the West had by degrees become English, but no English king had yet been sovereign of Wales. The people were Christians of the early British type; they spoke the old Celtic language, and the songs of their bards kept alive an ardent national spirit. They were threatening neighbors for the West-of-England shires, which the Norman kings had sought to protect by granting extraordinary powers to the border nobles—the earls of the marches. Thus the western families of Mortimer, Bohun, Marshall, and Clare rose to dangerous eminence, and were sometimes even found in league with the Welsh princes in their private feuds or against the king. Prince Llewellyn of Wales refused to pay homage to King Edward. In 1277 he was forced to admit the king's feudal supremacy, but he soon broke faith and invaded the western marches. The half-measures of the past fifty years had failed, and the time for thorough work had come. Edward's great army crossed the border, defeated the prince and his brother, and compelled the submission of the Celtic chieftains. It was long believed that the bards who had inspired the Welsh to resistance were ruthlessly massacred by his order. In 1284 the "Statute of Wales" proclaimed the annexation of the principality to England.[1]

The subjugation of Wales, 1284.

Soon after the pacification of the West confusion arose in the North. The death of the Scottish sovereign left thirteen claimants wrangling for the vacant throne. The English kings since William I. had claimed authority over Scotland. The disputed claim was now left to Edward to decide. John Balliol and Robert Bruce

Edward decides the Scottish succession, 1291.

[1] Edward's son, Edward of Carnarvon, who was born in this year, was acknowledged "Prince of Wales." According to the tradition, the Welsh chieftains, who had vowed never to serve an "English-speaking" prince, gave in their allegiance to this speechless babe.

were the leading candidates before the Scottish council which King Edward held in Norham Castle in 1291, and to the former, with the general assent of the Scots, the king awarded the crown. Balliol accepted the kingdom as a fief of England, and did homage for it in true feudal fashion. Yet both the Scots and their king fretted under this English sovereignty. They resisted Edward's decree that appeals from Scottish law courts be settled in his own council, and they disobeyed his summons to fight in the English wars. In fact, Balliol made a secret treaty with Edward's enemy, Philip IV. of France.

It was to invade France that Edward had summoned the Scottish barons. The sailors of the English Channel ports had quarreled with the Norman seamen, and King Philip, as Edward's feudal lord, had called him to account. Instead of going Edward sent his brother, offending thus His Majesty of France, who at once seized Guienne, one of the remnants of English territory on the Continent. War was inevitable. The defection of the Scots was the king's first care. He had learned of their alliance with France—the beginning of a connection which lasted until the eighteenth century—and demanded possession of their border castles as a pledge of good faith. When Balliol defied him, Edward's army sacked the border city of Berwick, captured Edinburgh, Stirling, and Perth, and forced the king to surrender. John Warrenne, Earl of Surrey, was left to pacify and organize the English rule. The conqueror took back with him to Westminster a sacred stone supposed to be the hard pillow on which the patriarch Jacob dreamed of the heaven-reaching ladder. Upon this stone in the Abbey of Scone each sovereign of Scotland had been crowned. Edward had it placed in the

War with France.

Invasion of Scotland.

The Stone of Scone.

English coronation chair which is still in use at Westminster. When James VI. of Scotland became James I. of England, the Scots saw in the event a new proof of the virtue of this relic.[1]

William Wallace.

THE ENGLISH CORONATION CHAIR.

Earl Warrenne was rudely checked in his work of organization by William Wallace, an outlawed Scottish knight. The baronage and the clergy obeyed Edward's lieutenant, but Wallace aroused the common people to win back the freedom which the nobility had surrendered. Such a tide of national feeling had not been seen before in Scotland, and its first waves were resistless.

Stirling, 1297.

Utterly routed in the battle of Stirling (September, 1297), Earl Warrenne abandoned the kingdom. Wallace was now hailed as "guardian of the realm," but Edward hastened against him with an overwhelming force. Two abler generals had not met before on British soil than Edward and the outlaw Wallace. The supe-

---

[1] The tradition is that this "Stone of Destiny" was brought to Ireland from the Continent and set up at Tara, as the coronation stone of the ancient Irish kings. It was later removed to Scotland and about 840 was installed at Scone. An old Latin distich ran:

"Where'er this stone may be, such is the Fates' decree,
There the Scottish race shall fill the highest place."

rior strength of the English archers carried the day at Falkirk, in July, 1298.[1] But not until 1304 did Edward consider the conquest of Scotland completed. Wallace was put to death as a traitor, and the government of his country was entrusted to a council of Scottish nobles. In the year before Edward's death (1307) the spirit of Scottish nationality flamed forth again, and a war was begun which eventually won the independence of that kingdom.

Falkirk, 1298.

The stirring events of the West and North must not obscure the political and legal activities of Edward's reign. The king's justices were now divided, for judicial purposes, into three courts: Exchequer, for trying revenue cases; King's Bench, where criminal suits are heard; and Common Pleas, the court of private litigation. A separate staff of judges was assigned to each division. As a source of revenue the Parliament of 1275 granted to the king an export duty upon wool—the first customs duty imposed on English goods. The Welsh and Scottish campaigns exhausted the royal coffers and frequent Parliaments were called to devise new methods of raising money. At first the innovations of Simon de Montfort were disregarded, and only the barons and clergy were represented in these gatherings. But the government was hard pressed for money, which the towns-people and county farmers could supply. In 1295 King Edward summoned the first perfect Parliament—"the clergy represented by their bishops, deans, etc.; the barons summoned severally in person by the king's special writ; and the commons summoned by

Courts of law.

The "Model Parliament," 1295.

[1] King Edward's tactics against the masses of Scottish infantry consisted in shaking the column by volleys of arrows and then throwing it into confusion by a charge of mailed knights on horseback. The English archers had by this time exchanged the old-fashioned shortbow (four-foot) for the six-foot weapon and cloth yard-shaft of the Welsh. With the longbow a sinewy yeoman could drive a heavy arrow through a plank door four inches thick. For centuries this was the national weapon of the English.

writs addressed to the sheriffs, directing them to send up two elected knights from each shire, two elected citizens from each city, and two elected burghers from each borough." The right of the barons to be summoned to Parliament became hereditary, and these members, with the bishops, made up the House of Lords. The other members, knights and commons, formed the House of Commons, though in Edward's time, and long after, this division of Parliament into two houses was unknown.[1]

It is not to be supposed that Edward granted these free institutions to his people from any philanthropic motives. Order and system were, in his mind, essential to good government, but it was no less essential that the king should be the source of all order and the center-point of the system. His obstinate persistence in taxing the church involved him in a quarrel with Winchelsey, archbishop of Canterbury, which was prolonged through several years, and which ended in 1297 by a compromise. In that year the king needed money and men for the invasion of Flanders. The barons, irritated by the king's assumptions of power, refused to follow him, and the clergy, led by the archbishop and backed by the pope, refused to be taxed. As the price of submission of both orders, Winchelsey obtained a confirmation of the old charters, and the promulgation of new decrees establishing the right of the people to determine all questions of taxation. This confirmation of the charters was repeated again and again, and twice a year the charters were to be read aloud in the cathedral churches, to remind the people of their political rights and obligations.

Controversy with Winchelsey.

Confirmation of the charters.

[1] The essential points of this "Model Parliament" are: (1) The knights and towns-people (burgesses) were represented; (2) they were genuine representatives of their class, being *elected*; (3) they met to *do* something to authorize taxation, not merely to debate and give advice; (4) the magnates and the clergy met with them. Thus the whole nation was represented.

The closing months of Edward's life are characteristic of the man. He was now nearly seventy years of age, and his magnificent physique had been shattered by the mental and physical strain of a busy life in camp and council hall. The government which he had inaugurated in Scotland had gone wrong. Robert Bruce, a grandson of the Bruce who had claimed the crown in 1290, was heading an insurrection. By combining strength with stealth he overcame the English interest, stabbing with his own hand John Comyn, the late regent. Bruce was crowned king of Scots at Scone, in March, 1306. To him rallied the elements which had made Wallace's rising momentarily successful; but his resources were slender, and had Edward been young and vigorous the end might have been otherwise. An English army beat the Bruce and drove him into the fastnesses of the Highlands; Edward himself hurried forward to assume the direction of affairs, but his infirmities bore him down, and on July 7, 1307, he succumbed, dying at Burgh-on-Sands, within sight of the Scottish border. Eleanor,[1] his first queen, whom he loved devotedly, had died seventeen years before, her sole surviving son, Edward, being Prince of Wales and heir to the crown of England.

<small>Robert Bruce.</small>

<small>Death of Edward I., 1307.</small>

England has had no more kingly king than the first Edward. His reign was not destitute of great men, but he towers above his earls and bishops as he over-topped them in life. Strong and steadfast in every crisis, the exemplar of his motto, "Keep troth" (*Pactum serva*), he was a genuine leader of the nation, a real king. Men have called him cruel, but his "massacre of the

<small>"Keep troth."</small>

---

[1] Eleanor, daughter of Alfonso X. of Castile, died near Lincoln in 1290. She was buried at Westminster, and at every town in which the body rested along the route of the funeral procession King Edward caused to be erected a monumental cross. The crosses at Northampton and Waltham are the best preserved.

Welsh bards" is a falsehood, his treatment of Wallace and the Scots was in his eyes just judgment upon oath-breakers, and his expulsion of the Jews from the kingdom (1290) was in answer to an undoubted popular demand.[1]

Edward II. of Carnarvon, 1307-1327.

Edward of Carnarvon, who succeeded his hard-headed father, was a gay and pleasure-loving gentleman of twenty-three. The burden of a centralized personal government, which the elder Edward had carried easily upon his sinewy shoulders, sent the son staggering to his fall.

Piers Gaveston.

The young Edward's devotion to a Gascon courtier, Piers Gaveston, was the spring of his misfortunes. The old king had warned his son that the nobles would be jealous of Piers, and before his death he had banished the favorite and pledged the prince not to recall him without the consent of Parliament. But this wise counsel was lost upon the flighty young king, who immediately recalled Gaveston to England, made him Earl of Cornwall, and, to the disgust of the English nobility, left this earl of a day regent of the kingdom while he went to France to claim the hand of Isabella, daughter of Philip the Fair. King and queen were crowned together (1308), the sovereign swearing "to keep the laws and righteous customs which the community of the realm shall have chosen, and to defend them and strengthen them to the honor of God, to the utmost of my power."

Foreign favorites.

[1] The Jews being the principal capitalists were hated by their debtors, the improvident landowners, and were offensive to the common people on other accounts. It seems to have been generally believed that on Good Friday their custom was to crucify a Christian lad. On account of such a report, in 1278 "manie Jewes at London, after Easter, were drawn at horses' tails and hanged." After 1275 Jews were compelled to wear a conspicuous badge of their nationality. In 1278 over two hundred of them were hanged for counterfeiting or otherwise debasing coin. In 1286 they were fined to raise a military fund. In 1290 the popular outcry prevailed. The Jews to the number of above 16,000 left the kingdom, not to return until the time of Cromwell, four centuries later.

The Plantagenet Kings. 121

The barons' opposition to Gaveston showed itself at once. The Scottish war was allowed to languish, and the king devoted himself to the protection of his unworthy favorite. The great Earls of Lancaster, Lincoln, and Warwick led the attack. Two months after the coronation Piers was forced into exile, but the shifty king soon had him back again. A revolution followed. The Parliament of 1310 took the government out of Edward's hands and gave it for one year to a commission of twenty-one "Ordainers." The "ordinances" proposed by this body in 1311 provided for the banishment of the foreign favorites, and the limitation of the king's authority by the barons in Parliament. Edward accepted these laws, but broke them at the first opportunity. The exasperated earls again took the law into their own hands, and put Gaveston to death. The weak king had to submit, and the Earl of Lancaster became the virtual master of the realm. *The "Ordainers."*

After the death of Edward I. the English commanders in Scotland won isolated successes, but no comprehensive plan of subjugation was made or followed. The fugitive Bruce, encouraged, says the tale, by the perseverance of a spider spinning and respinning its torn web, resumed his efforts. The English garrisons, left unsupported, surrendered one by one, until in 1314 Stirling, the only English stronghold left, was itself at the point of yielding. Edward tried to relieve the post, but Bruce's Scotchmen beat the king's knights at Bannockburn, June 24, 1314. This signal victory gave Bruce the absolute sovereignty of Scotland. *Scotland wins her independence at Bannockburn, 1314.*

The Earl of Lancaster was now almost supreme in England, but his use of his high position raised up powerful enemies. The weak king, craving support, adopted Hugh le Despenser, father and son, granting them such wealth and honors as his restricted means allowed. All the old jealousy of Gaveston was aroused against the new recipients of royal favor. Parliament sentenced the two Despensers to forfeiture and exile (1322). But the whirligig of fortune soon sent the earl to the block, despite his popularity.

The Despensers.

Lancaster's death left the national party without a leader, and for a few months the Despensers had their own way. The thunder-cloud which was to blast them gathered on the eastern shore of the Channel. The accession of a new king in France, Charles IV., made it necessary for Edward to renew in person his oath of fealty for his small continental dominions. But his mentors dared not trust him out of their hands, nor yet to accompany him, for England would rise against them in their absence, and there was more than one whetted dagger for them in the French court, swarming with English exiles. In 1325 the queen, herself a French princess, went over and persuaded her husband to send their son and heir, Prince Edward, to her. Mother and son straightway turned against the king. Roger Mortimer, an English lord who had escaped Lancaster's fate, hired troops for the invasion of England. They landed in September, 1326, the queen proclaiming herself the liberator of the realm from the king's false counselors. The Londoners joined her, and the king, after a weak resistance, abandoned the struggle. The Despensers, elder and younger, were put to death. A Parliament at Westminster (January, 1327) declared the king faithless and unfit to rule, and the broken-spirited monarch made no defense. He resigned the crown in favor of his thirteen-year-old son, whose mother, guided by Roger Mortimer, reigned until the death of the king. The unhappy Edward was confined

Fall of the Despensers.

Abdication of the king.

in Berkeley Castle, where he was murdered September 21, 1327.

Death of Edward II., 1327.

TOPICS FOR READING AND SPECIAL STUDY, WITH LIBRARY NOTES.

1. SIMON DE MONTFORT.
    Simon de Montfort. Pauli. (Epochs of English History.)
    The Rise of the People and Growth of Parliament. Rowley. (Epochs of English History.)
2. THE ENGLISH UNIVERSITIES.
    History of the University of Cambridge. J. B. Mullinger.
    History of the University of Oxford. G. C. Brodrick.
3. EDWARD I. AS A STATESMAN.
    Edward the First. T. F. Tout.
    The Early Plantagenets. W. Stubbs. (Epochs of Modern History.)
4. SCOTLAND'S STRUGGLE FOR INDEPENDENCE.
    History of Scotland. Burton.
    Story of Scotland. (Story of the Nations Series.)

FICTION, ETC.

Scottish Chiefs. Jane Porter.
Castle Dangerous. Scott.
Siege of Kenilworth. L. S. Stanhope.
Edward II. Marlowe.

CHAPTER VIII.

ENGLAND AND FRANCE, 1327 A. D.–1422 A. D. – FROM THE ACCESSION OF EDWARD III. TO THE DEATH OF HENRY V.

Edward III., 1327-1377.

THE reign of Edward III. began amid wretched conditions—the Scots plundering the northern marches, the French trespassing upon the English continental province, the deposed king a prisoner, the new king a child, and the regency controlled by Queen Isabella and her paramour, Mortimer. The regents made a disreputable peace with Scotland (1328), signing away at Northampton whatever feudal rights Edward III. might have been entitled to in that kingdom. Scotland was free, and Robert Bruce was its king.

Treaty of Northampton, 1328.

This disgraceful treaty of Northampton aroused the English nobles against Mortimer, but he was strongly intrenched. His destruction came when least expected. Edward was eighteen years of age in 1330—old enough to feel keenly the shame of the situation. He made entrance with an armed band of his close friends into Mortimer's presence in Nottingham Castle and seized the offender, who, once bereft of authority, was quickly sentenced by the lords in Parliament and hurried to a traitor's death at Tyburn.

Death of Mortimer.

Edward III. now assumed personal direction of the government. His attempt to reassert English authority over Scotland was frustrated by the outbreak of hostilities with France. This was the famous "Hundred Years' War," which lasted, with intervals of truce, from

1336 to the middle of the fifteenth century, from Edward III. to Henry VI. It opened with the claim of Edward to the crown of France; at its close Henry was master of the single French town of Calais. The waters of the Channel and the fields of France furnished battle-grounds, and England was not once invaded by her foreign enemies save when their allies, the Scots, broke over the northern border. The struggle extended over the reign of five English kings, glorified the names of Edward, the Black Prince, and Joan of Arc, and afforded the famous battles of Crecy, Poitiers, and Agincourt. This war, continuing through four generations, did much to deepen and perpetuate the national enmity between the people of the two kingdoms.

The Hundred Years' War.

VIEW OF WINDSOR CASTLE, SHOWING THE GREAT ROUND TOWER.

The first Plantagenet kings ruled wide domains in France, acquired by inheritance from their Norman and Angevin ancestors and by dowry of their French wives. The weakness of John had let most of these lands slip, and for several reigns previous to the accession of Edward III. Aquitaine, in Southern France, with a narrow coast-strip in the north, alone remained. Of this remnant the French kings were covetous. They had designs, moreover, upon the Flemish cities Ghent, Antwerp, and others, whose manufactures of wool com-

France and England.

mended them to the especial favor of sheep-raising England. With these existing grounds of hostility, but a slight provocation was needed to bring the two nations to actual war. Upon the death of Charles IV. of France leaving no direct male heir, Edward III. laid claim to the throne by right of his French mother, the sister of the late king.¹ The French lawyers, however, declared that by the Salic Law² no female might wear or transmit the crown. Edward was accordingly passed over, and Philip VI. of Valois succeeded peacefully (1328). Seven or eight years later, when Philip was encroaching upon the English holdings and succoring the Scots, Edward reasserted his right and abandoned the Scottish war for this greater struggle. Such European alliances as were possible he made, and with such German soldiers as he could hire from their peddling princes he recruited his ranks. In the great sea-fight off Sluys,³ in June, 1340, he won the first of his French

marginal notes: Edward III. claims the crown of France. — Sea-fight off Sluys, 1340.

---

¹ EDWARD'S CLAIM TO THE FRENCH CROWN.
(French sovereigns in italic.)

(1) *PHILIP III.*,
"THE BOLD,"
reigned 1270-1285.

(2) *PHILIP IV.*,   Charles,
"THE FAIR."   Count of Valois.

(3) *LOUIS X.*, (5) *PHILIP V.*, (6) *CHARLES IV.*, Isabel,   (7) *PHILIP VI.*
   d. 1316.   "THE TALL,"   "THE FAIR," wife of Ed. II.   OF VALOIS,
(4) *JOHN I.*,   d. 1322.   d. 1328.   of England.   r. 1328-1350.
   d. 1316.   (8) *JOHN II.*,
                                                      (7) **EDW'D III.**   "THE GOOD,"
                                                            of England.   r. 1350-1364.

² The sixty-second title of the ancient code of the Salian Franks restricted the succession of any except males to the lands allotted to vassals in return for military services. In the fourteenth century this provision was extended to the crown. It is clear that in a feudal state it was essential that the tenant should be an able-bodied fighting man.

³ This splendid victory gained for Edward the title "King of the Sea." He wrote on board his ship *Thomas* to his ten-year-old son Edward an account of the battle: "Soon after the hour of noon, with the tide, we, in the name of God, and in the confidence of our right quarrels, entered into the said port upon our enemies, who had placed their ships in very strong array, and who made a very noble defense all that day and the night after. But God, by his

successes, and indeed the brilliant record of the royal navy has had few more terrible triumphs.

The king's son Edward, feared in France and loved in England as "the Black Prince," was the hero of his father's wars. The campaign of 1346 was his first in the field, and on August 26 he—a youth of sixteen — commanded the right wing of his father's army in the battle of Crecy. The French, with an immensely superior force, made the attack. There was a striking difference between the two armies, as there was indeed between the two countries. France was wealthy, populous, and in the full flower of feudal splendor, and the men who fought under her banner were the proud barons and their mailed retainers and mercenaries. England was comparatively free; her soldiers were the stout yeomen of the shires, accustomed to draw their cloth-yard arrows to the head, and learning to fight for their country rather than for a feudal lord. The battle was a slaughter; the boy Edward fought with the skill and bravery of a veteran,

The Black Prince.

CANNON USED AT CRECY.

Crecy, 1346.

> While his most mighty father on a hill
> Stood smiling, to behold his lion's whelp
> Forage in blood of French nobility.

power and miracle, granted us the victory over our said enemies, for which we thank him as devoutly as we can. . . . The number of ships, galleys, and great barges of our enemies amounted to 190, which were all taken except twenty-four only. These fled and some of them have since been taken at sea. And the number of men-at-arms and other armed people amounted to 35,000, of which number, by estimation, 5,000 escaped. . . . Thus God our Lord has shown full favor, for which we and all our friends are ever bound to render him grace and thanks." In commemoration of his victory gold coins were struck, the design showing the king standing in a ship, in his right hand a sword, in his left a shield bearing the arms of France and England.

The French lost 1,200 knights and 30,000 footmen, more than the whole English army. King Philip fled in dismay, and King Edward, embracing the prince, exclaimed, "Fair son, my son you are in truth, for loyally have you acquitted yourself to-day!"[1]

Neville's Cross, 1346.

In the autumn an English army at Neville's Cross routed the Scottish king, David Bruce, whom his French allies had set on to invade England in the absence of its chief defender. In France the English power widened steadily; after a year the beleaguered port of Calais[2] was starved into surrender. Its stubborn resistance and its villainous reputation as a resort of Channel pirates had exasperated the king. Edward promised to spare the people if six leading citizens should give themselves up to him. Five patriots followed Eustace St. Pierre, who first volunteered, and the old chroniclers tell how the king's fierce anger melted under the warm tears of his queen, Philippa, who besought her lord to show mercy "for the sake of the merciful Lord Christ."

The fall of Calais.

In 1355 the struggle was renewed. The Black Prince sallied forth from Aquitaine, pillaging the pleasant farms of Central France, which had never known the sight of war. The plunder sufficed to fit

---

[1] At short range the English arrows could pierce plate armor; at three hundred yards they were fatal to horses and light-armed soldiers. At Crecy the English fought on foot, even the knights being dismounted. The French army, outnumbering the English five to one, advanced up a hill, the Genoese crossbowmen in the van, then the mailed horsemen, with the irregular militia in the rear. The English archers threw the Genoese into confusion by the rapidity and accuracy of their discharge. The charge of the French knights was stopped by the same deadly fire. For hours the knights "surged along the English front," but the line was inflexible, and without moving from their tracks the English slew more than a fourth of the enemy. This successful stand of the yeomen infantry against the feudal horsemen revolutionized the art of war.

[2] Gunpowder and cannon were just then coming into use. Edward had rude cannon at Calais, small pieces made of iron bars, welded and hooped. Cannon balls were of stone, and the larger bombards could be discharged not more than thrice in an hour. Nevertheless they soon displaced battering-rams for the demolition of fortifications, and the days of the Norman castle, so long considered impregnable, were numbered. It was not until the next century that heavy guns were employed for field service.

out another army in the following year, at whose head the prince ravaged the valley of the Loire and gained the road to Paris. The new king, John, called "the Good," rallied 60,000 Frenchmen to block the way. Young Edward, with 8,000 English and Gascons, entrapped at Poitiers, offered peace and a restoration of his conquests rather than to risk a fight. But John, sure of his prey, scorned the terms. The battle of Poitiers ensued September 19, 1356. By a reckless attack the Frenchmen threw away the advantage of superior numbers; and the skilful dispositions of the English and their fierce charges won the day for the Black Prince.[1] King John was taken captive and was exhibited to the Londoners in the triumphal procession over which England went wild in the spring of 1357. For two years more France was a prey to anarchy and Edward; then the regents consented to the treaty of Bretigny, which closed the first stage of the war. King John was to be released on the payment of 3,000,000 crowns in gold. King Edward renounced his empty claim to the throne of France and the duchy of Normandy, but he was confirmed in the possession of Aquitaine, Poitou, Guisnes, and Calais, and it is to be noted that he held these lands henceforth independently as king of England, not as a vassal of France.

Poitiers, 1356.

The captive king in London.

Treaty of Bretigny.

The Black Prince remained on the Continent as ruler of the English possessions, but his ambition could not be bridled. His own province being at peace, he

---

[1] Mindful of the fate of the mounted knights at Crecy, John dismounted his knights and sent them in armed with lances six feet long. The English were so well posted that his advance was up a hill covered with vines and underbrush, and crossed by hedges—rough country for warriors so overweighted with steel plate armor that if one of them lost his footing he could not rise without help. The English archers threw the first line back upon the second, and their mounted men-at-arms charging the confused masses completed the rout. "The French were so dismayed by the result of Crecy and Poitiers that for some years they would not accept battle, but shut themselves up behind walls in towns and castles."

sought employment for his sword in the broils of the neighboring peninsula of Spain. The expenses of this pastime were burdensome to Aquitaine, and the emissaries of the French passed in and out among his people, inciting them to rebellion. In 1369 France and England grappled again, but the Black Prince had won his last great battle. Broken in health, despairing of his own succession, and fearful lest his brothers should bar his son Richard from the throne, he became irritable and cruel. His ill health and the interests of the succession recalled him to England. His brother, John, Duke of Lancaster, famous from his Flemish birthplace as "John of Gaunt" (Ghent), led an English army into France, but accomplished nothing. Castle after castle of Aquitaine admitted French garrisons, and by the end of 1371 only two important towns, Bordeaux and Bayonne, remained to England of all her wide realm in Southern France. Within fifteen years the results of Crecy and Poitiers had vanished, and the bloody campaigns of the Black Prince had produced nothing but misery and lasting hatred between England and France.

John of Gaunt.

The reign of the third Edward has other claims to attention as important as the French wars. Within this period of fifty years Parliament acquired the form which it still wears. There was a time when its four orders—the clergy, barons, knights, and citizens—met separately, each considering such matters as concerned itself. But after the Parliament of 1341 the prelates of the church and the specially summoned barons or "peers" met as one body, while the elected members, both the knights of the shires and the borough or town representatives, met as another. So arose the Houses of Lords and Commons.

Two houses of Parliament.

The "Black Death,"[1] a horrible Asiatic pestilence which was ravaging Europe, swept over England in 1348, and broke out repeatedly at intervals throughout the century. No pestilence of modern times can be compared to it for destructiveness. Such a diminution of the population had a deep influence upon society, and particularly upon the condition of the laboring classes, as the troubles of the next reign will show.

The Black Death, 1348.

The plague and the wars with France told terribly upon the strength of England. The clergy suffered least. Their lands and houses, constituting a large share of the best property in England, were free from ordinary taxation, and their prelates and dependents had not to offer themselves as targets for French bowmen. The jealous baronage, led by the ambitious John of Gaunt, attacked the privileges of this class. In his father's lifetime he gained control at court and filled the high offices with laymen, ousting the bishops and abbots whom the king had raised to these positions. The incompetence of the new men and the failure of the French campaigns brought about an alliance of the clergy under William of Wykeham[2] and the commons. The last act of the Black Prince was to side with the people against his brother. In the Parliament of 1376 the commons had the audacity to protest against John's

Factions at court.

---

[1] The caravans of the China merchants introduced the germs of this bubonic plague into Europe. It first appeared in England in August, 1348, and before Christmas there were not priests enough in the infected diocese to shrive the dying. The symptoms were painful swellings of the glands, carbuncles on the fleshy parts, and ominous red spots, "God's tokens," on the breast and back. It often ran its course within twenty-four hours, and at least fifty per cent of the cases were fatal. It raged through all classes, in city and country alike. In London some 20,000 died and a new cemetery of thirteen acres was needed for their burial. Norwich, the second city of the kingdom, lost one third of its population. All England probably lost more than one third and did not make up the loss for two hundred years.

[2] This great churchman, politician, and architect (he was the rebuilder of Winchester Cathedral) was also founder of the English public school system. His model boys' school at Winchester still flourishes upon his endowment and in his buildings, and his "New College" at Oxford, which was instituted to counteract the teachings of Wyclif, is the model of many of the later colleges. His tomb and statue are in his cathedral church.

extravagance and mismanagement; for the first time in English history two of the royal ministers were accused, convicted, and condemned; the court was purged of its unpopular courtiers, and Alice Perrers, the favorite of the king, was banished. These and other reforms won for this Parliament the designation "the Good." No sooner was it dissolved than John of Gaunt resumed control, reversed its enactments, restored the favorites, and made a fresh assault on William of Wykeham and the clergy. Prince Edward died June 8, 1376, and Parliament acknowledged his little son, Richard, as heir. In June of the following year the king himself died.

WILLIAM OF WYKEHAM, BISHOP OF WINCHESTER.

"The Good Parliament," 1376.

Death of the Black Prince, 1376.

Death of Edward III., 1377.

The English language.

The intense hatred of Frenchmen which pervaded England in this century had one permanent effect. Until now it had been doubtful what language would prevail in the British Islands. The Romans had found a Celtic dialect there, and had introduced the Latin tongue. The Anglo-Saxon migration had driven the Celtic people into Wales and Scotland, and had established the Anglo-Saxon, or old English, language so firmly that the great infusion of Danes among the people of the islands left but an inappreciable number of

Danish words. The Norman Conquest in the eleventh century brought in the French language, and made it the common speech of the court and the aristocracy throughout the time of the Norman and Angevin sovereigns, while the Latin, now corrupted and fallen from the classical standards, was the language of the church and literature. Beneath this Norman-French upper-crust the masses of peasantry and towns-people clung to their English mother tongue. Its disuse by scholars suffered it to pass through many changes, until the Anglo-Saxon of King Alfred was no longer the English of the time of Edward III. By the close of the fourteenth century it had been changed in form and substance, and its vocabulary had been largely swollen with words from the French and Latin. No important books had until now been written in this dialect, which was ridiculed by the upper classes. But the Hundred Years' War brought all things French into disfavor. English began to displace other tongues in the schools; in 1362 courts of law began to use English, "because French had become unknown." William Langland wrote his homely poem, "The Vision of William concerning Piers Plowman," in English, that it might be more widely read. The poet Gower, and his contemporary, Chaucer,[1] who died in 1400, used the common country speech for their compositions. Chaucer's "Canterbury Tales" and the prose pamphlets and translated Bible of John Wyclif practically settled the question that the new English should be spoken and written by Englishmen.

Langland.

Gower.
Chaucer.

[1] **The dialects of English** varied so greatly among themselves that in Chaucer's time a north of England man and a southerner could scarcely understand each other's speech. The Midland dialect, which was fairly intelligible to all, gained the ascendancy in London, the common meeting-place of Englishmen. Chaucer the Londoner popularized this dialect by putting his poem into it, and Caxton, the first English printer, gave it greater currency, and assured its permanence.

John Wyclif,[1] sometimes called the first Protestant, was educated for the priesthood and became a famous teacher in Oxford University. His study of the Scriptures convinced him that the religion of England had drifted away from Christ. The clergy should preach the Gospel and lead Christ-like lives; he found them amassing fortunes, misusing the ecclesiastical courts, and seeking temporal rather than spiritual influence. To inculcate his own doctrines he sent out "poor preachers," clad in russet gowns, to labor among the lowly. His active mind did not stop at this reform; he denied the right of the pope to levy taxes upon England. The tribute which King John had pledged his kingdom to pay was thirty-three years in arrears, and Parliament boldly refused to pay it more. Wyclif applauded and defended this defiance of Rome. John of Gaunt, in his quarrel with William of Wykeham and the clergy, was thus brought for a time into sympathy with Wyclif, and protected him from the archbishop's

JOHN WYCLIF.

[1] Wyclif was convinced that the Bible was an all-sufficient rule of Christian faith and practice. He said: "Christen men and women, olde and young, shulde study fast in the New Testament, and no simple man of wit shulde be afered unmesurably to study in the text of Holy Writ. . . . The New Testament is of ful autoritie, and open to understanding of simple men, as to the poynts that ben most needful to salvation." One verse of the Magnificat will show the character of his version: "And Marye seyde, My soule worschipe the Lorde and my spirit joiede in God myn helpe."

England and France.

condemnation for heresy. Repudiation of the worldly ambition of the church led the free-thinking priest to an examination of its doctrines, and thence to his denial (1381) of the dogma of "transubstantiation." To explain his position he wrote a host of tracts, in English, written copies of which, even before the invention of printing, made their way among the people and helped the open-air preachers to found the sect called "Lollards," the forerunners of the English Reformation. Wyclif died in retirement as parish priest of Lutterworth. His later years were devoted to his grandest work, the translation of the Bible into the tongue of the common people of England. He died on the last day of the year 1384, reckoned a man of great note in his own day, and now esteemed among the first men of Christendom.[1] *The Lollards.*

Several sons of King Edward III. grew to manhood: (1) Edward, the Black Prince, who died just before his father, leaving a son, Prince Richard; (2) Lionel, Duke of Clarence (the poet Chaucer's patron), who died in 1368, leaving a daughter, Philippa, the ancestress of the earls of March; (3) John "of Gaunt," Duke of Lancaster, the ancestor of the Lancastrian kings; (4) Edmund of Langley, Duke of York, from whose line sprang the Yorkist kings; and (5) the Duke of Gloucester. *The sons of Edward III.*

Richard II., son of the Black Prince, ascended the throne at the age of eleven (1377), his uncle John of *Richard II., 1377-1399.*

---

[1] After his death Wyclif was excommunicated; his body was taken out of the churchyard and burnt, and the ashes scattered on the water of a running stream—the Avon—all by the pope's order. The great influence of this pioneer Protestant gave rise to this popular rhyme:

"The Avon to the Severn runs
 The Severn to the sea;
And Wyclif's dust shall spread abroad
 Wide as the waters be."

Richard II.'s queen, Anne of Bohemia, introduced Wyclif's works into Bohemia and so kindled the reforming spirit in the breast of John Huss.

Gaunt being in the prime of life. England was suffering from the war taxation and the ravages of the plague. Moreover, the common people were now fairly astir. The three Edwards had brought the nation to a consciousness of its unity and its independence of any foreign power; the development of Parliament had admitted a new class to a share in the government, and the spirit of Wyclif and his itinerant preachers was working among the stolid country folk, and teaching them to question for themselves their social and political system.

Social changes. A change had in due course come over the condition of the lower classes. Slavery no longer existed, and serfage and villeinage in its various forms had nearly passed away. The serf, or villein, who had lived upon his master's land in return for certain labor performed, had been released from this obligation, and now paid a certain rent in cash or produce for his holding, in place of the old manual labor. The Black Death appeared at the time when many villeins were winning, and many thought they had already won, their freedom from this degrading service. The great landowners saw their laborers dying off like sheep. The flocks strayed and grain rotted in the fields. To *The labor market.* secure herdsmen and harvesters the landowners obtained from king and Parliament, in the years following the plague, certain "Statutes of Laborers," requiring all landless men and women to work at a fixed low wage for any employer who should demand their service; and the laborer was forbidden to go beyond the limits of his parish in search of employment.

The proprietors, at their wits' end for labor, even reasserted their claims upon those villeins and serfs who had gained partial freedom. The sons and grandsons of freedmen were haled before justices and compelled to serve the family to which their ancestors had belonged. Bitter discontent and frequent local outbreaks mark these times. The protest of Wyclif against the luxury of the church was taken up by his disciples and pressed to its full extent. The hardworking peasants saw the nobles and bishops gorgeously arrayed while their tenants perished with hunger. John Ball, "a mad priest," as a courtier called him, seemed sane enough to the crowds of Kentishmen who listened to his socialistic sermons. Equality was his gospel, community of property the burden of his homilies.

Socialistic agitators.

> When Adam delved, and Eve span,
> Who was then the gentleman?

was a text with which he roused the jealousy and envy of his countrymen.[1]

In 1380 Parliament levied a heavy poll-tax on all above the age of fourteen, and the next summer the poor farmers and artisans, excited by the injustice which they had suffered, broke out in the rebellion known as "the Peasants' Revolt." Homely jingles in the common country people's English passed from mouth to mouth, giving the signals for the rising, and it seemed as if the whole nation had risen in one day. Wat Tyler and John Hales, with many thousand farm-hands at their backs, marched on Canterbury and dismantled the archbishop's palace, entered London, burning John of Gaunt's palace, breaking into the Tower, and killing

"The Peasants' Revolt," 1381.

Wat Tyler.

---

[1] Green ("Short History of the English People") quotes Ball's teaching: "Good people, things will never go well in England so long as goods be not common, and so long as there be villeins and gentlemen. By what right are they whom we call lords greater folk than we? On what grounds have they deserved it? Why do they hold us in serfage? If we all came of the same father and mother, Adam and Eve, how can they say or prove that they are better than we, if it be not that they make us gain for them by our toil what they spend in their pride?"

the archbishop and the poll-tax commissioner. Along the north bank of the Thames came another host from Essex, killing lawyers and burning deeds, charters, and mortgages as they advanced. King Richard, a lad of fifteen, sent the Essex men home with promises that serfage should exist no more. Two days afterward he dispersed Wat Tyler's men at Smithfield. The lord mayor stabbed the peasant leader for insulting his king, and Richard proclaimed himself captain of the rioters. They heard with joy his pledges of redress and then dispersed. The insurrection profited little. The king and nobles raised armies and stamped it out without mercy. Seven thousand of the poor peasantry were put to the sword or sent to the gallows before autumn.

The last of John Ball.

The socialist Ball was hanged, drawn, and quartered. Parliament, wherein sat scarcely a man who was not a landlord, declared that the king had no power or right to give away private property. So villeinage and serfage remained lawful, but the natural causes which had been at work before the pestilence soon revived, and by a rapid and peaceful revolution free labor took the place of the ancient form.[1]

Tyranny.

After eight years of subjection to his uncles—the regents Lancaster and Gloucester—the young king came to the throne. He soon abandoned all restraint and grasped at despotism. Submissive legislators, awed or paid by the king, granted him revenues for life, and appointed a commission of eight men to act in the place of Parliament.

Richard ruled henceforth with little respect for the rights of nobles, clergy, or commoners. Two power-

[1] To keep the peasants from improving their social condition, and maintain the supply of agricultural laborers, acts of Parliament "forbade the child of any tiller of the soil to learn a craft or trade in town." The king was even asked to prevent them from sending their sons to school. Oxford and Cambridge turned a cold shoulder upon the sons of the peasant-farmers.

England and France.

ful lords, Thomas Mowbray, Duke of Norfolk, and the ambitious Henry of Bolingbroke, he banished (1398). A few months later, when Bolingbroke's father, old John of Gaunt, died, the king seized his rich estates. Henry complained of this injustice and set about to recover his rights. The king was absent in Ireland when Bolingbroke landed in Yorkshire (1399) with other exiles, who made common cause against the tyrant. Percy of Northumberland and other northern nobles joined Henry. Even his uncle Edmund, Duke of York, regent in Richard's absence, turned from the setting to the rising sun. Upon the king's return he found himself forsaken and defenseless in the presence of a hostile army. Henry at first demanded his own inheritance and a share in the government; but this did not long appease his appetite for power. A Parliament at Westminster declared the king incapable of reigning and decreed his deposition. The nearest heir in direct descent was an Edmund Mortimer, great-grandson of Lionel, Duke of Clarence. But his tender years and lack of friends defrauded him of a hearing, when the victorious Henry of Bolingbroke, now in his forty-fourth year, demanded the crown by right of descent and by right of recovery from the evil government of Richard.[1] Parliament accepted Henry as the lawful sovereign. The wretched Richard was im-

Bolingbroke.

Deposition of Richard II., 1399.

Henry IV., 1399-1414.

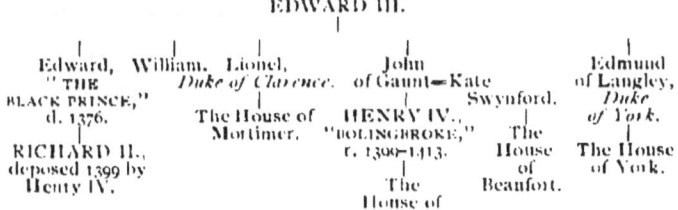

1 THE DESCENT OF HENRY IV.
EDWARD III.

Edward, "THE BLACK PRINCE," d. 1376.	William.	Lionel, Duke of Clarence.	John of Gaunt = Kate Swynford.		Edmund of Langley, Duke of York.
RICHARD II., deposed 1399 by Henry IV.		The House of Mortimer.	HENRY IV., "BOLINGBROKE," r. 1399-1413.	The House of Beaufort.	The House of York.
			The House of Lancaster.		

prisoned in the Castle of Pontefract, where not long after he died, or was murdered. He was the eighth and last of the Angevin kings in the direct line. The House of Plantagenet now divides among the descendants of Edward III.'s two younger sons, the Dukes of Lancaster and York. It was in Richard's reign that the Statute of Præmunire, originally framed in Edward III.'s time, was reënacted. This was one of the twists by which England shook off the hand of the pope. This law made it a grave crime for any person to bring into England any bull or letter of excommunication from the pope without the consent of the king.

Statute of Præmunire.

As Henry IV. had his own right to the throne to vindicate he could afford neither idleness nor oppression. He was under obligation to the northern nobles, who had helped him to win the crown, and to the archbishop, who had put it on his head. But the friendship with the Percys soon turned to open war. The Earl of Northumberland, with his son, that hotspur, Harry Percy, had expended blood and treasure in guarding the frontier against the Scots. For this the king did not reward them. Harry Percy had married into the family of Mortimer, and thus became related to Edmund Mortimer, Earl of March, already mentioned as Richard's lawful heir. Wales revolted in 1400 under Owen Glendower.[1] But the power of the king beat down all resistance.

The Percys crushed.

Welsh revolt, 1400. Glendower.

If the king, as the Percys charged, broke faith with

---

[1] Owen Glendower, the hero of the Welsh struggle for independence, was a man of education, property, and liberal ideas. His just quarrel with a neighboring noble was misrepresented to Henry, who used force against him. Upon this, Glendower rallied his countrymen in arms, and for five years, aided by the inclement weather and the uncommonly difficult country, foiled every attempt of the English to restore their authority. His own Celtic followers hailed him as "Prince of Wales," and the English soldiers dreaded him as a sorcerer who had the prince of the power of the air in his service. He never yielded, though his country was subdued. In the traditions of his race he is the sleeping hero who shall some day lead them to victory over the Saxon.

the barons, he kept it with the bishops. The lords of the church could not disregard the practical tendency of the Wyclifite teachings. Little as the abbots and deans may have cared for purity of doctrine, they had a very sensitive regard for the rights of property, which were recklessly assailed by the leveling Lollards. The first year of the fifteenth century (1401) is memorable for the passage of a "Statute of Heresy." King Henry had already urged the regular clergy to put a stop to the preaching of the "simple priests" of Wyclif's sect. This act of Parliament gave the church authority to arrest heretical preachers, teachers, and writers, to imprison them, and, on their persistent refusal to abjure their errors, to burn them alive in a public place, that the people might see and be admonished. The bishops were eager to begin their persecution. William Sautre (1401) and John Badby (1410), a priest and a tailor, were the first martyrs of the reign—the leaders in a procession of Englishmen, Catholic and Protestant, who furnished food for persecuting flames for two centuries.

The laws against Lollardry, 1401.

Two martyrs.

Henry's reign was brief and full of trouble. On May 20, 1413, he died in the Jerusalem Chamber of Westminster Abbey, leaving his kingdom to his son, the "Prince Hal" of Shakespeare.

Henry V. was twenty-five years old at the time of his father's death, and had already approved himself a soldier in the Welsh wars. Comely of face and figure, brave and skilful in war, and ambitious to restore the military reputation of England, Harry of Monmouth became a popular hero like Richard Lion-heart and Edward, the Black Prince.

Henry V., 1413-1422.

The Lollards troubled the first months of the reign. Sir John Oldcastle, Lord Cobham, an able soldier and a

Sir John Oldcastle.

trusted friend of the king, turned Wyclifite, and tried to protect his fellow-believers. He was denounced as a traitorous demagogue, and some of his actions convinced Henry that he was plotting the destruction of the king and the chief men of the council. Cobham was burned, and many Lollards perished with him.[1]

Second stage of the Hundred Years' War.

Henry's French campaigns mark the second period of the Hundred Years' War. The king of France, Charles VI., was insane and his nobles were fighting among themselves for the control of the government. Henry seized the opportunity to reassert his claim to the French crown, basing his pretensions upon the rights of his grandfather, Edward III. In 1415 he crossed to Calais with an army, intending to engage in turn with the contending factions. But at his approach contention ceased, and it was a united host far greater than his own which faced his bowmen at Agincourt, October 25, 1415. His peril was greater than that of Edward at Poitiers, for his men were sick and starving, and in his position defeat meant the utter destruction of his army. Before the combat the Earl of Westmoreland had wished that some of England's idle warriors might be in their ranks. Not so the king, as Shakespeare voices his reply:

Battle of Agincourt, 1415.

> No, my fair cousin:
> If we are marked to die, we are enow
> To do our country loss; and if to live,
> The fewer men the greater share of honor.
> God's will! I pray thee wish not one man more.

The battle was stubbornly contested. But at Agincourt, as at Crecy, no weapon could withstand the

---

[1] In his trial this general, popularly known as "the good Lord Cobham," declared: "Before God and man I profess solemnly here that I never abstained from sin until I knew Wyclif, whom ye so much disdain." He was suspended from a gallows by chains and roasted over a slow fire.

cloth-yard shafts from the English longbows. King
Henry fought in the thick of the battle, and had his
helmet split open by a French sword. His intrepid
courage inspired his men to exploits almost beyond
belief, and the sun set upon a field strewn with French
corpses.[1] The victors were so few and ill-provided that
they could not follow up their success. In 1417 Henry
returned to resume the conquest of Normandy, when a
sudden turn in French affairs threw open the doors to a
more splendid triumph. John, Duke of Burgundy, the
most powerful vassal of France, was murdered by partisans of the dauphin Charles. The vengeful Burgundians betrayed their country to the English. The treaty
of Troyes (1420) made Henry of England regent of
France during the life of Charles VI. and heir to the
French crown at his death. To cement the union
Henry married the Princess Catharine. The country
north of the Loire accepted him as regent, but in the
southern provinces the disinherited dauphin maintained
an ineffectual struggle.

Treaty of Troyes.

At King Henry's death (August, 1422) his son, a
babe in arms, was acknowledged King Henry VI. of
England and heir of France. Two months later the
mad Charles died also, and the baby king of England
was formally proclaimed king of France. Henry V.
had named his two brothers, Thomas, Duke of Gloucester, and John, Duke of Bedford, as regents of England and France respectively during the infancy of his
son.

Death of Henry V., 1422.

---

[1] In front of the English position at Agincourt stretched a mile of plowed ground, soft with recent rains. The dismounted French knights, heavily overweighted with their clumsy plate armor, were quite exhausted by their effort to advance on foot through the mire, and "stuck fast in the mud with the archery playing upon them." When the arrows gave out the whole English army charged, and the embogged, steel-cased knights were at their mercy.
The English loss was less than one hundred; the French lost 10,000 killed and
many prisoners. Indeed, their armored knights could not run if they tried.

TOPICS FOR READING AND SPECIAL STUDY.
WITH LIBRARY NOTES.

1. THE ENGLISH LANGUAGE.
    History of the English Language. T. R. Lounsbury.
    The English Language. R. Morris. (Article in Ency. Brit., Ninth Ed.)
2. WYCLIF AND THE LOLLARDS.
    John Wyclif. Lewis Sergeant. (Heroes of the Nations Series.)
    Wyclif and Movements for Reform. R. L. Poole. (Epochs of Church History.)
3. THE BLACK DEATH.
    History of Epidemics in Britain. C. Creighton.
    The Black Death in East Anglia. Jessopp. (In "Nineteenth Century," Vols. XVI., XVII.)
4. MANNERS AND CUSTOMS.
    English Wayfaring Life in the Middle Ages. Jusserand.
    Chronicles of Froissart. Lord Berners. (Trans.)

FICTION, ETC.

Coulyng Castle. Agnes Giberne.
The White Company. A. Conan Doyle.
Jock o' the Mill. W. Howitt.
Lances of Lynwood. C. M. Yonge.
Mistress Margery. Emily S. Holt.
The Dream of John Ball. W. Morris. (Poem.)

The Shakespearian plays of this period are: Richard II., Henry IV. (Parts 1 and 2), Henry V.

CHAPTER IX.

LANCASTER AND YORK, 1422 A. D.–1485 A. D.—
FROM THE ACCESSION OF HENRY VI. TO
THE DEPOSITION OF RICHARD III.

THE enormous power which Henry V. had wielded was jeopardized by his death. Even the arrangements which he had made for the management of the two kingdoms were disregarded. John, Duke of Bedford, was allowed to retain the regency of France and to continue the struggle with the dauphin, but while the other brother, Gloucester, was honored with the empty title of "protector," the government of England was really conducted by a council of lords—church and lay—directed by Gaunt's son, Henry Beaufort, bishop of Winchester, who for a generation was the "pillar of the state." Parliament retained little influence and the commons almost none. The baronage had grown rich from the plunder of France,[1] and the church from the taxes of England. Through their representatives in the council these two classes exercised almost absolute authority, and the liberties which the rise of the commonalty had brought almost within reach of the English nation were snatched away. *The regency and the council.* *Decadence of Parliament.*

The dauphin, whom the national party in France recognized as King Charles VII., occupied but a fragment of his father's dominions. By the provisions of the treaty of Troyes (1420) he inherited nothing, the *Affairs in France.*

[1] "The age of castle-building was past, and the newly enriched nobles built such houses as Hurstmonceaux in Sussex, a series of open courts with rooms built round them. The whole was surrounded by wall and moat and had the appearance of a castle but very little of the strength of a fortress."—*Hughes.*

whole realm passing to the English House of Lancaster, whose armies already occupied two thirds of France by virtue of Henry V.'s conquests and his alliance with the dukes of Burgundy. This foreign domination could not be popular, and the private grudge of the Burgundians against the French royal family was destined to die of itself, or to be smothered by other interests. Whenever Burgundy should withdraw her hand from England's friendly grasp the English power in France must fall.

Such was the French situation when John of Bedford became regent. Could he have depended, as did his brother, upon the united support of the nobility at home he might have given some degree of permanence to the English domination of France. *Charles VII. of France.* Charles VII. was weak in mind and appalled by the wreck of his kingdom. The South, which remained true to him, and the patriots who clung to the royal line could draw little inspiration from his feeble efforts to expel the foreigners. The Scots and Milanese who were sent to his assistance were terribly beaten at Verneuil *Verneuil.* (1424).[1] Orleans, the finest city remaining to Charles, was invested by an English army, and was on the point of yielding when—one of the most marvelous events in the world's history—a peasant girl stepped forth and saved France.

Joan of Arc, or "Jeanne d' Arc," was the daughter of *Joan of Arc.* a laboring man of Domremy, a hamlet on the borders of Lorraine. She was three or four years old when Henry of Monmouth's yeomen routed the French knights at Agincourt, and she was in her eighteenth

[1] In this year (1424) James I. of Scotland, who had been for eighteen years a political prisoner in England, was restored to his throne. During his captivity he fell in love with Lady Jane Beaufort, whom he married and in whose honor he wrote "The King's Quair," a celebrated poem in the manner of Chaucer.

year when the miseries of her nation called her from her father's cottage to the royal camp. She had been a quiet, thoughtful child, and in dreams and visions by day and by night she had held conversations with saints and angels. Mysterious "voices" told her what to do. When she grew to young womanhood and heard the neighbors speak of the war and the degradation of

The "voices."

JOAN OF ARC. From the painting by Bastien-Lepage.

France, the "voices" whispered to her that the King of Heaven had chosen her, the peasant girl of Domremy, to deliver the king of France from his enemies. Her father's threats could not make her disobey the sacred call. The priests and the captains who tried to stay her shrank before her unquestioning faith in her mission. Jeanne was not the only superstitious person in the realm, and her faith bred faith in others around her. They brought her to Charles, to whom she said: "Gentle sir, I am Jeanne the Maid. The heavenly King sent me to tell you that you shall be crowned in the town of Rheims, and you shall be lieutenant of the heavenly King, who is the King of France."

Rheims was then in English hands, and it was difficult to believe her words; but it was even more difficult to doubt her calm confidence, and the Maid was furnished with the armor and the troops that she required. By a bold maneuver she entered Orleans and brought succor to the besieged. At the head of the garrison she sallied forth and captured the English forts beyond the walls, liberating the city from its long constraint (1429). The French soldiery reverenced her courage and saintly purity; in the English camp her name was at first a by-word, but after her successes the men *A witch.* began to fear the "Maid of Orleans" as a witch, declaring that her guiding "voices" were of the devil.[1] The simple-hearted heroism of the Maid had at last kindled the patriotism of the people, and the force of the nation was rallying to the support of the dauphin. Before the end of the year Charles was crowned in the Cathedral of Rheims, and Jeanne, her mission accom- *The dauphin crowned.* plished, begged leave to go home. But the king, who had found her useful, denied her request. She fell into the hands of the Burgundians, whose duke sold her to the English. Being accused of witchcraft and heresy, she asserted her innocence and purity to the last. When the judges gave sentence against her she appealed to "her Judge, the King of heaven and earth,"

[1] The common soldiers were not the only ones who dreaded her power. Bedford himself spoke of her as a "disciple and limb of the fiend, called the Pucelle, that used false enchantments and sorcery."

saying, "in all my doings God has been my lord." They condemned her to be burned. The ungrateful French king, who might well have pledged his crown to ransom her, let the sentence take its course. In 1431, before she was yet twenty-one years old, Joan of Arc, praying aloud and crying "Jesus!" with her last painful breath, was burned at the stake in the city of Rouen.[1]

Death of the Maid, 1431

Four years after Joan's martyrdom England's grip upon France was loosened. The Duke of Burgundy swung over to King Charles. The regent Bedford died (1435), and the area of English influence on the Continent shrank with every campaign. In the year 1450 the last Norman town surrendered to France, and in 1453 Gascony also was lost. The Hundred Years' War was at an end. England lost not only her recent conquests, but all her lands and citadels in France, excepting Calais, were taken from her.

England loses hold of France.

Very little had Henry VI. to do with these reverses. During the first twenty years of his reign he was under guardianship as a minor, and the last ten were marked by long periods of imbecility. He was married to Margaret, Princess of Anjou, but until 1453 he had no heir and a vigorous controversy raged over the succession. Out of the disputed claims of the ducal families of Lancaster and York, called from the badges of their partisans the "Red Rose" and the "White," sprang the thirty years (1455-85) of civil uproar, which are

Henry VI., 1422-1471.

The "Roses."

---

[1] Joan was not the only victim of the credulity of the age. In 1439 the Duchess Eleanor, wife of the "Protector," was solemnly tried for consulting the fiend and using sorcery against the king, Henry IV., melting a wax image before the fire as a type of his wasting away. Her accomplices, Roger, "a magician," of Oxford University, and Margaret, "a witch," were put to death. Even the great lady herself must walk barefoot through London and die in prison. A generation later (1477) one Thomas Burdet, exasperated because the king had shot his favorite deer, was heard to wish that the head, horns, and all were on the man who had killed it. He was accused of poisoning, sorcery, and enchantment, duly tried, and executed.

known as the Wars of the Roses, and to whose history we have now come.¹

The vexed question of the royal inheritance will be better understood by reference to the genealogical table of the descendants of Edward III. (page 151). For three generations the crown had been in the family of Lancaster—the three Henrys (IV., V., and VI.) being son, grandson, and great grandson of John of Gaunt. Assuming that Henry VI. would die childless, the Lancastrian party selected to succeed him Edmund Beaufort, Duke of Somerset, grandson of John of Gaunt by his mistress, Catherine Swynford. Richard Plantagenet, Duke of York, was his principal rival. Richard had a double claim if he chose to press it. Through his mother, Ann Mortimer, he inherited the royal rights of the Earls of March, the descendants of Edward's third son, Lionel, and from his father he acquired the claims and titles of Edmund, Edward's fifth son. The illegitimate Beauforts had once been debarred from the succession by law; therefore, should the Lancastrian king have no children Richard Plantagenet would be his lawful heir; meanwhile his prior claim as Earl of March was kept in reserve.

The contest opened, therefore, with Edmund Beaufort, Lancastrian, and Richard Plantagenet, the Yorkist, striving for recognition as heir to Henry VI. In 1453 a son, Edward, Prince of Wales, was born to the king and Margaret, his queen. This offered a peaceful settlement for the quarrel by superseding the claims of

---

¹ Besides the question of the inheritance the Yorkist party, whose strength was chiefly in the South, represented the current dissatisfaction with the Lancastrian dynasty which had brought the French wars to a disgraceful end, and had plunged the nation into unprecedented debt. A popular rhyme against the party ran,
"We have made the king so poor,
That now he beggeth from door to door."
For Shakespeare's version of the Red and White Rose emblems, see "1 Henry VI.," Act ii., Sc. iv.

LANCASTER AND YORK.

EDWARD III.,
d. 1377.

(3.) Lionel, DUKE OF CLARENCE, d. 1368.

Philippa, m. Edmund Mortimer, EARL OF MARCH.

Roger Mortimer, EARL OF MARCH, d. 1398.

m. Catharine of France=m. Owen Tudor.

Edmund Mortimer, EARL OF MARCH, d. 1425.

Ann, m. *Richard*, EARL OF CAMBRIDGE. (See last column.)

(4.) John of Gaunt, = Catherine Swynford.
DUKE OF LANCASTER, d. 1399.

Blanche of Lancaster. ⟶ John of Gaunt,

John Beaufort, EARL OF SOMERSET.

HENRY IV., r. 1399-1413.

Edmund Beaufort, DUKE OF SOMERSET.

HENRY V., r. 1413-1422.

Edmund Tudor,=Margaret Beaufort.
EARL OF RICHMOND.

HENRY VI., r. 1422-1471, m. Margaret of Anjou.

Edward, PRINCE OF WALES, killed at Tewkesbury, 1471.
(Ending direct line of Lancaster, or "Red Rose.")

HENRY VII.,=*Elizabeth*.
d. 1509.

HENRY VIII.
("Union of Red and White Roses.")

(5.) *Edmund of Langley*,
DUKE OF YORK,
d. 1402.

Richard,
EARL OF CAMBRIDGE.
m. Ann Mortimer,
heiress of March (see 1st column).

Richard,
DUKE OF YORK,
d. 1460.

EDWARD IV.,
r. 1461-1483.

RICHARD III.,
r. 1483-1485.
DUKE OF YORK,
d. 1485.

George,
DUKE OF CLARENCE,
d. 1479.

(1.) *Edward V.*

(2.) *Richard*,
DUKE OF YORK.

Princes, murdered in the Tower, 1483.

NOTE.—House of York in Italic;
House of Lancaster in Roman.

both parties, and had Henry been a powerful monarch the nation might have escaped the civil wars; but his malady increased, and the periods of lethargy through which he passed made it necessary for the helm of the state to be in steadier hands. Duke Richard was appointed "Protector." Queen Margaret with an eye to her little son's prospects supported the Lancastrian, Edmund Beaufort. The king's disease came and went; in his periods of sanity he resumed the government, and, guided by Beaufort, took harsh measures against York. The strength of the Yorkist party lay in the Earls of Salisbury and Warwick. In 1455 the royal army was beaten by Richard and the two earls at St. Albans,[1] and Edmund Beaufort was slain. Richard resumed the regency, and the king relapsed into imbecility. At his next recovery, in 1458, there was another revolution. The Yorkist party defended itself, and in the battle of Northampton, 1460, captured the king.

Elated by his victory, and encouraged by his full possession of the throne, Richard now asserted his immediate claim to the crown as the descendant of Lionel, John of Gaunt's elder brother. This the Parliament refused to allow in full, but conceded that the Duke of York, and not the Prince of Wales, should succeed Henry at his death. This called the Red Rose into the field. A new Duke of Somerset had succeeded the fallen Edmund Beaufort, and with him stood Lord Clifford in the struggle for the inheri-

Duke Richard becomes "Protector."

The Wars of the Roses, 1455-1485.

---

[1] This engagement, the first of the fourteen battles of the Wars of the Roses, was a mere skirmish in which "only some sixscore" fell. The masses of the people were not moved by the issues of this civil war, which was fought between factions of the nobility at the head of mercenary troops. The end of the long war with France had turned loose in England a horde of professional soldiers, whose swords were at the service of the highest bidder. The smaller knights and squires took the livery or badge of the great nobles and espoused their quarrels.

tance of Prince Edward. They cut the Yorkist forces in pieces in the battle of Wakefield (1460). Duke Richard died on the field, and the Earl of Salisbury on the scaffold. The queen with grim humor crowned the severed head of her enemy, Richard, and exposed it on the walls of York. The duke's son, Edward, and Salisbury's son, the Earl of Warwick, continued to resist. They occupied London, gathered a great army in the East, and on Palm Sunday, 1461, met the Lancastrian army on Towton Field. Twenty thousand bloody corpses were strewn on the trampled snow at sunset, where the banner of the Red Rose had floated at dawn. The fiercest battle that had been fought in Britain in four centuries was won by Edward of York. The pitiable king fled to Scotland with his valiant queen and her little son, while Parliament and citizens alike hailed the Yorkist victor. In June he was crowned as King Edward IV. *Battle of Towton, 1461.*

Edward IV. was a strong man, handsome, brave, and a brilliant soldier, but with much of the tyrant in him. With Parliament he had small patience, and under him that body lost the strength which it had been accumulating since the death of Simon of Montfort. For years at a time he did not once summon the Lords and Commons, managing by various unconstitutional devices to raise, without legal taxation, the money which his ambitions required. The estates of conquered Lancastrians were forfeited to the crown; subsidies were granted and collected for wars which were never fought; and when Parliament was called together no more the king invited the rich citizens of London to give of their substance "benevolences" into the royal treasury. *Edward IV., 1461-1483.* *Edward's personal rule.* *"Benevolences."*

Such a royal invitation was not to be slighted. Beyond all these sources of revenue Edward was a moneymaker in a manner new to English sovereigns. The world was awakening from the sleep of the Middle Ages. The crusades had increased communication between the East and West, and trade had followed in their wake. The king became a merchant, owning and freighting a fleet of ships whose voyages turned fresh streams of gold into his treasure chests. Europe was all astir. Medieval customs, the feudal system, the temporal supremacy of the Catholic Church had passed their prime, and the old order was ready for a change. In Italy art was blossoming forth into its most perfect flower. In the courts of Western Europe a Genoese skipper was showing a roll of curious maps and begging for a chance to discover a new world. John Gutenberg in Germany was cutting types for the first printed book; and in every university and many a monastic library men read with wide-eyed wonderment the treasures of Greek and Latin literature which, long preserved in Constantinople, had been dispersed at its fall (1453). Art, science, letters, intellectual activity of every sort was born again. The Wars of the Roses held England back from the general advance. Her artists were rude imitators, she had no poets, her first printers learned their craft at German cases,[1] and Spain was quicker than London to prove that Columbus's dream was true.

King Edward's wars did not end with his accession. The great Lancastrian lords had lost their lives and

The world astir.

England behind the times.

---

[1] The first English printer was William Caxton, a native of Kent (1422), who was a cloth merchant at Bruges when the art of printing came into use. He probably learned the craft at Cologne and first practiced it at Bruges, where he issued the earliest English book, "The Recuyell of the Histories of Troye," about 1474. Caxton was translator, editor, corrector of the press, and printer. In 1477 he established his office in London, within the precincts of Westminster Abbey, and in November he issued "Dictes or Sayings of the Philosophers," the first book printed in England. Caxton's use of the English spoken by the Londoners did much to establish that dialect as the language of literature. He died about 1491.

their lands in the hour of defeat, but the great allies of York claimed unusual favors from the duke whom they had set upon a throne. The Earl of Warwick, the "king-maker," himself, was the most rebellious subject. After Towton battle the unconquerable Queen Margaret had roused her partisans to other futile efforts for her son. To these the battle of Hexham (1464) put an end, and Edward felt encouraged to show his independence. He offended the Yorkist lords by marrying a Lancastrian lady. To strengthen his position he betrothed his sister to Duke Charles the Bold, of Burgundy, the leading noble of France. The "king-maker's" rebellion.

The ambition and jealousy of the Duke of Clarence, the king's brother, furnished Warwick with a center for his plots. Clarence married the earl's daughter (1469), and the allied nobles seized the person of the king. But their proposition found no supporters. Edward, soon released and moving quickly, pressed the conspirators so hard that they were forced to new treasons. Queen Margaret, ready for any alliance which should benefit her house, promised the earl that her son should wed his daughter. Thus the remnant of the strength of Lancaster joined with the mainstay of the House of York to ruin Edward. Surprised by this sudden turn, the king escaped to France (1470), while the distracted Henry VI. emerged from his prison for a few weeks of empty royalty. The fugitive king.

The subtlety of the king-maker was surpassed by Edward. With French support he landed in England and rallied an army. Henry, the lawful sovereign, had been restored, and Edward declared that with the king he had no quarrel. His royal rights and title he would waive; only for his dukedom of York would he fight. This specious statement served its purpose. Even his brother, Clarence, took part in this vindication of the House of York. The Lancastrians lacked a leader. King Henry was but a shadow of a king; the Prince of Wales was a youth of seventeen; and the traitor Warwick, the strongest man in the party, had so identified himself with the Yorkist cause in the past that half his present host distrusted him. Edward IV. alone was kingly, and he was soon the only king. He struck his enemies before they could unite; Warwick's army was routed at Barnet, in April, 1471,[1] and three weeks later Margaret was defeated at Tewkesbury, and her son, the hope of the House of Lancaster, did not survive the fray. On May 22 the husband and father, Henry VI., died in his prison.

Barnet and Tewkesbury, 1471.

Death of Henry VI., 1471.

Edward IV. resumed the crown unchallenged. For twelve years he reigned securely. Diplomacy was the king's best weapon, and by its means he kept his kingdom free from serious foreign wars and gave it the peace which was needed after the disorder of the civil strife. His brother Clarence, whom he feared, was accused of treason and put to death in London Tower (1478) — drowned in a butt of malmsey, said the babblers of that time. Another brother remained, Richard, Duke of Gloucester, whom many believed to be guilty of the blood of Henry VI., and upon whom the sudden death of Edward IV., April 9, 1483, drew dark suspicions.

Clarence disappears, 1478.

Death of Edward IV., 1483.

The king left four children—the twelve-year-old Edward V.; the ill-fated Richard, Duke of York; Elizabeth, afterward queen of Henry VII., and Katharine. Again the accession of an infant tempted a usurper. The king's cruel uncle, Richard of Gloucester, gained

Edward V., 1483.

---

[1] The battle was fought on the foggy morning of Easter Sunday, and has been called "the battle of the mist." There was great confusion on the field and the Lancastrian archers fired by mistake into troops of their own party.

possession of the boy-king and his brother and seized the government. To give his usurpation a legal gloss he obtained a decree from a council of friendly nobles, annulling the marriage of Edward IV. and declaring their children illegitimate. That his elder brother, Clarence, had been condemned as a traitor tainted the blood of that branch, and thus Richard of Gloucester remained the next male heir of the House of York. Two months only were needed to consummate this iniquity; the duke hurried his nephews (Edward V. and Richard of York) to London Tower, and they were never seen again.[1]

THE TRAITOR'S GATE, TOWER OF LONDON.

The princes in the Tower.

In June, 1483, the usurper was crowned as King Richard III. But his deeds of blood could not establish him firmly upon the throne. The partisans of Lancaster were his natural enemies, and the best men of his own party were shocked by his heartless murders. The king saw that he must win popular favor by real

Richard III., 1483-1485.

---

[1] The Grey Friars' chronicle for the year said simply, " And the two sons of King Edward were put to silence." Two centuries later (1674) workmen engaged in repairing the Tower discovered under the old staircase the bones of two youths. These were believed to be the remains of the princes and were reinterred by order of the king, Charles II., in Westminster Abbey.

concessions. His brother, Edward IV., had erred on the side of tyranny. By neglecting Parliament, and by levying forced benevolences, he had habitually overstepped the bounds which the barons had laid down at Runnymede. By abandoning these forms of misrule Richard might still gain favor. The people of London declared in petition: "We be determined rather to adventure and to commit us to the peril of our lives and jeopardy of death, than to live in such thralldom and bondage as we have lived a long time heretofore, oppressed and injured by extortions and new impositions against the laws of God and man, and the laws and liberty of this realm, wherein every man is inherited." This and like addresses had due effect. Parliament was assembled; the oppressions and exactions of the late king were censured, and new and better laws were enacted. But this mildness failed to save Richard, secure though he deemed himself to be.

Petition of the Londoners.

The Princess Elizabeth, his niece, represented all that was left of the House of York, and her King Richard determined to wed. Another marriage had been planned for the maiden princess. A representative of the House of Lancaster still lived. This was Henry Tudor, Earl of Richmond. His grandfather, Owen Tudor, was a Welsh gentleman of little importance, save for his marriage with Catharine, the widowed queen of Henry V. From this marriage sprang Edmund Tudor, who, with his father's eye for an advantageous match, wedded Margaret Beaufort, of the ducal family of Somerset. Thus Henry Tudor, son of Edmund and Margaret, had in his veins, from his mother and his father's mother, the blood of John of Gaunt. As the hope of Lancaster he was an object of suspicion to the Yorkist kings, and prudence led him

Henry Tudor, Earl of Richmond.

to reside in France rather than in his own earldom. The Lancastrian politicians joined with those Yorkist partisans who had no stomach for Richard's usurpations to marry Henry Tudor to Elizabeth of York. Before the marriage could be compassed the conspiracy was discovered, and Buckingham, one of its leaders, was beheaded for his share in the plot. But Henry of Richmond kept beyond the king's reach until 1485, when despatches from England informed him that the plans were ripe. His reception showed Richard how insecure was his own footing. In all parts of the kingdom there were Lancastrian risings, while the friends of York, for the most part, rose with them or remained quietly in their homes. The last battle in the struggle of the Roses was fought August 22, 1485, on Bosworth Field, in Leicestershire. King Richard's men deserted him in the face of the enemy; he had no chance of flight, but—with the bravery of his Plantagenet blood—he sold his life at the cost of many, and fell in a vain attempt to kill the Tudor. The Red Rose triumphed over the White that day, as the White had vanquished the Red at Tewkesbury fourteen years before, but the union of the Red and White in the marriage of Henry and Elizabeth ended forever the strife of Lancaster and York. Henry of Richmond was accepted by Parliament as Henry VII., the first of the Tudor line of kings.

Bosworth Field, 1485.

Death of Richard III., 1485.

TOPICS FOR READING AND SPECIAL STUDY, WITH LIBRARY NOTES.

1. JOAN OF ARC.
    Joan of Arc. Francis C. Lowell.
    Jeanne d' Arc. M. O. W. Oliphant.

2. WARWICK, THE KING-MAKER.
   Warwick. C. W. Oman.
3. THE WARS OF THE ROSES.
   Richard III. J. Gairdner.
   Lancaster and York. J. Gairdner.
4. WILLIAM CAXTON AND THE BEGINNINGS OF ENGLISH PRINTING.
   Life of William Caxton. W. Blades.

FICTION, ETC.

The Earl Printer. L. E. Guernsey.
In the Days of Jeanne d' Arc. Mary H. Catherwood.
Personal Recollections of Joan of Arc, etc. "Mark Twain."
The Last of the Barons. Bulwer Lytton.
A Parish Priest of Barnet. A. J. Church.
Henry VI. and Richard III. Shakespeare.

CHAPTER X.

THE TUDOR DESPOTISM, 1485 A. D.–1547 A. D.— HENRY VII. AND HENRY VIII.

FOR one hundred and eighteen years the descendants of Owen Tudor and the widow of Henry V. occupied the English throne. This period marked the transformation of medieval England into a modern state, and the change was accompanied by a splendid outburst of those intellectual forces whose beginnings had thrilled Western Europe while the island kingdom stagnated under the curse of civil war. *Henry VII. of Richmond, 1485-1509.*

The Tudors were strong-willed monarchs, who opposed at every turn the efforts of their subjects to limit their personal authority. The checks which had gradually been placed upon the absolute power of the king previous to 1485, when Henry VII. ascended the throne, were essentially these, some of them as old as Magna Charta itself: (1) No new tax might be imposed upon the nation without the consent of a Parliament in which nobles, clergy, and commoners were represented. (2) The consent of such a Parliament was requisite for all new laws and all changes in the old laws. (3) Without legal warrant no man might be arrested and deprived of his liberty. (4) Accused persons were entitled to speedy trial by a fair jury in the county where the offense was committed. (5) All crown officers were liable to jury trial and punishment for injuries committed upon persons or property, even though such injuries should result from obedience of the king's orders. *Limitations on the royal power.*

These five safeguards secured to England the most liberal government in Europe. It is true that they had not always been respected by every king, but they were so well established that the king who disregarded any one of them branded himself as an oppressor. By force and guile Edward IV. had succeeded in strengthening his position at the expense of Parliament. Richard III. angled for a short-lived popularity with the bait of constitutional reform. Henry VII., when firmly seated on his throne, returned to Edward's policy, and worked with steady purpose to upbuild the personal power of the sovereign.

Despotic monarchs.

Henry's first care was to make firm his seat. As the representative of Lancaster he might serve as a rallying center for a faction, but his descent was by a devious line. He was king by force of arms as truly as Richard had been king by treason and murder, and the one had no clearer royal title than the other. Parliament decreed that Henry VII. and his heirs should rule England ("and France," as the vain title still ran), and on this parliamentary act, backed by the incontrovertible arguments of conquest and possession, the king's authority rested. The remnant of the family of York was a possible source of disturbance. The two sons of Edward IV. were dead, by Richard's order—or as good as dead—in the Tower dungeons. Elizabeth, their sister, the king married, uniting the blood of Lancaster and York. The young Earl of Warwick, son of the "malmsey" Duke of Clarence, and grandson of "the king-maker," was cousin and next of kin to Edward V.; him Henry hurried to the gloomy Tower. Such havoc was made among the Yorkist princes that the party was in straits for a standard-bearer. In this exigency two remarkable imposters appeared in England, reviving for a little the withered rose of York.

Securing his seat.

A headless party.

The first of these "pretenders," one Lambert Simnel,[1] claimed to be that young Earl of Warwick whom Henry held in prison. Men of note believed him to be Warwick, and gave their lives in battle for him at Stoke. He was defeated, captured, and was made a scullion in the palace kitchen. Little daunted by his fate, Perkin Warbeck, another claimant, more successful in his pretensions and more wretched in his end than Simnel, took up the banner of the White Rose. He claimed to be that Richard, Duke of York, whom Richard III. had smothered in the Tower, and his personal charm won powerful support. Profiting by Simnel's experience the managers of the later pretender showed their prize in foreign courts before bringing him to England. The Duchess of Burgundy, aunt of the real Richard, accepted him and kept him two years at her court. In 1496 Warbeck and the Scots' king in-

Lambert Simnel.

Perkin Warbeck.

THE PRINCES IN THE TOWER.
From the painting by Sir John Millais.

---

[1] Simnel was the son of an Oxford baker, and was trained for his part by a priest. The queen-mother, who resented the king's unwillingness to have the queen, her daughter, formally crowned, may have encouraged the imposture. The baker's boy was well received by the Yorkist partisans in Dublin, and was crowned in the cathedral as "King Edward the Sixth." The Earl of Lincoln and Lord Lovel were his chief adherents.

vaded England. The invasion came to nothing. Warbeck was captured in the following year and placed in the Tower with Henry's other enemies. His repeated attempts to escape made him a dangerous prisoner, and in 1499 he and his fellow-prisoner, Warwick, whom Simnel had personated, were put to death. Thus was the White Rose blasted.

<small>Tyrannous exactions.</small>
As soon as the enemies of his house were silenced the king entered upon the career of despotism which characterized the Tudor sovereigns. Parliament sat infrequently. Yet the crown had ample revenues, and the avaricious king amassed a private fortune independently of the consent of the Lords and Commons. Certain commercial duties—tonnage and poundage—were granted him for life by an early Parliament, and these increased in profit with the rapid extension of English trade. Wars with France proved as profitable to Henry as they had been to Edward IV. Money for the campaigns was obtained from the people, but the money went into the royal treasury, the French king at the same time paying well for peace.[1] As the landlords had revived forgotten bonds of servitude when the Black Death had depleted the labor market, so Henry, lacking the tax levies which only a Parliament might impose, revived ancient feudal rights of the crown over the landowners, and compelled the payment of fines and dues which had lain in desuetude for generations. Nobles paid dearly for exemption from the support of armed retainers, this method of punishment yielding profit to the king and depriving the feudal lords of the private armies with

---

[1] Besides the sums levied in England for an expedition against France, which lasted but twenty days, the king received $500,000 from France. It was murmured that Henry was willing "to plume his nobility and people to feather himself."

which they had formerly intimidated the royal power. The development of the art of warfare further strengthened the monarchy. In the simpler days, when bow and arrow, axe and spear, served for offensive armor, many a battle went by preponderance of numbers. Gunpowder had revolutionized the science of war. The Lancastrian kings owed much of their success in France to their use of cannon. The castles of the nobles, which were so many strongholds against the king in times of civil war, were at the mercy of the royal artillery, and the long castle-sieges of the early reigns do not figure in the records of the Tudors.[1]

Changes in warfare.

Landless merchants and other men of wealth had to share their gains with the grasping Henry. "Benevolences," forced contributions, were revived and collected with especial zeal. Morton, the royal officer who was charged with their collection, was so persistent in his search for wealth that men came to speak of "Morton's fork" of two tines. They said that if a man lived extravagantly he was mulcted of a "benevolence" on the ground of evident wealth, and if he sought to avoid this fate by an unostentatious way of life the sheriffs pounced upon him as a miser who must divide his hoard with the king.

"Morton's fork."

It would have been impracticable for the sovereign to use the ordinary jury-courts as a means of enforcing these projects for raising money; an impartial jury would have resisted such acts as tyrannous. So the king had recourse to a court composed of high officials and members of his council. This court—sometimes called "Star Chamber" from the decorated ceiling of

"Star Chamber."

---

[1] "It is hardly possible to exaggerate the advantage which the king had over rebels of all sorts through possessing the only parks of artillery within the four seas."—*Hassall.* Small firearms were coming into use, but the long-bow still remained the chief reliance of the English armies.

its meeting-room—heard cases concerning fraud, libel, feudal privileges, forgery, perjury, riotings, etc., and was in this reign and the next an instrument of the most hateful tyranny. Its judges being appointed by the crown, and no jury being present, the court became a facile tool.

<small>Henry VIII., 1509-1547.</small>

Henry VII. died in 1509, leaving to his burly son, Prince Henry, undisputed title to the throne, a treasure of $10,000,000, and, as he said, alluding to his marriage alliances with Scotland and Spain, "a wall of brass around England." Arthur, another son, had married Catharine of Aragon, daughter of Ferdinand and Isabella, the Spanish patrons of Columbus. His death six months later left her a widow, and the special dispensation of the pope was obtained for her marriage with Prince Henry (1509). The Princess Margaret Tudor found a royal husband in James IV. of Scotland, and in after years became grandmother of Mary Queen of Scots. Mary Tudor, the youngest of Henry's daughters, also wedded a king, Louis XII. of France. After his death she married an Englishman, Charles Brandon, and their grandchild was the unfortunate Lady Jane Grey. These several marriages figure prominently in the history of the sixteenth century in England.

<small>Royal marriages.</small>

Henry VIII.—"bluff King Hal"—was eighteen years old when he came into his father's noble inheritance in 1509. He was in ruddy health, tall, and of fine physique, excelling in every manner of English sport and not ill-trained in the learning of the schools. In him were united the families of Lancaster and York. From his father he received a splendid treasure and a peaceful and prosperous kingdom, whose long quiescence, stagnation indeed, was now giving place to an

<small>"Bluff King Hal."</small>

unprecedented activity in letters, art, and science.[1] His father, moreover, bequeathed to him a vigorous mind, a stubborn will, and a recklessness of life and law which served him well in his thirty-eight years of stormy rule.

The popular favor which greeted the new king was strengthened by an act which augured ill for the security of personal rights. Empson and Dudley, two officers who had aided Henry VII. in his harshest forms of tax-collection, were put to death upon a trumped-up charge.

Death of Empson and Dudley.

HENRY VIII.

Henry thirsted for war as a means of asserting England's place among the continental powers, as well as for the glory and emolument which personal success would bring to him. His marriage with his brother's widow, Catharine of Aragon, determined his place in the struggle which was vexing Europe. After the expulsion of the English from Normandy the French kings had steadily gained in power at the expense of their great feudatories. France was now a consolidated state, and outranked all

---

[1] The study of Greek and the noble literature of the ancient classics began in England in the last decade of the fifteenth century. William Grocyn and Thomas Linacre, who first taught Greek at Oxford, learned it at the universities of Northern Italy.

Henry joins the league, 1512.

other kingdoms in wealth and military power. To hold her in check and protect the pope's temporal possessions in Italy was the object of the Holy League, which was formed about the year 1511 by Ferdinand of Aragon, Queen Catharine's father, with the pope and the Venetian Republic. Henry joined this alliance and drove the French cavalry from the field of Guinegate so swiftly that the day has ever since been called "the

"The Battle of the Spurs," 1513.

Battle of the Spurs" (1513). In the same year the Scots, always on the side of France, were beaten on

Flodden, 1513.

CARDINAL WOLSEY.

Thomas, Cardinal Wolsey

Flodden Field and their king, James IV., was slain. Peace with both countries followed--a peace which the diplomatic ability of Thomas Wolsey prolonged for seven years (1514–21).

Wolsey was the son of a wealthy commoner of Ipswich. Graduating at Oxford at the age of fifteen he was known as "the boy bachelor." By fidelity and adroitness he had worked his way up in the civil service of the state and into the heart of the king's favor. Henry gave him rich offices in the church, and he became bishop of Lincoln and archbishop of York. He was politician first and prelate afterward. He now (1513) took charge of the foreign policy of England and formed a passive alliance with France, where Francis I. began to reign.

Ferdinand of Aragon died, and his famous grandson, Charles V., succeeded to the kingdom of Spain. With kings like these to deal with Wolsey needed every resource, and his master indeed spared none. The pope sent the commoner's son a cardinal's hat and a legate's commission. This placed him at the head of the English Church. He was already foreign minister, and as chancellor of the realm he controlled the judicial machinery of the nation. In his personal revenues, the magnificence of his palaces, the splendor of his household,[1] he was little behind royalty itself.

Charles V., Queen Catharine's nephew, had now, as German emperor and Spanish king, possessions which surrounded and overshadowed those of France. With such an ally the House of Tudor might regain the crown of France. Charles came to England in person to urge immediate action. Francis foresaw his peril, and in a fruitless interview with Henry near Calais sought to recover his friendship, on "the Field of the Cloth of Gold."[2] Henry, Charles, and the pope again joined hands in secret against Francis—Charles promising to marry Henry's daughter, the Princess Mary, his own cousin though she was. Mary was formally recognized as heir to the English throne.

"Field of the Cloth of Gold."

The approach of a foreign war perplexed Cardinal Wolsey. During seven peaceful years he had succeeded in governing England and raising sufficient

Exactions.

---

[1] Wolsey enjoyed the revenues of three bishoprics and a rich abbey. He had eight hundred personal dependents in his household, and was vulgar and ostentatious in his display of wealth.

[2] The description of Henry's costume by an eye-witness warrants the name: "Then the king of England showed himself . . . in beauty and personage, the most goodliest prince that ever reigned over the realm of England. His grace was appareled in a garment of cloth of silver, of Damaske, ribbed with cloth of gold, so thick as may be. The garment was large and plaited very thick. . . . Marvelous to behold. [The trappings of his steed] were of fine gold in bullion, curiously wrought, pounced, and set with antique work in Roman figures." This was extraordinary, even in an age when the dress of the men of rank was splendid.

revenue without recourse to a Parliament. Now a Parliament, with all its possible interference in the king's business, must be called to vote money for the war. It assembled (1523) and voted less than half the sum demanded.[1] In 1525 the government again asked for the detestable "benevolences." Bold voices were heard protesting against the lawless extortion. Bolder hands drove the king's agents from their towns. The levy failed. Meanwhile the war had begun. Charles was winning victories from Francis and spending Henry's hard-wrung gold for his own benefit. England went out shearing and came back shorn; she helped to pay for humbling France, but lost her money for her pains. Charles repudiated his pledge to marry Mary Tudor, and Henry in dismay transferred his friendship to the French king.

<small>The royal divorce.</small>

The course of events has now brought us to the central event of Henry's reign—his divorce from Catharine. This single act led to the fall of Wolsey, the elevation of Cromwell, the quarrel with the pope, and the final separation of the Church of England from the Church of Rome. The royal pair had been married by special permission of the pope—their relationship being ordinarily a bar to such a union. Catharine was some years older than her husband, and it was unlikely that she should leave him any other heir than the Princess Mary. The king was naturally anxious concerning the succession. He now (1525) suspected that the untimely death of his sons was a sign that Heaven was

---

[1] Wolsey's conception of the function of Parliament appears in this anecdote: The pompous cardinal addressed the House of Commons on the needs of the royal treasury, and asked the members to give their opinions. None answering, the cardinal demanded answer from Sir Thomas More, the speaker. More knelt before the great minister and "excused the silence of the House as abashed by the sublimity of the cardinal's presence among them, and showed him that it was neither expedient nor agreeable with their ancient privileges to comply with the cardinal's demands." Whereupon Wolsey took himself out, greatly displeased.

displeased with his marriage; he had, moreover, been
attracted by the wit and beauty of Anne Boleyn, a lady Anne Boleyn.
of the queen's household. Superstition or passion
prompted him to put away his faithful wife, however
serious the obstacles. Only a papal divorce might
dissolve the union which the pope had blessed. The
pope, Clement VII., was under the thumb of the
Emperor Charles and
dared not disgrace
that monarch's un-
happy aunt. The
queen protested that
she had been a true
and loyal wife and
could not be put away
without sin. In 1529
an Italian cardinal
was sent by the pope
to judge the case with
Cardinal Wolsey, but
before the court could
give sentence the
pope transferred the
case to Rome. Mad-
dened at this turn of

ANNE BOLEYN.

affairs the king stripped his favorite of his offices, honors,
and wealth (1529), and would have brought him to the Wolsey's fall.
block on charge of treason had not disease claimed the
broken-spirited man. Wolsey's dying words have been
put into immortal form by Shakespeare:

> O Cromwell, Cromwell!
> Had I but served my God with half the zeal
> I served my king, he would not in mine age
> Have left me naked to mine enemies.

The great cardinal's successor in the royal favor was Thomas Cromwell, a man of obscure origin who had attached himself to Wolsey's fortunes and clung to his master to the end. He combined shrewdness with audacity to a degree which made him the ideal minister of a determined man like Henry, who fixed his mind on definite objects and suffered no earthly obstacle to block his path.

Thomas Cromwell.

The opposition of the pope had now shut the king from his dearest wish—divorce and a new marriage. Cromwell audaciously advised the king to disavow the pope's authority, and to decree the divorce himself as the head of the national church. At first Henry shrank from such a step, and by the advice of Cranmer, whom he was rapidly advancing to the archbishopric of Canterbury, he called upon the universities of Europe to pronounce upon the validity of his marriage with his brother's widow. By unblushing bribery he obtained a favorable opinion from a portion of these scholars, although the best men were unanimous against the divorce. This flimsy endorsement served the purpose. Archbishop Cranmer pronounced the divorce (May, 1533). The king had already (January) married Anne Boleyn, the gay maid of honor.

The king weds Anne Boleyn, 1533.

The pope, thus openly defied, declared the king excommunicated and annulled the divorce; but Henry's will, upheld by the statesman Cromwell and the prelate Cranmer, was inflexible. His Parliament of 1534 passed the Acts of Supremacy and Succession, the former declaring the king to be the "only supreme head on earth of the Church of England," the latter disinheriting the Princess Mary and naming Elizabeth, the new-born daughter of Anne Boleyn, as heir to Henry's throne. Henceforth no appeals from English ecclesiastical courts should be decided in Rome; the papal revenues from English churches were stopped, and the king became

The Act of Supremacy, 1534.

what the pope had been since St. Augustine entered Canterbury, the spiritual and temporal master of the English Church. To Thomas Cromwell, as vicar-general, the king deputed this limitless ecclesiastical power. *Cromwell, vicar-general.*

Refusal to accept the Act of Succession was declared to be treason, and this act included recognition of the validity of the divorce, an admission which no devout Catholic could make. The law became in Cromwell's hands a terrible weapon. With it he convicted the leading Catholics of treason. Sir Thomas More,[1] the lord chancellor, was among the earliest, as he was among the noblest, victims. John Fisher, bishop of Rochester, was beheaded for obedience to his conscience (1535).[2]

SIR THOMAS MORE.

Death of More and Fisher.

[1] More was the most illustrious Englishman of the reign, a great lawyer, a fine scholar, a polished writer, the friend of Erasmus, and a man of singularly pure and noble character. Being unable to countenance the divorce, he resigned the chancellorship and absented himself from the Boleyn wedding. Charges of treason were trumped up against him, but they failed repeatedly. He would not take the oath of supremacy, his conscience forbidding, and on the perjured testimony of one witness the crown attorney—he was convicted. A week later his severed head was exposed to the crowds on London Bridge.

[2] Fisher, who was venerable in years and in character, was kept for a year in the Tower, under circumstances of especial misery. When the pope, hearing of his fortitude, created him a cardinal, the king in his rage had him beheaded at once. When the king heard that the cardinal's hat was coming from Rome he brutally exclaimed: "He shall wear it on his shoulders, then, for I will leave him never a head to set it on."

Cromwell was not content with striking here and there a leader among the opposite party. He served his king with a zeal surpassing that which the dying Wolsey lamented. The church which Henry had now separated from Rome by law must be made thoroughly subservient to the king. Its revenues, its courts, its offices, its lands, its very doctrines must be at his disposal. The power delegated to the vicar-general was sufficient to accomplish this design. Fresh enactments gave the monarch the appointment of all bishops, and a new and startling movement brought its property and revenues under royal control; this was the dissolution of the monasteries.

Reorganization of the church.

The dissolution of the monasteries, 1536.

Several hundred of these monkish cloisters existed in the kingdom. They had originated in a fervent desire to spread the Gospel and cultivate holiness of life. Through the Dark Ages they preserved whatever was preserved of art, science, and literature. But many of them had lost their high aims. The monks of the sixteenth century were rich and worldly. By purchase and bequest they had acquired one fifth of the soil of England, and the pursuit of wealth and luxury had superseded the quest for heavenly things. Popular report said that the convents were the abodes of luxury and vice. The commissioners whom Cromwell sent to investigate the affairs of these religious houses reported early in 1536 that drunkenness and vice prevailed in two thirds of the number. The smaller establishments (376 in number) were now suppressed, their revenues some $160,000—being turned into the royal treasury.

"The Pilgrimage of Grace," 1536.

In the north of England the monasteries were in favor with the common people, and the bitterness caused by their abolition became the revolt called "the Pilgrimage of Grace" (1536), and many Catholic lords and Yorkist nobles openly or in secret abetted the uprising. Thirty thousand armed men protested against the arbitrary rule of Cromwell, the separation from Rome, and the disinheritance of Mary. Henry's minister dealt with the rebels as Richard II. had dealt with Wat Tyler and the insurgent peasantry of Kent and Essex. The army at his disposal was weak, but at his promise to

RUINS OF THE CISTERCIAN ABBEY OF FOUNTAINS.

comply with their demands the "pilgrims" dispersed joyfully to their homes. Then Cromwell swept through the North with an avenging sword. He broke his pledges of reform and hunted the rebels to exile or death.[1]

A fresh campaign was begun against the greater monasteries. The abbots, fearing the consequences of

The distribution of the plunder.

[1] Lord Darcy, a veteran soldier and leading noble of Yorkshire, was among the nearly twoscore victims sent to the block, the gallows, or the stake. On his trial he burst out against the king's iron-handed minister, "Cromwell, thou art the cause of this rebellion. I trust ere thou die there shall remain one noble hand to strike off thy head."

delay, surrendered their estates to the king—some had already fallen to him by the treason of their occupants.[1]

To the monks thus deprived of their homes pensions were granted. Some of the church lands were sold, others granted to favorites of the king—all went to increase the holdings of nobles and gentry, and to strengthen these classes against a restoration of monasticism.[2]

Henry VIII. and Martin Luther.

The Protestant Reformation was at hand. By the year 1546, the date of Luther's death, Protestantism had reached its fullest extent on the Continent. This reform had its influence upon England, where Wyclif's Bible and Lollardry had prepared the soil. The early years of Henry VIII. coincided with the period of greatest excitement over the Lutheran revolt,[3] and in the controversy of those times the king was the ally of the pope. In 1522 Henry put forth a book in defense of Catholic doctrine, for which the pope dubbed him "Defender of the Faith," and which called out Luther's remark, "When God wants a fool he lets a king teach theology." Wolsey as a faithful Catholic attempted by persecution to prevent the spread of the new ideas in

"Defender of the Faith."

---

[1] For example, the Carthusian monks of the Charterhouse, London, lived exemplary lives under the prior, John Houghton, a man of really noble character. Houghton spent six weeks in the Tower (1534) for his scruples against taking the oath of succession, which involved approval of the divorce. The next year the prior with others notified Cromwell that they could never take the oath of supremacy, which put Henry in the place of the pope. For this new sort of treason they were tried, condemned, and executed. The arm of the sturdy prior was nailed over the gate of the Charterhouse as a warning. Most of the inmates refused to be intimidated, and were eventually dispossessed. The noble property was bestowed on Sir Thomas Audley.

[2] Cromwell himself received the income of four great monasteries. The Duke of Suffolk received no less than thirty grants of church lands in a single county. A new nobility was thus built up to replace the ancient Norman baronial families, among whom the War of the Roses had played sad havoc.

[3] After 1517 Lutheran books and tracts found their way into England every year in increasing numbers. About 1521 a club of Cambridge students who met in the White Horse Inn to read the latest religious pamphlets from the Continent were nicknamed "the Germans" and suspected of heresy. Among them were Coverdale and Tyndale, the fathers of the English Bible, and Hugh Latimer, soon to win fame and martyrdom by his eloquence and boldness in the Protestant cause.

England. Norfolk and More, his immediate successors, continued this part of his policy, but Cromwell reversed it.

Whatever were the vicar-general's beliefs, his influence certainly favored the Protestants. His ally, Cranmer, was infected with Lutheran doctrines, though he would not force them on the church in opposition to the royal will. For a time the king let himself be ruled by the vicar-general and the archbishop. Miles Coverdale's edition of the English Bible, which William Tyndale had translated, was not only published in England but by royal command appointed to be read in the churches (1538).[1] Two years before, new articles of religion were set forth, by the king's own hand, prescribing what Christians should believe. They simplified the Roman formula, but retained its most important features, lagging far behind Luther and the Swiss and French reformers. Henry himself was no Protestant. Only necessity had forced him to break with the papacy, and he hated Luther as soundly after the divorce as before it.

The Bible in English, 1538.

The outrageous conduct of the people, who broke the windows of the abbey churches and insulted the priests at mass, caused the king to draw back from all reforms of doctrine which looked toward Protestantism. In 1539 the "Six Articles," the hateful "whip of six strings" for the correction of Protestants, were enacted in accordance with his wish by Parliament. It declared six points of doctrine, the denial of any one being heresy; the heretic punishable with death on the sec-

"The whip of six strings."

---

[1] Tyndale's New Testament was printed at Mainz, in Germany, in 1525, in a small octavo volume. It was full of errors, and the bishop of London, in the hope of suppressing it, bought up the edition and burned it in St. Paul's churchyard, a silly piece of business, which enabled Tyndale to bring out other editions. Coverdale's first complete Bible in English appeared in October, 1535, Matthew's Bible in 1537, and, in 1539, Coverdale's "Great Bible," a copy of which was commanded by the king to be placed in every parish church for the common use of the people. The reaction came soon, and in 1542 we find the bishop of London forbidding "all crowding to read, or commenting on what is read."

ond, if not the first, offense. The six strings were: (1) transubstantiation—the dogma that the blessing of the priests at communion transforms the bread and wine into the actual body and blood of Christ; (2) communion in only one kind (bread) for laymen; (3) celibacy of the priesthood (Luther and his preachers might marry); (4) inviolability of vows of chastity made by monks and nuns; (5) necessity of private masses; (6) necessity of confession of sins to a priest. The heavy penalties consequent upon infraction of these articles were for a time kept off by the hand of the vicar-general.

HAMPTON COURT PALACE.

Cromwell, whose policy had won him the nickname "the hammer of the monks," was beset by enemies. The despoiled abbots, the subjected clergy, the proud nobles, who chafed at the supremacy of a commoner, all strove to ruin him with the king. As Cromwell's advice in regard to the divorce of one queen was the means of his rise, his recommendation of another hastened his fall.

In 1536 Anne Boleyn, whose family were of the Protestant faction, incurred the king's displeasure, and a subservient Parliament declared the marriage void. She was executed as a traitor,[1] and her bereaved hus-

[1] The unfortunate queen seems to have been free from the guilt of unfaithfulness, with which she was charged. She kept up a show of gaiety to the end. "The executioner," she said to the lieutenant of the Tower, "is very skilful and my neck is very slender," smiling as she spanned it with her fingers. She left one child, the Lady Elizabeth, afterward "the virgin queen."

band solaced himself next day by marrying Jane Seymour. Jane died in 1537, giving birth to a son, Edward, who was declared heir to the throne, his half-sisters, Mary the Catholic and Elizabeth, having been debarred from the succession on the ground of illegitimacy. For three years the sovereign lived single, taking his fourth wife, in 1540, on the recommendation of Cromwell. This marriage was a device of this prudent minister to gain a political alliance with the Protestant princes of Germany. The lady was a sister of the elector of Saxony. The foreign princess proved to be tall, coarse, and ill-featured—"a Flanders mare!" the king said when he first saw her. Her homely face was Cromwell's death-warrant. Henry withdrew his support from the man who, as he thought, had trifled with him. The Catholic Howard, Duke of Norfolk, the leading noble, accused the vicar-general of treason. Conviction, without a hearing, and execution followed in a few days, and in July, 1540, one of the strongest heads that ever directed English affairs fell beneath the axeman's stroke.[1] As for poor German Anne, the king soon cast her off, and married in her stead Catharine Howard, a niece of the Duke of Norfolk. The Howards remained in great influence at court until near the close of the reign, although Henry kept the government well in hand and through his ministers exercised greater powers than had been wielded by any king since Magna Charta.

Parliament met, it is true, with considerable regularity, but neither House dared, or cared, to oppose the

Henry marries Jane Seymour, 1536.

Fall of Cromwell, 1540.

Queen Catharine Howard.

---

[1] Cromwell in the pursuit of his ends had once propounded to the judges the question whether "if Parliament should condemn a man to die for treason without hearing him in his own defense the attainder could ever be disputed." The subservient judges, suspecting what reply was wanted, answered that the decree of Parliament could never be reversed. It was afterward noted, says Hallam, that Cromwell was himself the earliest to suffer under this monstrous interpretation of justice. He was disposed of by a bill of attainder jammed through Parliament without his knowledge.

Subservience of Parliament.

will of the sovereign. In the House of Lords the power of the church had been crushed; for the mitered abbots sat there no longer, and the bishops were the nominees of the king. The temporal peers were equally submissive. Gibbet and block had removed the men who might have led an opposition, and liberal grants from the church lands had bound the others to their royal patron. A new landed aristocracy had been founded by the distribution of the broad acres of the monks, and far more of the leading families of England date their prominence from the conquest of the English Church by Henry than from the conquest of the island by William the Norman. The Commons were scarcely behind the Lords in their subservience to the wishes of the sovereign, for the members of the lower house knew the color of Henry's gold and had shared in the plunder of the convents.

Bills of attainder.

Thus constituted, Parliament, established as a check upon royal authority, became a tool of tyranny. The king's own court of Star Chamber was not so quick to pass sentence on his enemies as this Parliament, whose bills of attainder—at an hour's notice, and without a hearing—tried, condemned, and sentenced to confiscation and death whomsoever the king would destroy.

Doctrinal reforms.

Although the Howards were Catholics, none dared whisper to the king the possibility of restoring the papal authority in the English Church. Henry had not gone far toward Protestantism, but he had settled this one point: that no pope of Rome should supplant an English king in any department of church or state. In continental politics his sympathies were with the pope against the Protestants. Reform in the church he undoubtedly desired, and to some extent he carried his desire into execution. The service in English churches was pruned of certain superstitious practices; the litany and prayers were revised and printed in English, and, with some restrictions, the English Bible was recommended to the people as the ground of their faith and life.

The king and the men who stood with him against the Lutheran Reformation hoped that a universal council of Christendom might peacefully incorporate these moderate changes in the Roman Church, and thus stay, if not close, the schism which was rending the

WESTMINSTER ABBEY.

Council of Trent, 1545

Catholics of Western Europe. In 1543 Henry is again found in alliance with the Emperor Charles V. for a war with France. Leagued with Charles he hoped to sway the proposed Catholic council to his moderate schedule of reform; but the council held at Trent in 1545 blasted this hope. It denounced the heresies of England as well as those of the German reformers, and it reasserted the beliefs and practices against which Luther had protested, and those which the English had abandoned. The Council of Trent determined that there should be no compromise between Rome and Protestantism.

But the theologians had no terrors for the English king. He refused to retrace a single step which separated him from the papacy, nor would he advance further toward the Protestantism which was growing around him. While lines between the two parties were being more strictly drawn, the Howards and Bishop Gardiner leading the Catholics, and Cranmer and Latimer showing more of the Protestant color, King Henry stood by himself, leaning toward neither faction. Anne Askew[1] and three others, who denied the first of the "Six Articles," were burned for their heresy; but on the other side Bishop Latimer, "downright Father Hugh," the leader of Protestant thought and the raciest and most eloquent preacher of his time, was acquitted of heretical guilt.

Protestant martyrs.

Shortly before his death the king changed ministers again; the Howards went to the Tower, and the Seymours, the Earl of Hertford at their head, came to the council-board. Henry VIII. breathed his last January 28, 1547. Catharine Howard had already been beheaded for most unwifely conduct, which was accounted treason, and the king had taken a sixth wife, Catharine Parr, who outlived her much-married lord.

Palace revolutions.

Death of Henry VIII., 1547.

Later marriage.

The wars of Henry's later years had been of slight importance. In Scotland the authority of the pope was still acknowledged, and the influence of France was ever present to keep alive the old hatred of England. Henry VII. had married his daughter, Margaret, to James IV., king of Scots, in the hope of forming a

The Scottish marriage.

---

[1] Anne Askew was young, beautiful, and popular with the queen and her court ladies. For denying the "real presence" of God in the mass she was imprisoned and put to the rack. Barbarous torture failed to draw from her an accusation against others, or to force from her a recantation. When tied to the stake she was informed that her pardon was ready signed, awaiting her disavowal of heretical doctrines. She welcomed death in preference. In all twenty-eight persons were put to death for heresy under the "whip with six strings."

blood-bond between the sister kingdoms; but the Scots continued to take their cue from France, and Margaret's son (James V.) even invaded his uncle's realm, albeit without success. One condition of the treaty of peace was the marriage of James's little daughter, Mary Stuart, with Prince Edward, son and heir of Henry VIII. Had this been consummated the union of the two kingdoms might have been anticipated by fifty years. But it was not to be. The French party in the northern kingdom defeated the negotiation. *Scotland allied with France.*

It was in this reign that Wales was incorporated with England (1536), and no distinction held henceforth between Welshmen and Englishmen.

TOPICS FOR READING AND SPECIAL STUDY, WITH LIBRARY NOTES.

1. THE ENGLISH CHURCH UNDER HENRY VIII.
    The History of the Reformation in England. G. G. Perry.
    The Early Tudors. C. E. Moberly.
2. WILLIAM TYNDALE AND THE FIRST PRINTED ENGLISH BIBLE.
    The English Bible. John Eadie.
    The History of the English Bible. W. F. Moulton.
3. WOLSEY.
    Wolsey. Creighton.
    History of England. J. A. Froude.
4. THE DISSOLUTION OF THE MONASTERIES.
    Henry VIII. and the English Monasteries. F. A. Gasquet.
    See also Froude's History of England.

FICTION, ETC.

The Household of Sir Thomas More. Anne Manning.
The Cloister and the Hearth. C. Reade.
The Fair Gospeller: Anne Askew. Anne Manning.
Henry VIII. Shakespeare.

CHAPTER XI.

THE LATER TUDORS, 1547 A. D.–1603 A. D.
FROM THE ACCESSION OF EDWARD VI.
TO THE DEATH OF ELIZABETH.

Edward VI., 1547-1553.

THREE children of Henry VIII. survived him: the Lady Mary, daughter of Catharine of Aragon; the Lady Elizabeth, Anne Boleyn's daughter, and Edward, the nine-year-old son of Jane Seymour. He had finally named his son as his heir, and in case Edward should die without issue directed that the inheritance should pass in order to the Princess Mary, the Princess Elizabeth, and then to the heirs of Henry VII.'s daughter Mary Brandon, Duchess of Suffolk. The will furthermore appointed a commission of sixteen men to govern the kingdom during Edward's minority.

The regency.

Unwilling to commit the government wholly either to the Reformation or to Rome, the king had shrewdly mingled the two English parties in the composition of this council of regency, but the ambition of one of its members, Edward Seymour, Earl of Hertford, frustrated the plans of the king. Seymour, who was in sympathy with the Reformation, was uncle of the boy monarch and executor of the royal will. Making the most of his advantages he excluded Gardiner, the strongest of the Catholics, from the council, gained possession of the person of the boy-king, and had himself declared Duke of Somerset and "Protector of the Realm." Under this title he exercised full royal power in the name of his nephew, Edward VI.

Somerset, "Protector of the Realm."

To complete the work which King Henry had undertaken in Scotland was Somerset's first care. The marriage treaty which was to unite King Edward with Mary Stuart was yet unfulfilled, and the benefits which would accrue from its consummation seemed to warrant every endeavor to attain that end. The safety of England was continually imperiled by the proximity of Scotland, the ally of France and Rome. The Protector led an army across the border to enforce the marriage treaty, and defeated the Scottish lords at Pinkie Cleugh (1547).[1] But Queen Mary was well guarded by the Catholic party, who took her to France (1548) and destroyed Somerset's hopes by betrothing her to the dauphin, afterward Francis II.

Pinkie, 1547.

Mary Stuart betrothed to Francis.

The Protestant party was unchecked throughout Edward's reign. Somerset was its natural leader and Cranmer his willing assistant in all matters of church reform. In Henry's time the archbishop, though inclining toward the new doctrines, had allowed himself to be governed by the royal will, and had not permitted his Protestantism to injure him in the king's favor. He had married a wife in Germany, but at a crack of the "whip of six strings" had ignominiously deserted her. Yet Protestant he was at heart, and Edward's accession left him free to bring the English Church into conformity with the reformed doctrines. Other bishops—the learned Ridley of London, the eloquent Latimer of Worcester—and such theologians as Bucer and Peter Martyr assisted in

Cranmer's reforms.

---

[1] In the battle of Pinkie the English with field artillery, 6,000 horse and 10,000 foot, few of whom had firearms, attacked the 30,000 Scottish pikemen on a side hill. The Scots "stood at defense, shoulders nigh together, the fore ranks stooping low, well nigh to kneeling, their fellows behind holding their pikes in both hands, the one end of the pike against the right foot, the other against the enemy's breast, . . . so thick that a bare finger shall as easily pierce through the bristles of an angry hedgehog as any encounter the front of their pikes." The first charge was checked by this bristling wall, but cannon soon made gaps in the array and the horsemen rallying put the Scots to flight, "leaving the hillside like a woodyard," strewn with pike-staves.

the work. Hallam sums up in six paragraphs the innovations which were forced upon the English Church in the reign of Edward VI.

Hallam's summary.

1. English supplanted Latin as the language of the service. Prayer, homily, and hymn were henceforth in a speech understood of the people. From the Romish missal and breviary, with such excisions and additions as the revised creed required, Cranmer translated the first "Book of Common Prayer" (1548).

"The Book of Common Prayer."

2. Statues, paintings, windows, and altars, which the ignorant populace had regarded with a veneration which approached idolatry, were now destroyed, and ceremonials, such as the use of incense, tapers, and holy water, were forbidden.[1]

3. The adoration of the saints and the Virgin Mary was forbidden, the doctrine of purgatory was denied, and prayers for the souls of the dead were given up.

4. Auricular confession was made optional. Henceforth the believer might or might not confess his sins in the ear of the priest and receive absolution. This liberty soon put an end to the use of the confessional in England.

5. The Catholic doctrine of transubstantiation was abandoned, and "the doctrine of the real presence of the body and blood in the bread and wine of the communion-table was explicitly denied."

6. Lastly, priests were allowed to marry.[2]

The "Six Articles" were repealed. The harsh laws against Lollardry were erased from the statute books,

---

[1] "The favorites of the court were endowed with the estates of the church until, as Latimer complained, "The clergy, kept to sorry pittances, were forced to put themselves into gentlemen's houses and serve as clerks of kitchens, etc.," to keep from starving. Another says that the houses of private citizens were hung "with altar cloths, their tables and beds covered with copes, that some at dinner drank from chalices."

[2] "It was said that the married priests had the altar vestments made over into dresses for their wives."

for the leaders of the church had at last caught up with the principles of the persecuted Wyclifites. Forty-two "articles of religion" were set forth in 1552 by Cranmer, embodying the principles of the Reformation.[1]

<small>The Forty-two Articles.</small>

These changes were forced down into the church from the top. A few statesmen and prelates, the merchants of London, and the large towns of the East, the scholars of the universities, were heartily in favor of reform. The peasantry wanted back their old priests, the mysterious ceremonies, Latin chants, and wonder-working relics which had been the attractive part of their religion. With the destruction of the monasteries, now followed by the suppression of several thousand chantries, chapels, and colleges, hard times had dawned for the peasants, for the new landowners living in London were more exacting than the monkish landlords.

<small>Reform from the top down.</small>

Moreover a new industry was supplanting agriculture. The value of English wool, rising steadily with the growth of cloth manufacture in Flanders, turned the English plow-land into sheep farms. Tenants were evicted from their holdings to make room for these pastures, and common-land was seized by the manor lords and enclosed for private use. Wages dropped as the price of food mounted higher.

<small>Agricultural discontent.</small>

It was natural for the ignorant to believe—as their discontented priests doubtless told them—that these

---

[1] The following entries in the diary of Bishop Blandford of Worcester show the gradual transformation of the church service in these years:

"1547.—Candlemas day: No candles hallowed or borne. Ash Wednesday: No ashes.

"1548.—Palm Sunday: No palms or cross borne in procession. Easter eve.: No fire, but the Paschal Taper and the Font. Easter day: The Pix with the Sacrament taken out of the Sepulchre, they singing 'Christ is risen' without procession. Good Friday: No creeping to the cross. Oct. 26: The cup with the body of Christ was taken away from the Altars.

"1549.—Good Friday: No Sepulchre, or service of Sepulchre. Easter Eve.: No Paschal Taper, or Fire, or Incense, or Font. Apr. 23: Mass, Matins, Evensong, and all other services in English.

"All Mass Books, Graduals, Pies, Portasses, and Legends, brought to the Bishop and Burnt."

miseries sprang from the new religion. This they did believe, and became riotous in their demonstration against their "heretical" rulers.[1] The Catholics—a quiet but numerous party in the council—had always opposed Somerset, and when these troubles broke out in Norfolk his enemies combined to give the chief command to their colleague, John Dudley, Earl of Warwick, son of that magistrate Dudley who had perished with Empson, in the first months of Henry VIII. Soon after (1550) he was made Duke of Northumberland and "Protector of the Kingdom."[2]

Fall of Somerset.

Northumberland Protector.

Though a mere boy, and in delicate health, King Edward was wonderfully precocious. In books and study, especially the ponderous theological works with which the age abounded, he took strange delight. He loved to listen to the sermons of Ridley and the sharp-tongued Latimer, and in what way he could he was zealous to bring in the Reformation. By his order twenty grammar schools were founded in English towns, and the old house of the Grey Friars in London was given up to Christ's Hospital for the famous school of the Bluecoat boys.[3] At the age of sixteen his frail constitution yielded to consumption and he died on July 6, 1553.

Edward's foundations.

Death of Edward VI., 1553.

[1] Sheep-grazing became almost a mania with English landholders in this century, and the dispossessed tenants and unemployed farm laborers were bitter against the landlords. In Norfolk one Robert Ket, a tanner, led a riotous demonstration. The insurgents demanded that gentlemen should not enclose common lands, that bondmen should be set free, and that the power of the landlord to turn out a tenant-farmer should be restricted.

[2] Somerset was accused of treason and felony, acquitted of the former and condemned upon the latter charge, and beheaded January 22, 1552.

[3] This dissolution of the monasteries had broken up most of the best schools in England, and even the universities were crippled. Some of the confiscated property of the chapels and chantries was applied by Edward VI. to the foundation of these grammar schools. A writer of the time touches upon the discredit of learning: "There were none that had any heart to put their children to any school, any farther than to learn to write, to make them apprentices or lawyers. The 'two wells of learning, Oxford and Cambridge, are dried up,' students decayed, of which scarce an hundred left of a thousand, and if in seven years more they should decay so fast there would be almost none at all." In his plundering of church property, the Protector Somerset would have destroyed Westminster Abbey had not the citizens of London and the vestry taken measures to protect the time-honored sanctuary.

Foreseeing the king's untimely end, Northumberland had formed a plan for the succession. By the terms of Henry's settlement the Princess Mary—Catholic and papist though she was—must be queen. This daughter of Catharine of Spain had refused to accept the new tenets and practices, and had clung to the old religion with true Tudor obstinacy. Northumberland, who had a private advantage to serve, persuaded Edward to change the order of succession. Both princesses were set aside as illegitimate, and the crown was passed over to the descendants of Henry's sister Mary, Duchess of Suffolk. The heiress thus designated was Lady Jane Grey, a beautiful and high-minded Protestant girl—the wife of the scheming Protector's son.

Lady Jane Grey.

The death of Edward brought these plots to light. Eluding the Protector's grasp the Princess Mary rallied her friends in Norfolk. Northumberland proclaimed his daughter-in-law queen and for ten days (June 10-19, 1553) she bore the title,[1] but she had no national support. The Protector's men deserted him, and with tears of chagrin on his cheeks he was forced to accept the triumph of Mary Tudor. The daughter of Henry VIII. was hailed with joy in London. Lady Jane and her husband were placed in the Tower, and Northumberland was beheaded. The papists were in the saddle. The Catholic bishops were restored to their cathedrals, Latimer, Ridley, and Cranmer were deposed, and the two latter cast into prison. Bishop Gardiner became chancellor and leader of the council.

Queen Mary, 1553-1558.

Fall of Northumberland.

Queen Mary's heart was set upon a complete restora-

---

[1] Lady Jane Grey had been the friend and companion of her cousin, the late king, who was of her own age and studious tastes. She protested against her father-in-law's ambitious program for her and entered upon it only in response to the entreaties of Northumberland and his son, her beloved husband. When her ten days of tedious glory ended in Mary's triumph the gentle girl returned to her home and her books, asking only to be let alone.

tion of the papal power in England. She was her father's daughter in the firmness of her will, but otherwise she was the true child of her Spanish mother. Her cousin, the king and emperor Charles V., of Spain, was her political mentor.

The pope's partisan.

MARY TUDOR.

The counter-revolution.

The counter-revolution was cautiously begun.[1] The first backward step was the restoration of the religious system to its condition at the death of Henry VIII. The anti-Lollard legislation was revived; again the six-stringed whip became the test of orthodoxy. Mass was said in the churches and Cranmer's prayer-book gave way to the Latin missals and breviaries. Married priests were hooted out of their parishes and images of the saints and Virgin were brought in. For the most part this reaction took place quietly; in some quarters it was hailed with delight, for the populace had not kept pace with the bishops, and the commands to believe this doctrine and discard that dogma had often fallen upon uncomprehending ears. So far the queen was satisfied with the

[1] Latin mass was restored at her coronation and she had already shown her hand by a proclamation forbidding her subjects to use "the devilish terms of Papist, Heretic, and such like," together with "private interpretation of God's Word by men's own brains." In 1554 the religion of the realm was declared to be the same as existed in 1529 before the breach with Rome.

progress of her reign; the sagacious emperor counseled her against forcing her people to accept the pope's supremacy again or to give back the lands and revenues which they derived from the distribution of the property of the church. As long as she was content with this moderation Mary retained a measure of popularity. It was the project of the "Spanish marriage" which first turned her subjects from her.

The emperor urged the queen to fortify her position by marrying his son Philip, heir to his possessions in Spain, Italy, and the Low Countries. Philip was a papist of the bigoted stripe,[1] and Mary's union with him would insure the supremacy of the pope in England, and might eventually found a Catholic league, which should overpower the Protestant princes of Germany, and close by force the schism in Christendom. All English Protestants who lived in the hope of better times ahead, all English patriots who dreaded the interference of foreign pope or king in England's government, all selfish lords and commons whose share in the monastery lands bound them to uphold the system of King Henry VIII., were united against the proposed match. There were isolated risings in the West against the marriage with the Catholic prince, and in Kent fifteen thousand men gathered under Sir Thomas Wyatt and swooped down on London. The personal courage of Mary Tudor called twenty thousand Londoners to her defense. "Stand fast against these rebels," she cried in her harsh man's voice. "Fear them not, for I assure you I fear them nothing at all."

---

[1] Philip's father, Charles V., regretted to the day of his death that he had not put Luther to death. Philip himself, the persecutor of the Dutch Protestants, once burnt thirteen persons as a thank-offering for deliverance from shipwreck. To the entreaties of the kinsmen of some of his victims he said "he would carry fagots to the pile of his own son if the prince should ever become a Lutheran."

Wyatt was captured and beheaded. There had been talk of putting Lady Jane Grey in Mary's place; her execution,[1] with that of Lord Dudley, her husband, dispelled such treasonable dreams. Some of the rebels had cheered for the Princess Elizabeth and Edward Courtenay, and Mary deemed best to lodge them in the Tower. The emperor thought the scaffold a fitter place for them, but Mary's English advisers dared not tempt English loyalty too far, and after a time Courtenay went abroad, and Elizabeth, in the seclusion of Chaucer's Woodstock, studied book-lore with Roger Ascham, and romped with the country squires.

<small>Death of Lady Jane Grey.</small>

The queen took confidence to go forward. Parliament consented to the unpopular match and in midsummer of 1554 Philip of Spain married his English bride at Winchester. But the council, though impotent to prevent the union, had influence enough to rob it of its most threatening consequences. The Spaniard was called by courtesy "king of England," but the jealous Parliament never crowned him, and denied his right to the throne in case the queen should die childless.

<small>Philip in England. 1554.</small>

Mary's policy unfolded rapidly. To restore the realm completely to the bosom of "mother church" was her cherished aim. Parliament reversed the sentence of treason which stood against Cardinal Pole, who now came back as the pope's legate. This was followed by a formal declaration in favor of reunion with Rome. Queen Mary, Philip, and the lords and commons of

---

[1] The self-possession and strength of mind of this remarkable princess never deserted her. From her window in the Tower she witnessed her husband taken to the block and saw his headless body brought back in a cart. The tidings of his calm demeanor on the scaffold reassured her. Her last words addressed to the bystanders, at the closing scene, were mild and uncomplaining. Instead of denouncing the queen's government she accepted the blame of having allowed herself, however unwillingly, to be used as the tool of ambitious men, and hoped "that the story of her life might at least be useful, by proving that innocence excuses not great misdeeds, if they tend anywise to the destruction of the commonwealth." Then with the utmost serenity she submitted herself to the headsman.

England went down on their knees in the presence of the pope's representative on November 30, 1554, and, humbly confessing their sin of schism and rebellion, received the church's absolution and the pontifical blessing. Save for the dismantled abbeys, whose lands could not well be restored, the English Church now stood where it had been before Luther dreamed of "justification by faith," or Henry Tudor cast off the pope's authority that he might wed the lady of his fancy. *At the feet of the pope.*

The latter half of Mary's reign is black with memories for England. She undertook to blot out the Protestant stain from her people with blood. The surviving leaders of the Reformation paid dearly for their acts. Bishops Hooper and Ferrar were condemned for heresy and burned. John Rogers, who had helped Tyndale translate the Scriptures, died exulting amid the flames. Rowland Taylor, pious and beloved, was burned in his own parish of Hadley. The learning of Ridley and the wit of the noble Latimer availed nothing. These two bishops perished in one fire in Oxford, October 16, 1555.[1] The gray-haired Cranmer had double claims to Mary's hatred, for he not only stood first among the reforming clergy, but it was his decree which divorced Mary's mother and broke her Spanish heart. The irresolute archbishop renounced his faith to save his life. But Mary was relentless. Six times the wavering Cranmer avowed and disavowed his heresy, but when *Burnings at Smithfield and Oxford.* *Cranmer burned.*

---

[1] Latimer, the Protestant hero of three reigns, died grandly. "Three things," said his chaplain, "he did specially pray. First, for grace to stand till death. Second, that God would restore the Gospel to England once again; and these words 'once again, once again' he did so inculcate and beat into the ears of the Lord God, as though he had seen God before him and spake face to face. Third, he prayed for the Lady Elizabeth, whom with tears he desired for a comfort to this comfortless England." It is said that "he received the flame as if embracing it, and stroking his face with his hands, bathed them in the fire, crying out vehemently in his own English tone, 'Father in heaven, receive my soul!'"

they bound him to the stake his spirit rose, and, thrusting his right hand into the hottest flame, he exclaimed, "This hand wrote the recantation, and it shall be the first to suffer punishment."

These names were not alone among the English martyrs. Smithfield fires burned often in 1556 and 1557, and in other market-places throughout the kingdom men and women gathered to see how the heretics would die. Their heroism in death did more than pamphlet and preacher to spread the principles for which they suffered. "Play the man, Master Ridley," the dying Latimer had been heard to cry to his fellow among the fagots. "We shall this day light such a candle by God's grace in England as I trust shall never be put out."

Ridley and Latimer burned.

For three years these horrid burnings continued, the "bloody" Queen Mary pursuing her policy to the end.[1] Yet Protestantism grew with each new act of repression, and the miserable queen saw with dismay the failure of the terrible policy by which she had hoped to purify her realm.

Bloody Mary's failure.

Philip, whom Mary loved almost fiercely, cared nothing for her, and on receiving his European inheritance from his father (1556) had quitted England, where he was thoroughly detested. Mary's most fervent prayer had been that a son of hers should maintain the Catholic cause; but she was childless. The pope,

A disappointed queen.

[1] Under "Bloody" Mary 277 persons were put to death for their religion, besides 68 who died in prison. Many of the victims bear foreign names and were perhaps Lutheran refugees from the Continent. The persecution began by striking down only the Protestant leaders, thinking thus to terrify the rank and file, but it soon reached all grades of society, from bishops to the rural clergy, and from country gentlemen to day laborers. It is reckoned that the Marian martyrs included 5 bishops, 21 clergymen, 8 lay gentlemen, 84 tradesmen, 100 husbandmen and servants, 55 women, and 4 children. Some of the most impressive instances of heroism were furnished by women like Rose Allen, who said "the more it burnt the less it felt," and the dauntless boy William Hunter, who surrendered himself to save his father, and expired declaring that he was not afraid. Such constancy was more powerful than many sermons.

whom she wished heartily to serve, would not be pacified without money and the restoration of the church lands. The portion that remained in the possession of the crown she did restore, but to reclaim from her powerful subjects their lands would have been to stir up a rebellion in which all that she had gained for Rome would be swept away forever. Gardiner, her best adviser, was dead, and Cardinal Pole, his successor, was deemed a heretic by Pope Paul IV. and stripped of his churchly honors.

The haughty Philip yielded once to his wife's desire for his return. But his brief visit to England added to Mary's misfortunes. She sent an army to his aid against France. But the English could not even defend their own. Calais, the last remnant of the English empire on the Continent, was surprised and taken by the French in January, 1558. "It was the chiefest jewel of the realm," said Mary. "When I die you will find 'Calais' written on my heart," was one of the pitiful outbursts of the closing months of her life. Her body spent with sickness, her spirit bruised by her terrible disappointments, with scarcely a friend in the world, poor Queen Mary died November 17, 1558.

The loss of Calais, 1558.

Death of Queen Mary, 1558.

Elizabeth Tudor, daughter of Henry VIII. and Anne Boleyn, immediately succeeded to the throne. During the reigns of Edward VI. and Mary she had held prudently aloof from religious and political controversies,[1] devoting herself with unusual energy to serious

Queen Elizabeth, 1558-1603.

---

[1] Queen Mary's attitude toward her popular half-sister was one of bitter hatred. It is said that evil-disposed persons once laid a trap for Lady Elizabeth, hoping to obtain convincing evidence of her heretical opinions on the crucial question of the "real presence" of the blood and body of Christ in the sacrament. She was asked what she thought of the words of Christ at the last supper, "This is my body," etc. After a brief pause she replied,
  "Christ was the word that spake it,
  He took the bread and brake it,
  And what the word did make it,
  That I believe and take it,"
a response from which her enemies got no satisfaction.

study of ancient and modern languages and to archery, horsemanship, and the chase—the sports of young men of her own age.

This busy student of Greek now became a woman of the great world; fond of the pomp of courts, coveting finery, having gowns by the hundred in her wardrobe, and with all her personal vanity craving the flattery of her courtiers. She had the stature and shoulders of her burly father, the voice of a man, and a coarse manner of speech.[1] Elizabeth's character was peculiarly adapted for the situation which confronted her when she ascended the throne, and which faced her during the first thirty years of her reign. She was a hard, cold, intellectual woman, devoid of strong attachments and prejudices, shrewd of discernment,[2] and full of tact in devising and applying policies. The new queen was accepted without openly expressed

QUEEN ELIZABETH.

[1] "Elizabeth spat at a courtier whose coat offended her taste; she boxed the ears of another; she tickled the back of a great nobleman's neck when he knelt to receive his earldom at her hands; she thought it effeminate and ridiculous not to swear, and besides her great oaths her tongue was noted for its sharp and witty sallies, from which no one was safe."

[2] This trait was displayed in her choice of counselors, Cecil, Bacon, Burleigh, etc., laymen of property and education, the forerunners of the line of professional statesmen who have ever since been at the front of public affairs. Hitherto the chief ministers of the crown had been great ecclesiastics or nobles.

dissent in any quarter of her realm. Although there was no English rival for the crown, the outlook, both in England and on the Continent, boded a stormy reign. Mary's popish policy, with the bloody persecutions into which it had carried her, had not exterminated Protestantism, but it had aroused a bitter hatred between the partisans of the old and the reformed religion.

Under her Protestant brother, Edward, Elizabeth had accepted the forty-two articles of religion as drawn up by Cranmer, and at Mary's accession she had with as little difficulty conformed to the Catholic service. For herself she had no vital sympathy with either, and it was her aim to restore the moderate system which her father had established. On one point, however, her mind was made up: the Church of England, Catholic or Protestant, must be united. Circumstances which the imperious queen vainly strove to control forced her more and more to the side of the reformers, and obliged her to make changes in her father's creed; indeed, her most tyrannical measures were those by which she endeavored to impose the reformed doctrines and usages upon her reluctant subjects. *Forced toward the Reformation.*

The key-note of Elizabeth's purpose was struck by the repeal of the laws which had reëstablished the authority of the popes and lighted the fires of persecution. The church's independence of Rome was reasserted. The queen was declared the supreme governor of the church and all priests were ordered to conform to the new rules. The second prayer-book of King Edward and Cranmer (1552) was revised and made the common book of devotion. Parker, a man of her own conservative views, was made archbishop of Canterbury. Under his direction (1559-1575) religious matters settled themselves peacefully, or would have *Ecclesiastical independence.*

done so had it not been for the religious condition of Europe.

The power of Philip.

That Philip whose marriage with Mary had aroused England had now inherited the possessions of his father, Charles V. He was king of Spain, and afterward of Portugal, of Italy and the Netherlands, and the precious metals and rich merchandise of India, Africa, and America supplied his treasury. On sea and land the Spanish forces were the most formidable in Europe. The king who exercised absolute power over this vast realm was a bigoted Romanist, the chosen champion of papistry. The church was reviving from the shock of the Lutheran attack. The limits of Protestant territory were now pretty well defined, and they have scarcely been altered since. Northern Germany, the Scandinavian countries, Holland, and to a certain degree England and Scotland, no longer looked to the pope for guidance. There had been Protestants in Italy, but Philip's hand was there upheld by the Inquisition, and the "heresy" vanished before him.

The Catholic reaction.

Jesuits.

A new fervor inspired the priests and princes of Catholicism. The "Society of Jesus," better known as "Jesuits," founded by Loyola, devoted itself with a complete consecration, unmatched since the early days of the church, to the task of redeeming the world from heresy. In the Spanish Netherlands the iconoclasm of the Protestants went to such extremes that Philip was obliged to send an army against them. France, which ranked next to Spain among Catholic lands, was weakened by the incompetence of its king and by the religious wars upon the French Protestants, or Huguenots, as they were called. The Catholics of Scotland, few in numbers but ably led, could count upon the support of France, at whose court their queen resided.

The circumstances above narrated determined Elizabeth's course. She could not be a Catholic, for no English Catholic would recognize her, Anne Boleyn's daughter, as the lawful successor of Mary Tudor. Philip offered her his hand in the hope of impressing England into the troop of papal countries which he had united to the Spanish crown. She put him off for a year and then denied him—her people had had enough of Spanish marriages. Then he sought a political alliance with her until he might take by force what he might not win by favor. But France feared his ambition, and France, too, sought an alliance with the queen. Catherine de Medici, the queen-mother, offered her first one prince and then another (Anjou and Alençon) in marriage, but Elizabeth, after long coquetry, rejected both, for a league with Catholic France was almost as threatening to the peace of England as a connection with Spain. *Coquetting with the Catholic courts.*

Still another arrangement was possible. William Cecil, Lord Burleigh, Elizabeth's most trusted adviser, favored war. He wanted England, as champion of all the Protestant states and factions, to take up the gauntlet that Philip had thrown down. But the frugal queen started the council with her emphatic words, "No war, no war! my Lords!" She preferred to use diplomacy. *Burleigh's policy.*

Through the confusion of the time the queen's eye saw England's need of peace, and she determined to postpone as long as possible the inevitable war. Meanwhile she covertly sent aid to the Presbyterian lords of Scotland, who were struggling against a French regency, shrewdly hindered Philip in his war against the Dutch, and afforded scanty sustenance to the Huguenots. So long as she could keep the Catholics of Spain, France, and Scotland from joining hands against her, she was safe. *Diplomacy.*

200   Twenty Centuries of English History.

The northern peril was most embarrassing. Her young cousin, Mary Stuart, Queen of Scots and wife of the king of France, was a devout Catholic, and the hope of the papal party who scoffed at Elizabeth's title. At the French court Mary allowed herself to be

BEDROOM OF QUEEN MARY AT HOLYROOD.

addressed as "Queen of England," and upon the death of her youthful husband (1560) she returned to Edinburgh. Elizabeth's fleet failed to intercept her in the Channel and her arrival was hailed with rejoicing—tempered somewhat when the Presbyterian elders who were in control of the government learned of her intention of attending mass with all the elaborate ceremonial of Rome.¹ The relations between the royal cousins were violently strained. Elizabeth could not publicly

Mary Stuart in Scotland, 1561.

---

¹ The Queen of Scots, accustomed to the gaiety of the French court, soon became an abomination in the eyes of the Presbyterian preachers, the reformer John Knox most of all. To them the service of the mass was idolatry, and "idolater" was the gentlest name they could find for this girl-widow of nineteen years. The Church Assembly addressed a solemn protest to her. The populace desecrated her chapel, and Knox publicly berated this "Jezebel" until she broke down and wept unqueenly tears in his presence.

admit Mary's right to succession in England, for the probability of another "Mary the Catholic" would have endangered her own throne. Neither dared she select any successor nor inspire hopes of an heir by marrying one of her many suitors. For England's sake she must remain unmarried and let her hand be used as a piece in the deep game of statecraft which she played. *Elizabeth's perplexities.*

Mary Stuart's presence in Scotland brought trouble for the English Catholics. Most of the bishops and nearly two hundred parish priests had left their cathedrals and churches, rather than adopt the book of common prayer and the other adjuncts of the reformed service, but most of the clergy had accepted the changes without demur. In 1562, however, when Mary's plans seemed to augur success and the Catholic prospects brightened, the pope lent his aid to increase Elizabeth's perplexities. He forbade Catholics to attend any service in which the prayer-book was used (1562). Parliament first fined all who refused to attend church and in 1563 passed the "Test Act," which compelled all persons holding office in church or state to swear to obey the queen rather than the pope. At the same time the forty-two articles of Cranmer's creed were cut down to the "Thirty-nine Articles," which, with slight revision, still remain the standard of Anglican belief. Thus Elizabeth had been forced from the ground on which her father stood to the advanced Protestant position of Edward. *The Test Act, 1563.* *The Thirty-nine Articles.*

Mary Stuart caught a new inspiration from the news of Catholic dissatisfaction in England. She had not undertaken to force her own religion upon Scotland, but she now gained strength with English papists by marrying her cousin Henry Stuart, Lord Darnley, who, next to Mary herself, was the presumptive heir of Elizabeth.

Birth of James Stuart.

The fruit of their union was a son, James Stuart, who was eventually to unite the crowns of the two kingdoms.[1]

Mary proceeded toward her aim with suicidal recklessness. Her husband, Darnley, had won her hatred by murdering in her own apartment one David Rizzio, an Italian, in whom she trusted much. The next year the house in which her husband slept was blown to pieces with gunpowder, and Darnley's body was found near the ruins.

Death of Darnley.

The Earl of Bothwell, for whom she had a guilty love, was accused of the murder, and many believed that Mary was not innocent. "Black" Bothwell's trial was a farce, and his marriage with the queen, which followed closely upon his acquittal, ended their career in Scotland. A national uprising drove the odious Bothwell from the kingdom. Mary was deposed and imprisoned at Lochleven. Her babe was crowned as James VI. of Scotland, her half-brother, James Douglas, the Protestant Earl of Murray, acting as regent. Escaping from her captors, she soon found supporters, but the regent defeated her in battle. She turned, and entered England alone (May, 1568), as a queen in distress, asking Elizabeth[2] to restore her to her rightful Scottish throne.

The Queen of Scots seeks refuge in England, 1568.

[1] The news of the birth of this royal babe reached Elizabeth in the midst of a ball in her palace of Greenwich. The messenger noticed that all her joy and high spirits were dampened by the tidings. "She was sunk in melancholy, and said to her attendants that 'the Queen of Scots was the mother of a fair son, while she herself was but a barren stock.'"

[2] The personal relations of the two queens had long been strained. Mary had resented Elizabeth's interference in Scottish politics. In 1561 she had said to the English ambassador at Paris: "Perhaps she [Elizabeth] bears a better inclination to my rebellious subjects than to me, their sovereign, her equal in royal dignity, her near relation, and the undoubted heir to her kingdoms. . . . She is pleased to upbraid me as a person little experienced in the world. I freely own it; but age will cure that defect. However, I am already old enough to acquit myself honestly and courteously to my friends and relations, and to encourage no reports of your mistress, which would misbecome a queen and her kinswoman. I would also say, by her leave, that I am a queen as well as she, and not altogether friendless; and perhaps I have as great a soul too; so that methinks we should be upon a level in our treatment of each other." After her return to Scotland Mary agreed to renounce her present claim to the English crown if Elizabeth would declare her the successor, but both public policy and the Tudor jealousy forbade. The unbounded vanity of the Englishwoman was injured by the comparison of her meager personal charms with the beauty, grace, and winning manner of the younger queen.

What to do with the fugitive Queen of Scots was the question which puzzled the English government for nineteen years. The regent Murray was gladly rid of her, and refused to take her back unless she would submit to trial. This she declined to do, and England could not force a Catholic sovereign upon a country so thoroughly Protestant as Scotland had become under the fierce preaching of John Knox and the Calvinists. Mary next demanded safe conduct to the Continent. But from France or Spain she would have plotted with advantage against England. At that very moment the Duke of Alva, a general of Philip of Spain, was massacring the Protestants of the Low Countries with a merciless zeal which has made his name accursed.[1] His presence gave hope to the English Catholics, menaced the Huguenots, and challenged English Protestants to succor their suffering brothers in the faith. As Elizabeth could do nothing with safety, she did nothing at all. She would not give up Mary for trial in Scotland, nor try her in England, nor conduct her into France, nor set her on her throne, nor admit her right, or that of her son, to succeed to the throne of England. Under pretense of guarding her from her enemies, Elizabeth had Mary held as a prisoner. The royal captive became a personal center for Catholic plots. The pope launched his most terrible weapon, the Bull of Deposition (1569), absolving Elizabeth's subjects from their obedience. In 1570 the Duke of Norfolk, who had previously proposed marriage with the Queen of Scots as the prelude to a papist rising, became involved in a new conspiracy: Philip II. was to send 10,000 men of Alva's army to aid in putting

A puzzling problem.

---

[1] England was the gainer by this campaign, for many Dutch Protestants sought refuge in England, introducing new industries.

Mary in Elizabeth's seat. This conspiracy, known from the name of its agent as "Ridolfi's Plot," was discovered by Lord Burleigh's detectives. Its English accomplices were arrested, and Norfolk was beheaded (June, 1572).

Ridolfi's Plot.

As the excommunication encouraged Elizabeth's enemies, it nerved her also to more stringent measures against all persons refusing to worship in the legal manner. These recusants were of two classes. Besides the Romanists, who objected to the reforms in the service, there were the Puritans, who complained that the reform stopped too soon. They accepted the Presbyterian teachings of John Calvin and the extreme Genevan Protestants, and were dissatisfied because the English Church retained the rule of bishops, the surplice for the priests, and other relics of the Roman ritual. These people did not wish to withdraw from the communion, but they were clamorously in favor of purifying the national church while remaining in it. These efforts gained them the derisive nickname of "Puritans." Puritans and Catholics were alike excluded from Elizabeth's scheme of uniformity, and the Court of High Commission, which she created in 1583 to try ecclesiastical causes, soon had its docket crowded.

The Puritans.

Presbyterians.

Punishment by fines and imprisonment failed to check the rise of Puritanism. Toward the close of the reign it advanced a stage farther, until some stayed away from church altogether, worshiping by themselves out of doors, and in dwellings, barns, or warehouses. They were called Separatists[1] and Independents, and some of

Independents.

---

[1] These Separatists abhorred the very idea of a state church. Their "church" was a congregation of spiritually-minded persons associated for purposes of worship. Barrowe, one of their boldest champions (the reputed author of the savage "Martin Mar-Prelate" tracts against the episcopacy), wrote of the state church in 1590: "Never hath all kind of sinne and wickedness more universally reigned in any nation at any time, yet all are received into the church, all made members of Christ. All these people with all these manners were in one daye, with the blast of Queen Elizabeth's trumpet, of ignorant papistes and grosse idolaters, made faithful Christians and true professors!"

these sects gained peculiar names, as, for example, the "Brownists," a body of Congregationalists, among whose leaders was one Robert Brown.

Congregationalism.

While the rise of new sects showed activity in one school of religious thought, the work of the Jesuits in England exhibited the zeal of the opposing party. The Catholic leaders perceived that their religion must eventually lose its hold upon the mind and heart of the common people, for the old priests were with few exceptions conforming to the reformed order or being displaced by Anglican clergymen. The universities had come so thoroughly under Protestant influence that they no longer recruited the priesthood. Accordingly zealous English Catholics founded a school at Douay on the Continent—another was soon planted at Rome— for the training of Englishmen to preach the Catholic religion in the island. These "seminary priests" were men of unusual, even fanatical, enthusiasm for the work to which they devoted their lives.

Progress of Protestantism.

It was declared treasonable to land or shelter the new teachers. Parsons and Campion were the first Jesuits to brave the law (1580). They traveled in disguise, preached in secret, and did effectively reclaim Catholics of high and low degree who would otherwise have drifted into conformity. The strict enforcement of the laws against them deterred them no more than Mary's burnings had dismayed the Protestants. Campion died a traitor's death, and several hundred priests and teachers suffered a like fate, and were revered as martyrs by the Catholics, even as their persecutors reverenced Latimer and Ridley and the other stouthearted victims of Smithfield and Oxford fires.

Jesuits in England, 1580.

After the death of Norfolk Elizabeth had a brief respite. Her cousin Mary remained in custody, still

Breathing spell.

proud and hopeful, still the hope of all Catholics who yearned for the reclamation of England. Strange news came from the Continent. A dozen dangerous years had passed and Elizabeth had until now staved off the necessity of answering that hard question of a royal marriage. Neither France nor Spain could yet free its hands from home affairs long enough to deal out to England the chastisement which the pope had ordered.

An age of great endeavor.

As the nation grew in wealth and in unity it was swept by new enthusiasms. The cheap books which had followed the invention of printing, the resultant mental awakening, the penetrating force of the Reformation, which stirred all men to their depths, all these were bearing fruit in a generation of brilliant Englishmen. Great exploits were rewarded at Elizabeth's court, and among her courtiers were many doers of great deeds. Although there was no open war with Spain there was the bitterest hatred and the overhanging certainty that, once freed from its entanglements in Holland, the whole force of the Spanish monarchy would descend upon the Protestant island.[1]

The sea-rovers.

This was enough for the young Englishmen, who could not sit quietly at their school-books while the Dutch "sea beggars" were harassing the Spanish galleons. Philip's vast possessions in America formed a rich prey for English buccaneers. They plundered the cities of the Spanish main, intercepted the treasure-ships, darted into Spanish harbors, and cut out rich prizes from under the guns of the forts. Francis Drake, one of the boldest of these lawless sailors, had faced worse perils than Philip's gibbet. His was the first English ship in the Pacific Ocean, and his little vessel was the first to

---

[1] See Tennyson's ballad, "The Revenge," for a description of the spirit of the time.

carry the English flag around the world. Men of like daring were Davis and Frobisher, who explored the icy channels of America in vain quest for a "northwest passage" to India.

The depredations of sea-rovers like Drake[1] and Hawkins[2] hastened the outbreak of war with Spain. The queen accepted the inevitable. Brave little Holland was fainting in its struggle against the strongest state in Europe. William the Silent had been killed by an assassin (1584), and France and Philip had formed the "League" (1585) to keep the Huguenot, Henry of Navarre, from the French throne, and to put an end to Dutch Protestantism. The union of the two Catholic countries was the signal for England's neutrality to cease.

War with Spain.

HATFIELD, AN ELIZABETHAN MANOR.

Formation of the Catholic League.

However reluctant to risk the fortunes of war, the same instinct of self-preservation which had maintained a nominal peace for nearly thirty years now prompted the queen to vigorous action. The two Catholic king-

[1] Drake's buccaneering exploits gave him great celebrity. The Spaniards called him "The Dragon," playing upon his name, which in its Latin form, Draco, signifies "dragon."

[2] Sir John Hawkins, who was knighted for his successful voyages in the slave-trade, concluded his sailing orders thus: "Serve God daily; love one another; preserve your victuals; beware of fire; and keep good company." He evidently had no doubts of the propriety of slave-stealing as a calling, for on one occasion, having escaped death at the hands of an outraged African tribe, he said: "God, who worketh all things for the best, would not have it so, and by him we escaped without danger. His name be praised for it!" and again, becalmed and starving in the middle passage, a favoring gale came from "Almighty God, who never suffereth his elect to perish." His favorite ship was the *Jesus*.

doms would turn upon England the moment their bloody work in Holland was completed. Six thousand English troops crossed to the Low Countries under command of Robert Dudley, Earl of Leicester, Elizabeth's handsome favorite. But the gay man of courts fared ill against Philip's seasoned generals and Leicester came home in disgrace after his defeat at Zutphen, where fell that knightly poet, Sir Philip Sidney.

<small>Leicester's expedition to Holland.</small>

Every east wind wafted tidings of danger to Elizabeth. Her succors had not relieved the Hollanders; Henry of Navarre, to whom she paid a begrudged subsidy, could scarcely hold his own against the league; and there was rumor, and unmistakable evidence, too, of fresh conspiracies among the Catholic refugees upon the Continent. The hope of each nest of intriguers was, willingly or unwillingly, the imprisoned queen.

In 1586 the threads of a Catholic plot of which one Anthony Babington[1] held the English end were found and followed up. Walsingham, Elizabeth's secretary, whose spies were everywhere, secured evidence of Mary's guilty complicity in their design against the queen. Babington was executed with thirteen accomplices; still Elizabeth hesitated to do violence to her Scottish prisoner. Due regard for her own safety left no alternative. A special court tried, condemned, and sentenced the Queen of Scots for treasonable connection with Babington's plot "for the hurt, death, and destruction of the royal person." Even then, although she had signed the death warrant, Elizabeth would not order its execution, leaving that duty to her secretary.

<small>Babington's Plot.</small>

---

[1] Babington was an enthusiastic young Englishman of good family, who was devoted to the Catholic religion. Mary's emissaries in Paris fired his ardor in her behalf, and a personal letter from the royal prisoner herself bound him forever to her service. He threw himself zealously into the plot of a priest named Ballard to murder Elizabeth and deliver Mary.

On February 8, 1587, Mary Stuart was beheaded in the court of Fotheringay Castle, bequeathing to Philip of Spain her enmity to Elizabeth and her claims to the English crown.

Execution of Mary Stuart, 1587.

Philip was ready to move. For months his fleets had been building and assembling for the conquest of England and the Netherlands. Drake, plunging into Cadiz Harbor (1587), put back the preparations, and, as the rough sailor said, "gave the Spanish king's beard a singe." But in 1588 the league had won a notable triumph over the Huguenots, and the Duke of Parma had arranged matters in the Spanish Netherlands so that he, with 17,000 men, could be spared for heavy work in England. In May, 1588, "the most fortunate and invincible armada"—so the Spaniards fondly named their fleet—set sail on its double errand of invasion and conversion. The pope blessed the expedition as heaven's chosen instrument for the chastisement and redemption of the apostate realm. The Duke of Medina-Sidonia commanded the armament, which was thus made up: "132 war-ships, manned by 8,766 sailors and 2,088 galley-slaves, and carrying 21,555 soldiers, as well as 300 monks and inquisitors." The fleet was first to proceed to Dunkirk, where Parma's army was to be taken on board for the descent on the Thames.

The "Invincible Armada," 1588.

The navy[1] of England, swollen by volunteers, numbered at least as many vessels, most of them light

The English navy.

---

[1] The *Triumph*, which was for thirty years the most powerful ship in the English navy, was of somewhat over 1,000 tons burden. She carried 750 men, of whom 50 were gunners and 200 soldiers. In her armory (1578) were 250 harquebuses, 50 bows, 100 sheaves of arrows, 200 pikes, and 100 corselets. "Her heavy guns were 4 60-pounder cannon, 3 33-pounder demi-cannon, 17 18-pounder culverins, 8 9-pounder demi-culverins, 6 5½-pounder sakers, and 30 smaller pieces, falconets, serpentines, and rabinets." The towering Spanish ships furnished a fine mark for the English gunners, while their own shot could not be depressed sufficiently to strike the English hulls. The chief reliance of the Spaniards was in boarding, which the English were able to avoid by skilful handling of their lighter craft.

tonnage and slightly armed. With the admiral, Lord Howard, were Drake, Frobisher, Hawkins, and other hearts of oak, the heroes of many a rough bout with the Spaniards on the high seas. These gathered in Plymouth Sound. At Tilbury Fort the English volunteers, Catholic[1] and Protestant and Puritan, rallying to the defense of their common country, mustered in thronging companies, and flung their caps in the air when Elizabeth Tudor rode among them and with a few queenly words exhorted them to save their common country: "I am come among you, resolved in the midst and heat of battle to live or die among you all. I know that I have the body but of a weak and feeble woman, but I have the heart of a king, and of a king of England, too!"

Elizabeth at Tilbury.

RUINS OF KENILWORTH CASTLE.

English naval tactics.

On Friday, July 19, the Armada was sighted off the Lizard and beacon fires flashed the news over the kingdom, and on Saturday Howard went out, not to meet but to follow the foe. Until July 27 the Englishmen hung upon the flanks and rear of the great crescent-shaped Spanish fleet, attacking straggling or

---

[1] The conduct of the English Catholics at this juncture was most patriotic. The Armada came as the scourge of the pope for the chastisement of heretic England, yet so far from aiding it by raising revolt they loyally supported the queen's government, serving in her armies as volunteers, the rich even equipping ships for the navy. The admiral, Lord Howard of Effingham, was himself a Catholic.

disabled vessels and maneuvering for delay. On the 28th, at midnight, eight English fire ships bore down upon the Spanish vessels crowded in Calais roads. In the confusion which ensued Lord Howard gave battle. All day Monday, the 29th, the valiant English, reenforced by new arrivals, fought for their queen, their country, their religion. Their powder was almost gone when the "Invincible Armada" gave up the battle.

Howard gave chase for several days, making havoc of the stragglers; a great storm completed the destruction. The coasts of Norway, Scotland, and Ireland were strewn with wreckage, for the Spaniards, cut off from retreat through Dover Straits, endeavored to return by sailing northward around Great Britain. In October Philip's shattered fleet dropped anchor in the harbors whence it had sailed in pomp five months before. Fourscore vessels and 20,000 men were missing. "I sent them forth," said the phlegmatic king, "against man, not against the ocean," and he thanked God that he still had the power to send a larger armament. England thanked God for her great deliverance. *Destruction of the Armada.*

Philip's attack on England was not renewed. His far-reaching plans remained unfulfilled. England now struck back. Descents were made upon Corunna and Lisbon and privateers ravaged the Spanish ocean commerce. While Philip's authority upon the seas declined he saw his other plans collapse. The popularity and finally the apostasy of Henry of Navarre to Catholicism gave him the crown of France as Henry IV. and shut out Spanish influence. The death of his best general left the Netherlands unpacified, and so they continued until 1607, when their freedom was acknowledged. Philip himself was then nine years dead. He had died in 1598, at the age of seventy-one. *Collapse of Philip's plans.*

The dispersion of the Armada lifted a cloud that had hung over England for a quarter of a century. The leadership of Spain was ended forever. Protestant England took her rightful place among great nations. The sagacity, the patience, the diplomacy, and finally the courage, of Elizabeth and her staff of devoted ministers, Burleigh, Bacon, and Walsingham, had foiled the domestic plots of the Catholics, had postponed and in the end defeated the onslaught of Catholic Spain. Relieved of her fears England sprang forward with an exultant bound. Men were eager for opportunities to win renown for their country and their "virgin queen." The young Earl of Essex, Elizabeth's latest favorite, captured the Spanish port of Cadiz. Raleigh in rivalry pounced upon one of the Azores Islands, and Elizabeth sent him to jail for the affront to her pet commander.

An age of great endeavor.

Ireland rose in revolt. This kingdom, long divided and chaotic, had found a point of union. The English Parliament had established by law the Protestant religion in Ireland. The Irish were absolutely opposed to the new faith, and the attempt to force it upon them compacted them into a nation. The corrective measures of England failed utterly. The colonies of Englishmen, who were settled upon confiscated lands, formed "Saxon" communities detested by their Celtic neighbors. Spain aided, and the pope blessed, every insurrection of the Catholic Irish. Essex, who was Elizabeth's choice for every arduous task, was sent to quell the revolt of Hugh O'Neill, Earl of Tyrone. His failure disgraced him at court, and his audacious attempts to save his head angered the aged queen. She approved the sentence of treason which was passed upon him, and he was executed February 25, 1601. His successor firmly but mercilessly crushed the Irish

Essex in Ireland.

Repressive acts.

rebellion, and established English laws, language, and customs at the point of the sword.

Elizabeth did not neglect Parliament altogether, as most of her Tudor predecessors had done, but it did not often oppose her. Her Test Act excluded the Catholic members, who might have formed an obstructive force, and the common peril of queen and nation and the prevalent belief that her policy was the best for all doubtless smoothed her path. Moreover, her thrift and her love of peace spared her those constant appeals for money which always aroused the opposition of the people. Yet the national spirit, which grew with the successes of Elizabeth, sometimes asserted itself in the House of Commons. A part of the royal revenues was derived from monopolies of salt, wines, and other commodities. By patent from the sovereign the sole right to deal in these articles was granted to individuals or corporations, conditioned upon the payment of a "royalty" to the government. These taxes became so oppressive that in 1601 the Commons indignantly protested, and the queen revoked her patents.[1] *Parliament.*

Royalties.

Many charters for trade in America and Asia were granted during this reign, and on the last day of the fifteenth century an association of London[2] merchants *Commerce— America; India.*

[1] When the Commons thanked her for thus yielding, she made this characteristic address: "I have more cause to thank you all than you me; for had I not received a knowledge from you, I might have fallen into the lap of an error, only for lack of true information. I have ever used to set the last judgment day before mine eyes, and so to rule as I shall be judged to answer before a higher Judge—to whose judgment-seat I do appeal, that never thought was cherished in my heart that tended not to my people's good. Though you have had, and may have, many princes more mighty and wise, sitting in this seat, yet you never had, or ever shall have, any that shall be more careful and loving."

[2] Sir Walter Besant claims that the wisdom and foresight of Sir Thomas Gresham made London the world's commercial center. The religious wars in the Low Countries shook the supremacy of Antwerp and Gresham seized England's opportunity by building the Bourse or Royal Exchange in London, as "the city's brain, a place where merchants could receive news and consult together." The establishment of the exchange was followed by an unprecedented development of commercial enterprise, and London entered upon her career as the mart of the world.

was chartered as the East India Company, the corporation which conquered, and for a time controlled, the British Indian Empire.

Death of Elizabeth, 1603.

In the last years of her life the famous queen became fretful and nervous; she who had known no fear kept a sword continually in her chamber, and at times thrust it through the hangings in quest of concealed assassins. Her trusted counselors were dead. Robert Cecil, son of the good Lord Burleigh, became her chief secretary, and he it was who told, from the signs which she made on her death-bed, that she would have as her successor the son of her arch-enemy, Mary Stuart. Elizabeth Tudor died at Richmond, March 24, 1603, in the seventieth year of her age.

England's golden age.

The reign of "good Queen Bess" is reckoned the golden age of England. The patriotic feeling of the time is embodied in Shakespeare's panegyric:

> This royal throne of kings, this sceptered isle,
> This earth of majesty, this seat of Mars,
> This other Eden, demi-paradise;
> This fastness built by nature for herself
> Against infection, and the hand of war;
> This happy breed of men, this little world;
> This precious stone, set in the silver sea,
> Which serves it in the office of a wall,
> Or as a moat defensive to a house
> Against the envy of less happier lands.

TOPICS FOR READING AND SPECIAL STUDY, WITH LIBRARY NOTES.

1. THE ENGLISH MARTYRS.
   History of England. J. A. Froude.
   Book of Martyrs. Fox.

2. SHAKESPEARE AND THE ENGLISH DRAMA.
    English Writers. H. Morley.
    Shakespeare's Predecessors. J. A. Symonds.
    The People for Whom Shakespeare Wrote. C. D. Warner.
    English Dramatic Literature. A. W. Ward.

3. MARY QUEEN OF SCOTS.
    Mary Stuart. Robertson.

4. THE ENGLISH SEAMEN OF THE SIXTEENTH CENTURY.
    English Seamen of the Sixteenth Century. Froude.
    English Seamen under the Tudors. Fox Bourne.
    The Spanish Story of the Armada. Froude.
    Drake and the Tudor Navy. Corbett.

FICTION, ETC.

Queen Mary. Tennyson.
Marie Stuart. Schiller.
Kenilworth. Scott.
Westward Ho! Kingsley.
Isoult Barry of Wynscote. Emily S. Holt.
Judith Shakspeare. William Black.

CHAPTER XII.

CAVALIER AND ROUNDHEAD, 1603 A. D.–1649 A. D.
–FROM THE ACCESSION OF JAMES I. TO THE EXECUTION OF CHARLES I.

HENRY VIII. had desired that Elizabeth's successor be taken from the family of his younger sister, the Duchess of Suffolk; but at Elizabeth's death the royal council invited the king of Scotland to ascend the English throne.

James I., 1603-1625.

James I. (James VI. of Scotland) was the only son of Mary Stuart and Darnley. His Catholic mother had been allowed no voice in his education, which was strictly Protestant, and even Presbyterian. Weak and ungainly of body and slovenly in manner, the king really had a mind of considerable keenness, though one of the Scots divines had called him "God's silly vassal." He was especially learned in theology—"the wisest fool in Christendom," sneered Henry of Navarre —and was inordinately proud of his acquirements. A man of such parts—physical cowardice was a marked feature of his character, and a Scotch accent marred his speech to delicate ears—cut a sorry figure before the subjects of "bluff King Hal" and "good Queen Bess."

A crowned pedant.

The Puritan agitation was the first subject which was brought to King James's attention. As he passed southward toward London (1603), the "Millenary Petition," signed by about 1,000 Puritan pastors, was

The Millenary Petition.

offered to him.[1] It urged him to purify the English ecclesiastical system from the lingering taint of Romanism. It will be remembered that the reformers of Edward VI.'s reign—Cranmer and his supporters—were the high officers of the church, enlightened men, who introduced changes more rapidly than the common people were ready to receive them. Hence the Catholic reaction under Mary had been easy. The long reign of Elizabeth had spanned two generations. The English Bible had become for the first time the one household book in thousands of families, and its influence had contributed to an enormous growth of the Puritans. The situation of Edward's reign was now reversed. The bishops, appointed by the crown, were conservative, pledged to maintain the church, as established by law, and subject to rebuke and discipline if lenient toward innovators; the people, on the other hand, with many of the lesser clergy, were strongly Puritanical, and to King James they came with their petition.

Clergy and people.

JAMES I.

The petitioners had their trouble and something worse for their pains. In 1604 the king summoned

Hampton Court Council, 1604.

---

[1] The popery protested against consisted in such minor matters as the words "absolution" and "priest" in the prayer book, the use of the sign of the cross in baptism and of the ring in marriage. They decried "longsomeness of service and the abuse of church songes and music." They would have the power of excommunication restricted, and demanded that none should be ordained who could not preach.

four Puritans to a conference at Hampton Court [1] with eighteen prelates of the church. This famous conference denied the petition, and the king, after a savage denunciation of Presbyterian government (which he knew by bitter experience at home), ordered the bishops to compel their clergy to conform strictly to the rules of the church. Star Chamber Court adjudged signers of the great petition guilty of misdemeanor, and ten of them were imprisoned. Three hundred Puritan preachers were expelled from their livings for failing to obey the rules at which their consciences rebelled. The measures against the "Independents"—those extreme Puritans who, despairing of reform within the church, had left it altogether—drove some of them out of the country. They took refuge in Holland. Among them the earliest Baptist churches were gathered, and other fugitives under Brewster and Robinson from the village of Scrooby in Nottinghamshire became the Pilgrim Fathers of New England.

The petition denied.

Baptists.

The Pilgrim Fathers.

King James's Bible, 1611.

A new translation of the Bible, "the King James's version," was authorized by the Hampton Court Conference and published in 1611.[2]

---

[1] The king was very outspoken in favor of the Tudor system of church government. "A Scottish Presbytery agreeth as well with monarchy as God and the devil," he declared in this conference, remembering how the General Assembly dominated his paternal kingdom of Scotland. To the suggestion that it would be difficult to bring the Puritans back to the High Church theories, he flew into a rage and broke up the conference, saying, "I will make them conform, or I will harry them out of the land."

[2] The first "authorized" version of the English Bible was the so-called "Great Bible" of 1539. Its price, about $30 of our money, limited its circulation, though it was placed in most of the parish churches. In 1560 certain English scholars who had taken refuge at Geneva from the Marian persecutions brought out a small quarto revision of the Great Bible. It was printed in plain Roman, instead of black-letter; it was divided into chapters and verses; it had a running marginal commentary of a Puritan savor, and it was both handy and cheap. This "Geneva" or "Breeches Bible" (the word "breeches" is used for "aprons" in Gen. iii.: 7) became the family Bible of England. To displace it the "Bishop's Bible" in folio (1568) and quarto (1569) was brought out, but was never popular. King James's version was the work of a commission composed of the most learned men of both universities, and the Puritans and High Church party were equally represented. The king hoped that it would prove a unifying bond in the church. It was popular from the first and has proved a bond of union for the entire English-speaking race.

The first Parliament of the reign assembled in March, 1604, and its sessions marked the beginning of a new era. The dearest dogma of this theorizing monarch was "the divine right of the king to rule." He denied that the people were the source of law and of kingly power. His authority, he declared, was from heaven, and his prerogative was above the law, which he might of his own will alter as the welfare of his people required. Divine right of kings.

A resolute spirit of independence was evident in the first Parliament of James. He asked it to sanction a close union of England and Scotland, which had now separate governments under the same king. This they refused, and the king, in turn, slighted their wish to concede the Puritan demands for reform. The first session of Parliament closed fruitlessly. The session of 1605 narrowly missed a tragic opening. First Parliament.

James had promised to relieve the Catholics of the heaviest burdens with which Elizabeth's reign had weighted them, but his ear soon caught whispers of Catholic plots against him and he broke his promises. Robert Catesby and a few desperate papists planned to blow up the Parliament buildings on the day of the joint assembly of the two Houses to hear the king's opening speech. Gunpowder was placed in a vault under the House of Lords and all was in readiness to massacre king, princes, lords, and commons at a blow. Guy Fawkes was the agent of the conspirators. November 5 was the day for the king to meet the two Houses; but the secret transpired at the last moment.[1] Fawkes, Gunpowder Plot, 1605.
Guy Fawkes.

[1] Fawkes was a native of York, well born, and brought up among Catholics. His personal reputation was that of mildness, temperance, and fidelity to his friends. Like most of his associates he seems to have entered upon this atrocious work with a clear conscience, believing that he was doing God's will in clearing the way for the restoration of "heretic" England to the bosom of Holy Church. The plot leaked out when an anonymous letter warned one of the Catholic lords to keep away from the Parliament on opening day. Nearly all the conspirators were put to death. The Jesuits were seriously implicated in the business, and Garnet, the head of the order in England, was executed for his share in it.

arrested among his powder kegs, was executed with others, and November 5, the anniversary of the "Gunpowder Treason," was long celebrated by English Protestants with songs and festive processions.

Revenue. The question of crown revenues, for which Elizabeth's thrift had found ready solution, kept her successor in continual trouble. His expensive household, his pensions, and his foreign diplomacy used up vast sums. The only lawful way by which an English king might raise money was by taxation voted by the representatives of the people in Parliament. James had found Parliament a two-edged sword, which he feared *"Impositions."* to handle. Without asking its consent he accordingly laid a tax on certain imported articles. One Bate, an importer of currants, refused to pay, and was tried before the Court of Exchequer. The judges gave the startling opinion that the king, as regulator of commerce and foreign affairs, might lawfully lay and collect such customs duties without consent of Parliament.

This invaded the rights of Parliament. In 1610 James offered to relinquish certain feudal claims of the crown, in return for an annual grant of money. But *The "Great Contract."* the haggling over this "Great Contract" disgusted both parties, and the king dissolved Parliament, hoping to pay his way by means of the hated "impositions." But the way was hard, and after footing it for three years he summoned a second Parliament in 1614. The Commons refused to grant a farthing until the king should redress their grievances by renouncing the impositions and purifying the church. After the deadlock had lasted a month James ordered the Commons to go *The "Addled Parliament."* home, whereupon the "Addled Parliament" dissolved without enacting a single law. Among the participants in that stormy session were John Eliot and

Thomas Wentworth, memorable names in the history of the constitutional struggle of the following reign.

Robert Cecil, Earl of Salisbury, and son of that Burleigh who had given Elizabeth a life of faithful service, was the first adviser of the king, and the only real minister that James tolerated. After Cecil's death James cultivated court favorites in the place of serious counselors. The first was a page, one Robert Carr, a young Scot, who had neither ability nor character. James made him his companion and private secretary, loaded him with wealth and honors which ruined him. Young George Villiers, better known by his later title, Duke of Buckingham, next gained the royal favor. The king entrusted to him the distribution of offices and peerages, and his purse was soon stuffed with enormous bribes. "Steenie," as the king called Buckingham, was a handsome, genial fellow, with fine taste for art and very poor for virtue. To Prince Charles, heir-apparent to the crown, the favorite attached himself, even more closely than to the father.

Robert Cecil.
Robert Carr.
Buckingham.

Meanwhile James followed his own will in the administration of the realm. His plantation of Ulster[1] in the north of Ireland, with Scottish and Irish families, was accomplished at great expense. The question of revenue was variously met. The "impositions" proving insufficient, a "benevolence" was asked, but only a small sum resulted. "Baronets," a new order of nobility, were created, and patents of this new rank and seats in the House of Lords were sold for cash. The effort of the king to interfere with the proceedings of the law-courts was resisted by the chief-justice, Sir

Baronets.

---

[1] The estates of the Catholic Earls of Tyrone and Tyrconnel, together with other lands—the choicest in the six counties of Ulster—were confiscated (750,000,000 acres in all). A part of these lands were granted to English and Scotch undertakers, who agreed to people them with Protestant tenants from Great Britain. The native Irish were with few exceptions turned out of their homes, with their hearts burning against the Protestant intruder.

Edward Coke, and that great lawyer was dismissed from the bench (1616).[1] The lawless extortions of the crown were imitated by the officials of the court. Buckingham lived upon bribes. Judges received no salaries, and a premium was thus placed upon official corruption. In 1621 Francis Bacon himself, "the wisest, brightest, meanest of mankind," the chancellor of the realm, was impeached by the House of Commons for taking bribes. He acknowledged that he had received money from suitors, but denied that such payments had influenced his decisions.

Official corruption.

Coke and Bacon.

The Parliament which condemned Bacon was called for a very different purpose—one which brings the student to the perverse foreign policy of the Stuart kings. Elizabeth's reign had shown that England was the natural leader of Protestant Europe against Spain, the champion of papistry. The first armed conflict of the two religions had settled this. France and the Netherlands had furnished the battle-ground for that struggle. After a generation a fresh outbreak was imminent, and Germany was to be the field.

Foreign affairs.

England was Protestant, but the wilful king believed that an alliance with Spain would restrain both countries from the war and insure a European peace. To confirm the amity of the two naturally distrustful nations he proposed (1617) that Prince Charles should wed Isabella, the Spanish infanta. The prince's sister Elizabeth had married Frederick, the Elector Palatine, the

A Spanish marriage.

---

[1] Coke was the greatest lawyer of his time, and a man of sturdy independence. The offense which called down the king's displeasure was much to his credit. James had commanded the judges to delay judgment in a certain case until he had seen them personally. The chief-justice obtained their signatures to a paper declaring such an interference illegal. The king called them before him and lectured them on his "prerogative" until they fell on their knees to sue for pardon. Coke, however, protested that their action was proper, and when asked whether in the future he would delay a case at the king's order he would only say that "he would do what became a judge." For this "disrespect" he was dismissed from all his offices. He was afterward a member of Parliament and a champion of free speech.

leader of the German Protestants. James thought the best way to protect her and her children was to ally himself to Spain, the leading Catholic state. To this design he sacrificed Sir Walter Raleigh,[1] whose exploits in America made him odious to Spain.

Death of Raleigh.

The negotiation of the Spanish marriage proceeded slowly. The English denounced it, and Spain stipulated that the English Catholics should henceforth be unmolested in their worship. The parleyings were disturbed by the clash of arms in Germany. Bohemia called King James's son-in-law Frederick to its throne, expelling King Ferdinand, the Catholic relative of the Spanish king. This revolt opened the Thirty Years' War (1618-1648). Frederick maintained his position only a few months. The Catholic League drove him from Bohemia, and the Spaniards occupied his home dominions in the Palatinate (1620).

Thirty Years' War.

A small force of English volunteers set out to aid the Elector, with the permission of James, and in 1621 the third Parliament of the reign was summoned to grant supplies for a war in Germany. When the Commons found that the king wanted cash, but would give no definite plan of war, their ardor cooled. They voted a meager sum, but pledged themselves to aid the king with their fortunes and their lives if he would adopt a

---

[1] Raleigh was a representative Englishman of Elizabeth's reign. Leaving Oxford a mere youth he served as a soldier in several lands and learned navigation. The queen took him into favor and enriched him with offices and monopolies. His restless energy led him into unsuccessful attempts to colonize America, of which the name "Virginia" is the only memorial—if we except the potato and tobacco, which he brought to the knowledge of Europeans. None surpassed him in loyalty and energy in the "Armada year" and to him are attributed the tactics which dispersed the "invincible fleet." From that time he was the uncompromising foe of Spain, and James, who wished to maintain friendly relations with the Catholic powers, had no use for him. He was condemned to death for some wild utterance (1603), but the sentence was commuted to imprisonment in the Tower. In 1616 he was released on parole that he might accompany an expedition to Guiana—the El Dorado of the Spaniards—in quest of gold. No gold was found, but a Spanish village was taken and burnt, and on his return Raleigh was recommitted to the Tower and in 1618 executed on the sentence passed fifteen years before. This as a favor to Spain.

war policy in earnest. Still he temporized with Spain, and while the last shreds of his son-in-law's power were being seized by the Catholics he still swam about the tempting bait of the Spanish marriage.

The Protestation. When a committee of Parliament asked the king to declare war on Spain the monarch was furious. "Bring stools for these ambassadors," he cried, when the commoners made known their errand, and he bade them meddle no more with affairs of state. To this the House entered its Protestation, solemnly and prayerfully declaring "that the liberties of Parliament are the ancient and undoubted birthright and inheritance of the subjects of England, and that the arduous and urgent affairs concerning the king, state and defense of the realm, and of the Church of England, and the making and maintenance of laws and redress of grievances . . . are proper subjects of debate in Parliament." With his own hand the king tore the Protestation from the journal of the House, and sent the members to their homes.

The failure of the Spanish match. The shameful quiescence of England in the presence of the suffering German Protestant states at length aroused James to a final effort to vindicate his foreign policy. In 1623 Buckingham and Prince Charles set out together for Madrid to bring about the marriage which had been delayed so long. They were sumptuously entertained at Madrid, but every obstacle was placed in the way of the match. The infanta was averse to a "heretic" husband, and the Spanish king and the pope devised all manner of iron-clad oaths to compel King James to reopen the way for the restoration of England to Catholicism. Charles promised everything; still the marriage was delayed. Thwarted in his design to bring the infanta to England as his bride, the humiliated prince returned in 1624 and broke off the engagement.

James despaired of the Spanish alliance and summoned a fourth Parliament (1624) to prepare for war with Spain in defense of his daughter Elizabeth. But the Commons were wary of the king's purposes and chary of supplies; they made a small appropriation and then rested to study the movements of the king. His heart was fixed upon marrying his son to a princess who should secure to England a Catholic ally on the Continent. By Buckingham's advice he selected the Princess Henrietta Maria of France, and agreed to a marriage treaty which granted substantial liberties to English Catholics. With such an unpopular deed to answer for it was folly to ask Parliament for money. Buckingham undertook to open hostilities without an appropriation, but disease carried off the troops which he sent to the Continent. *Fourth Parliament, 1624.*

In the midst of these disasters James died, March 27, 1625, leaving his son to face the rising storm of resistance to tyranny.

Charles I. immediately succeeded his father. Courtly presence, pleasing address, dignity of manner, serious mind, and cultivated tastes combined to recommend him. In his household, as in society, Charles was a polished gentleman, but in his theory of kingly power he was a tyrant. The principles of absolute authority in which James had believed were inherited by the son, and pressed with a persistency which led to war, dethronement, and death. *Charles I., 1625-1649.*

Charles's hatred of Spain and zeal for his sister Elizabeth promised that England should soon resume her place among the Protestant nations. Parliament was asked to appropriate sums for the prosecution of

Protestant and Catholic.

the war for the recovery of the Palatinate. But a few months had altered the temper of the nation. Two months before (May, 1625) the king had married the

CHARLES I.

French princess, Henrietta Maria. It was suspected that the marriage was a prelude to a milder attitude of the government toward the English Catholics. Until the monarch should declare his intentions in this regard the Commons would not satisfy his demands. They voted him one sixth of the desired amount; but the tonnage and poundage duties, heretofore granted for the lifetime of the sovereign, were assigned to Charles for one year only. This Parliament was dissolved two months after its first meeting.

Struggle with Parliament.

Before a year had passed a second obstinate Parliament had met and been sent home (February to June, 1626). The Commons were intractable. Led by Sir John Eliot[1] they defied the king's claims to absolute power. When he cast Eliot and Digges into prison their col-

[1] Eliot had his eyes early opened to the corruption of the government, when in 1623 as vice-admiral of Devon he succeeded in capturing the notorious pirate Nutt. The pirate's gold properly placed among the highest officials gained his release, while Eliot himself was imprisoned for four months. His vigor, spirit, and dauntless courage made him the leader of the Commons in their attacks on the favorite, Buckingham, and it was for a bold speech comparing the favorite to Sejanus, the false favorite of the Emperor Tiberius, that he was sent to the Tower in 1626. The more he was singled out for the king's shafts the more popular he became.

leagues refused to transact business until the members were released. They would even have impeached Buckingham had not the king put an end to the session.

Two years had passed; two Parliaments had come and gone without filling the royal purse. The half-hearted war with Spain was a total failure. To conciliate the Protestants, the king now broke the pledges of Catholic toleration by which he had bound himself to France.

Cardinal Richelieu was the French statesman who directed the policy of Louis XIII. Late in 1626 war broke out between the two countries. The independent Huguenot seaport of Rochelle—"proud city of the waters"—was besieged by the French, and Buckingham's expedition for its relief (1627) ended in inglorious defeat. "Since England was England it had not received so dishonorable a blow."

Richelieu.

Rochelle.

JOHN HAMPDEN.

The king had secured the money for the war by a "forced loan." Men who refused to contribute were imprisoned without trial. Among them was John Hampden, a country squire, who said he did not begrudge the money, but he dared not incur the curse of Magna Charta by disobedience of its rules. Five of the prisoners asked for trial on a writ of *habeas corpus*, but the servile judges buttressed the royal power by declaring that it was for the king to say whether or not men should be tried. This decision

John Hampden.

violated another provision of the Great Charter. One after another the hard-won liberties of centuries were being extinguished.

The third Parliament of this reign met in March, 1628. Sir John Eliot, according to whose theory the king was the servant of Parliament, was its uncompromising leader. Sir Thomas Wentworth, keen and practical, but of aristocratic bias, stood with Eliot. In the rank and file of the House were John Hampden, John Pym, Denzil Holles, and another country squire, a cousin of the "stiff-necked" Hampden—Oliver Cromwell, a Puritan of the straitest sect.

Such earnest men did not wait for another to open the subject which was uppermost in all minds. With zealous care they drew up a "Petition of Right," reciting the hitherto acknowledged liberties of the kingdom and the divers manners in which they had been trampled upon by the House of Stuarts. Four especially odious acts were specified: the laying of taxes without consent of Parliament, the billeting of troops upon private families, the employment of martial law in time of peace, and the imprisonment of citizens without specified accusation. Charles was reluctant to accept this document which proposed to curtail his authority, but he was in sad financial straits and his fawning judges told him how to nullify the parliamentary proposals. With extensive mental reservations he set his signature to the bill, and was rewarded with an abundant subsidy.

The Commons followed up their victory by another assault upon the favorite.[1] "We will perish together,"

marginalia: Wentworth. Cromwell. Petition of Right.

---

[1] When the Commons proposed to rid the nation of the baneful influence of the unscrupulous Buckingham by bringing him to trial on charges, the king warned them "that he would not tolerate any aspersions upon his ministers." When Eliot would have spoken, the speaker, acting under the king's orders, declared him out of order. "Amid a deadly stillness" the champion of freedom sat down and burst into tears. The silence was soon broken by the voices of Prynne, Coke, and others, urging the rights of the nation in defiance of the tyrant.

said King Charles. But Buckingham fell first. He was at Portsmouth, superintending the embarkation of the forces with which he hoped to retrieve his fortunes at Rochelle, when John Felton, a disappointed lieutenant, spurred by motives of revenge and patriotism, stabbed him to the heart. *Assassination of Buckingham.*

While Parliament was training its guns on the throne for its unlawful taxes and its High Church sympathies, the king did his best to control its deliberations. The speaker, Finch, had precise orders from him which motions to entertain and when to adjourn. The Commons were justly indignant. They took counsel over Sunday what to do. On Monday, March 2, 1629, they met, with their minds made up. The speaker had the king's command to adjourn forthwith, but the House would not adjourn. When Finch would have left the chair young Holles and another held him in his seat, swearing, "He shall sit there till it please the House to rise." The doors were hastily barred and Eliot moved, amid the assenting shouts of the Commons, three resolutions, stating plainly that whoever introduced new religious opinions or services, whoever advised the levy of unparliamentary taxes, and whoever voluntarily paid such taxes, was an enemy of England. A few days later (March 10) this Parliament was dissolved. Sir John Eliot, Holles, and other actors in that famous scene were arrested; when Eliot died of consumption in the Tower (1632) the spiteful king refused his body to his mourning family for burial. *Arrest of members.*

King Charles concluded that much unpleasantness might be avoided by having no more Parliaments in which these impudent Puritans meddled with affairs of church and state. Three men were his main reliance in the period of personal government which now opened: *The king's men.*

Wentworth, Laud, and Weston. Sir Thomas Wentworth, Eliot's former colleague, had gone over to the king. He was president of the Council of the North, which administered the government of the northern counties and in civil matters was a loyal and faithful counselor. William Laud, a churchman of the narrowest type, was bishop of London. Within his diocese he allowed no deviation from the established rules, and when (1633) his elevation to the archbishopric of Canterbury made all England his parish he enforced the laws of conformity mercilessly against the Puritans. Weston, the lord treasurer, was less conspicuous, though it was his financial ability, the fertility and audacity of his invention which furnished the means by which the unparliamentary rule was supported. To save expense he persuaded his master to make peace with both France and Spain (1630).

"Thorough" was Wentworth's name for his system of administration. A definite purpose—to achieve good government by strengthening the power of the king—ruled all his movements, and in Laud he found a willing and efficient coadjutor. Together they set about the administration of church and state in such high-handed fashion that, between tax-gatherers and clergy, the Puritans had no peace. In 1629 the Massachusetts Bay Colony was chartered by a company of Englishmen in quest of religious liberty.[1] They founded Salem and Boston in New England. The tide of emigration ebbed and flowed in sympathy with the rigor or relaxation of Wentworth and Laud, but it never entirely ceased, and within a dozen years from the issue

---

[1] In August, 1629, twelve leading Puritan gentlemen met at Cambridge and laid plans for establishing a Puritan colony in New England. In April, 1630, their first expedition sailed for Massachusetts Bay and before the end of the year seventeen shiploads of emigrants had been despatched thither. By the year 1634 the settlers numbered 4,000.

of the charter 20,000 English Puritans left the mother country for the New England wilderness.

The Puritan exodus.

The problem of raising revenue was most immediate and puzzling. The illegal tonnage and poundage customs furnished a portion; extensive monopolies of commodities fed another financial rill; landholders were knighted and made to pay well for the enforced honor; obsolete feudal fines and dues to the crown were revived and collected; Catholics were mulcted for staying away from the national church. The king's court of Star Chamber, which had no jury, was the treasurer's instrument of oppression in these matters.

Ways and means.

The need of a fleet to protect commerce put a new idea into the heads of the crown officers. An ancient usage of commanding the maritime counties to furnish ships for the navy was revived and worked so well that in 1636 the inland counties also were ordered to pay a new tax, "ship-money," to be used in furnishing forth the fleet. Servile judges upheld the levy and the government thought that deliverance from its hardships had dawned at last. If this tax were lawful why be vexed by another Parliament? John Hampden, the commoner of Buckinghamshire, comprehended the importance of the principle and almost alone took stand against it. He was not a poor man, but he would not pay the twenty shillings of ship-money which the royal commissioners levied on him (1637). Try him they might and convict him they did (1638), but not until the nation had gained courage from the example of one plain citizen who had not bowed his neck to the scepter. Hampden was applauded; his slavish judges were reviled. But the new shackles which the ship-money decision placed upon English freemen increased the numbers who longed for rest from tyranny. A

Ship-money.

Prosecution of Hampden.

royal prohibition was required to check the emigration to New England.

Laud's persecutions.

What the Star Chamber Court was to the civil government the Court of High Commission was to Archbishop Laud. Outward conformity to the church laws was his aim, and in attaining it he was as thorough as Strafford could wish. For the numerous body of thoughtful Puritan Englishmen whose conscience rebelled at the copes, the robes, the crossings, bowings, and kneelings of the church service Laud had neither sympathy nor mercy. With absolute intolerance he drove Puritan ministers from their pulpits, forced the established worship upon unwilling congregations, making it even more outrageous to Calvinists by innovations which, in their sensitive nostrils, savored of ever-dreaded Rome. "Dr. Alabaster preached flat popery," said young Mr. Cromwell to the Commons.

WILLIAM LAUD, ARCHBISHOP OF CANTERBURY.

Not only were non-conformist preachers cast out, but laymen suffered for alleged lapses in morals and attacks upon the clergy. William Prynne, a barrister with a caustic quill, had his ears cropped for a libelous writing, "Histriomastix," condemning the the-

Prynne's "Histriomastix."

ater.¹ Other men who criticized the church for its loose Sabbath-keeping and its tendency toward papistry stood in the pillory, or sat in the stocks, while the common people stood by pitying.

In 1636 King Charles gave Archbishop Laud permission to carry his measures of reform across the border, and bring the Scottish Kirk into uniformity with the Church of England. The kirk had been modeled by John Knox and his fellow Calvinists upon strict Presbyterian principles, and the General Assembly was the most powerful organization in the northern kingdom.² Little wonder that James was charmed by contrast with the subservience of the English bishops to him as "the head of the church." *Laud and kirk.*

He upheld the Church of England against the Puritans for fear that Puritanism would lead to Presbyterianism. The bishops were a main reliance of his theory of absolute power, and in 1610 he forced upon the Scottish Kirk an anomalous system, bishops being appointed to preside in the Presbyterian synods. James had a wholesome fear of his canny countrymen, and he rejected Laud's early schemes to complete the reorganization of the Scottish Kirk. "He does not know the stomach of that people," was his comment on the bishop's plan for "thorough" reform. Charles Stuart knew less of the Scottish "dourness" or he would have been satisfied with his father's progress. He let Laud place the full control of the kirk in the hands of the *Presbyterian bishops.*

---

¹ Prynne worked seven years collecting materials for this book, which showed that all actors, playwrights, and theater-goers were "sinful, heathenish, lewd, and ungodly." He reserved his choicest denunciation for women actors, which brought the queen and her private theatricals into the affair. It was for this covert attack upon the queen that he suffered mutilation.

² "I tell you, sir," one of the preachers, Andrew Melville, had said to James, "there are two kings and two kingdoms in Scotland. There is Christ Jesus the King and his kingdom the kirk, whose subject James VI. is, and of whose kingdom not a king, nor a lord, nor a head, but a member. And they whom Christ hath called to watch over his kirk and govern his spiritual kingdom have sufficient power and authority so to do."

bishops, and force upon the Presbyterian preachers a liturgy based upon the English prayer-book. The Scots stopped their ears rather than listen to the new service. Jenny Geddes, a market woman, cried out, "Villain, dost thou say mass at my lug?" and threw her stool at the head of the dean who read service in St. Giles's Kirk, Edinburgh (July 23, 1637), and at the bishop who thought to quell the tumult the riotous congregation yelled "A pape, a pape!" and "Stane him!" It was impossible to use the new service-book there or elsewhere. No "Canterbury pope" for Scotland![1]

Jenny Geddes.

The king raged, but the Scots organized committees—"the Tables"—who, on February 28, 1638, signed the Covenant[2] to recover and maintain the purity and liberty of the Gospel. To regain his slipping grasp upon his ancestral kingdom Charles sent the Marquis of Hamilton to Edinburgh with slight concessions. A general assembly of the kirk was to be held and the service-book withdrawn. The assembly met at Glasgow, November, 1638, but in defiance of Hamilton and his master the Scottish bishops were deposed,

The Covenant of 1638.

---

[1] When the news of the Scottish uproar reached London, Archbishop Laud was met on the way to the council by Archie Armstrong, the king's fool, with the question, "Wha's fule now? Doth not your grace hear the news about the liturgy?" Laud, who was in no mood for jesting, had Armstrong disgraced and banished from the court, "for certain scandalous words of a high nature." Some one who met the sharp-tongued Scot clad in a black coat, and inquired what had become of his fool's motley, received this reply: "O, my lord of Canterbury hath taken it from me, because either he or some of the Scotch bishops may have use for it themselves."

[2] The day of the signing was marked with great solemnity. A solemn fast was kept. An impressive sermon was preached in the Grey Friars Church at Edinburgh. Then the Covenant, by which their ancestors had declared their purpose to preserve the reformed church from innovation and prelacy, was read. The Earl of London exhorted all to stand firm for God and Scotland. Rev. Alexander Henderson offered prayer. Then the noblemen signed the parchment and took the oath to defend the Covenant to the last. The other classes pressed forward to the table and the great sheet was soon crowded with signatures. The throngs in the churchyard and throughout the city were filled with rapturous enthusiasm over the new birth of the nation. Similar scenes were repeated throughout the kingdom. Thousands wept as they signed; some wrote their names in their own blood.

and the whole Presbyterian system was reëstablished.[1]

The overthrow of the royal and episcopal authority in Scotland was a serious reverse for the policy of Thorough. With John Hampden's resistance before them, and the Scots' example of stiffneckedness, the English Puritans might rise against the king—Parliament or no Parliament. Obviously the only consistent course for Charles and his archbishop was to reduce the Scots to submission. Money was scraped together in odd ways for the first "Bishops' War" (1639). The Covenanters rushed to arms. But a peace was patched up with little bloodshed by the "Pacification of Dunse"[2]; the Scots, however, refused to modify the decision of the Glasgow General Assembly. The king knew not what to do next, and Wentworth hastened from Ireland to give him counsel.

The Bishops' War, 1639.

Wentworth had been sent to govern Ireland in 1633, and had set up in that distracted kingdom the thoroughgoing policy which was his prescription for all political ills. With supreme confidence in himself and in his own wisdom he decided what would be best for the Irish—and the king; then he went to work to effect

Wentworth in Ireland.

[1] No sooner had Hamilton perceived the uncompromising temper of the General Assembly than he declared it dissolved. It thereupon denied his jurisdiction, and went about its work "in the name of the Lord Jesus Christ, the only head and monarch of his church." Alexander Henderson, its moderator, indicated its spirit when he said: "Whatsoever is ours we shall render to His Majesty, . . . but for that which is God's and the liberties of his house, we do think, neither will His Majesty's piety suffer him to crave, neither may we grant them, although he should crave it." When their work was done they sang the 133d psalm, and then having set the king at defiance, they were dismissed with the benediction and by the moderator's solemn words: "We have now cast down the walls of Jericho; let him that rebuildeth them beware of the curse of Hiel the Bethelite!"

[2] Baillie, who was a chaplain in the covenanting army, says of their camp at Dunse Law: "Every company had flying at the captain's tent-door a brave new color stamped with the Scottish arms, and this motto, 'FOR CHRIST'S CROWN AND COVENANT,' in golden letters. . . . Had you lent your ear in the morning and especially at even, and heard in the tents the sound of some singing psalms, some praying, and some reading the Scriptures, ye would have been refreshed." The commander of this wonderful host was an "old little crooked soldier," General Leslie, a veteran of the wars of Gustavus Adolphus. Against such an array Charles could oppose only a half-paid levy of impressed men, disgusted with fighting in such a cause.

that result, using indifferently any method—persuasion, cajolery, bribery, force—which would bring him most quickly to his destination. Thus he established order in Ireland, introduced the culture of flax and the linen trade, summoned an Irish Parliament, and with its aid maintained a small standing army. In fact he exhibited on a small scale the absolutism to which Charles so fondly aspired.

Wentworth's advice was to summon Parliament. Letters had been intercepted which showed that Scotland and France were ominously drawing together. Possibly he expected this disclosure to rouse the nation to the pitch of voting the money which must be had if Scotland were not to be lost.

The Short Parliament, 1640. Parliament met at Westminster, April 13, 1640, and, heedless of the intercepted letters, immediately demanded the redress of grievances as a prelude to the passage of the supply bills. "Till the liberties of the House and kingdom were cleared they knew not whether they had anything to give or no." Evidently nothing was to be done with such advisers, and on May 5 the "Short Parliament" was dissolved.

The second Bishops' War. Spurred on by Wentworth (who had been made Earl of Strafford) and Laud, the king renewed hostilities with Scotland—the second "Bishops' War"—but his untrained soldiers fled from the field at Newburn. The army of the Covenanters encamped on English soil, prepared to march on to London to extort favorable terms of peace. Charles shrank from another conflict with the Commons; the Lords had been less insolent, perhaps they would help him now. A council of peers was summoned in September, but their only recommendation was to call a Parliament. He could do no other. The Scottish army was only held off by his promise to pay £850 a day until a permanent settlement should be reached, and without help from Parliament he could not raise that amount of money. Writs of election were accordingly issued, and Royalist and opposition plunged into the contest for members.

The Scots in England.

John Hampden, the "ship-money" hero, rode through the country with John Pym, who had grown gray in resistance to the Stuart pretensions, arousing the people to their opportunity to fling off the tyranny of the crown. The crown candidates were beaten everywhere, and the Commons, who met at Westminster on the 3d of November, 1640, came with resolute purpose not to separate until they had set certain bounds to the royal power. Pym and Hampden were there—the former the leader of the House. The silent Cromwell was there from Cambridge town; young Holles, who had held the speaker in his great chair (and lain in prison for it), was there, with Lucius Carey and Edward Hyde, who, in the troublesome times ensuing, chose the king's side and quitted Parliament, the one to become Lord Falkland and perish in the civil wars, the other to figure as Lord Clarendon and write a ponderous Royalist history of what he termed the "Rebellion." This was the famous—or, if you will, infamous—"Long Parliament," which through many vicissitudes and adjournments, purgings, and restorations, existed until March 16, 1660, twenty years lacking eight months.

The Long Parliament, 1641–1660.

All that Charles asked of Parliament was to furnish money to pay the Scottish army its £850 a day and equip an army of Englishmen. But Parliament had a longer bill of items against the king. It proposed to settle forever the matters of arbitrary imprisonments, of unauthorized taxation, and of Laud's ecclesiastical

The king's need and Commons' demands.

innovations. It was in the main Puritan, with an infusion of extreme Independent members. The portentous presence of the Covenanters in the North gave to Parliament a power over the king which was pushed to the utmost extent. The Scots would stay until the stipend should be paid.

<small>Proceedings against Strafford.</small>

The Commons put the thumb-screws on the king. On the eighth day of the session they impeached Strafford of high treason, and a few days later Archbishop Laud was imprisoned on the same accusation. In an impeachment trial the House of Lords sat as judges. Treason was crime against the king and the Lords objected to condemning the king's most sincere friend on such a charge ; so the accusers hastily changed their plans and, relinquishing the trial, pushed a bill of attainder against Strafford through both Houses. Charles wept like a child when the bill which was aimed at the life of his faithful supporter "as a public enemy" was placed in his hands ; but to save himself he must sign, and the great earl, who had trusted in his ability to establish the absolute supremacy of his monarch over Parliament and nation, was executed on May 12, 1641. "Put not your trust in princes," he exclaimed when a messenger brought him word that the king had yielded to the popular clamor for his head.[1]

<small>Strafford's execution, 1641.</small>

The purpose of the Parliament-men was to tie the hands of the monarch until they should secure the reforms which he had denied. In February, 1641, they compelled his assent to the Triennial Act, providing that Parliament should meet every three years,

<small>The Triennial Act.</small>

---

[1] On his way to the block the earl stopped at the cell of his old friend Laud and besought the help of his prayers for strength in the last moment, and the aged archbishop with sobs and tears bestowed his benediction. On the scaffold the prisoner said : " The omen was bad for the intended reformation of the state that it commenced with the shedding of blood. . . . I thank God that I am no way afraid of death nor am daunted with any terrors ; but do as cheerfully lay down my head at this time as ever I did when going to repose ! " He was in his forty-ninth year.

whether summoned by the crown or not. There were to be no more eleven-year periods of personal rule. Two months later he consented, under pressure, to an enactment that the Parliament then in session should be neither adjourned nor dissolved without its own consent. The day of "addled" and "short" Parliaments was over; the one now in session was both brainy and long-lived. Assured of their continuance in power, the Commons struck out boldly. Tonnage and poundage taxes were condemned, ship-money was pronounced unlawful, the courts of Star Chamber and High Commission, by which the king had been able to cloak his tyranny with the robe of the law, were abolished. This work done, the Scots were paid off and peace restored between the two kingdoms (August, 1641).

Tools of tyranny broken

Of its own free will Parliament took an autumnal recess of six weeks, leaving a committee of each House on guard. Pym was chairman of the Commons committee. His name was first in all that the Commons did; the Royalists, who were much grieved by these doings, ridiculed the plain name of the man, and mockingly called him "King Pym." Parliament reassembled October 20, 1641, in a nervous condition. Charles had been in Scotland, and had made some bargain, the country scarcely knew what, with the great Duke of Argyle.

"King Pym."

In November horrible tidings came from Ireland. When Strafford's strong hand was withdrawn, the Roman Catholics, infuriated by the loss of their lands and by generations of English injustice, rose in savage insurrection and massacred the Protestant population of Ulster—strong men, defenseless women, and helpless children. Some believed that the king had caused the revolt that he might obtain from Parliament an army. With an army he might perhaps disperse other enemies

The Ulster massacres.

besides Irish rebels. However, no troops were granted to him; on the contrary, the Commons drew up, after serious debate, a Grand Remonstrance—206 articles long—itemizing the unlawful acts of the reign. The majority for it was small, and an old story has it that Mr. Cromwell was heard to say as he left the hall that "if the Remonstrance had not passed he would have sold all and gone to New England." This paper, printed and read in every English parish, molded opinion in support of the Commons against the sovereign.

<small>The "Grand Remonstrance."</small>

The church organization had been attacked at the spring session, when the Commons had made an unsuccessful attempt to oust the bishops from the House of Lords, where they acted with the Royalist majority. In December an unguarded act of the bishops themselves enabled the Commons to imprison them. This was followed by a law depriving them of their seat in the upper house.

<small>The bishops excluded from the House of Lords.</small>

January 4, 1642, was one of the memorable days of the session. The king's patience had given out. Against Lord Kimbolton and four commoners, "King" Pym, "ship-money" Hampden, Holles, and Strode, was raised royal accusation of treasonable correspondence with Scotland. Charles kissed his queen good-by and went to Westminster with five hundred men to arrest the five. "The birds were flown"—to use his own surprised expression—when he entered the House, and their colleagues deafened the ears of their royal master as he retired with cries of "privilege," "privilege," meaning that they considered his act a breach of their privilege of immunity as legislators.[1]

<small>Attempted arrest of the five members.</small>

[1] When the baffled king was scanning the House in quest of the offensive members he demanded of the speaker whether any of these persons were in the house. Said the speaker, "I have, sir, neither eyes to see nor tongue to speak in this place, but as the House is pleased to direct me, whose servant I am."

On the 10th of January Charles quitted his palace of Whitehall for the north of England, where he was safer than in the Puritan capital. The queen crossed to Holland to pawn the crown jewels for artillery and small arms. Civil war had become inevitable, and each party set about strengthening itself. The Royalist members of the two Houses, to the number of ninety-seven, left their places and joined the king at York. Since Parliament could no longer obtain the royal signature to its enactments, it decided to do without it. "Ordinances" was the name given to these unapproved laws. *[Charles leaves London. "Ordinances."]*

On June 2 Nineteen Propositions were submitted by the Commons to the king. They required him to surrender to Parliament the control of the militia, the possession of the forts and arsenals, the reformation of the church, and the appointment of his royal ministers. Upon the rejection of these demands Parliament assumed control of the militia, made the Earl of Essex its chief commander, and selected a committee of public safety to undertake the defense. Charles raised the royal standard at Nottingham (August 22, 1642). Before the close of the summer the rival powers, the king and the Parliament, were in arms. *[The Nineteen Propositions. Beginning of civil war, 1642.]*

The fighting of the first year of the civil war went against the parliamentary armies. Their soldiers were chiefly the peasantry and the city trades-people, while the cavalry, the pride of the royal camp, was composed of gentlemen of spirit, well armed, well fed, and superbly mounted. Prince Rupert, son of James Stuart's daughter, Elizabeth of Bohemia, was the dashing leader of these Cavaliers, and he made short work of the "roundhead" train-bands, as the short-haired Puritans were *[Character of the combatants. "Roundheads" and "Cavaliers."]*

called by the curled fops of Charles's court.[1] The first battle, at Edgehill, October 23, 1642, was indecisive, but the Royalists marched on London, and only the bold front of London train-bands kept them out of the city. Neither party ventured upon pitched battles; the northern, western, and midland counties were steadfastly Royalist. The counties of the South and East bound themselves in associations to support the parliamentary cause. Oliver Cromwell, now a colonel of horse, had become a leading spirit in the Eastern Association, which was the best organized of all.

Associations.

Throughout the second year of the war the Royalists gained ground. Something ailed the Parliament's troops; Cromwell told his cousin, Hampden, that they were 'prentices and tapsters, sure to run from the gentlemen who opposed them. If he had his way he would meet these men of honor with "sober men of religion." Patriot Hampden fell (June, 1643) in fight, but Colonel Cromwell put his theory into practice. His own regiment of horse, "Ironsides," becomes noted for its religious zeal. The men pray before battle, and never retreat. "Truly they were never beaten at all," said their leader.

Death of Hampden.

Cromwell's "Ironsides."

Parliament was not inactive, whatever may be said of its armies. An assembly of Puritan divines, in session by its side at Westminster since July 1, 1643, was con-

The Westminster Assembly.

[1] When the king and his train visited London in 1641 the Puritan bystanders jeeringly called the mounted men "cavaliers," and the name stuck to the court party throughout the troubles. It was an age of great extravagance in dress. When Buckingham went to Paris in 1625 he had twenty-seven suits of clothes made, one of which was white uncut velvet, set all over with diamonds valued at £14,000, besides a great plume encrusted with diamonds. The Puritans testified their contempt of the world by opposing its fashions. The men wore plain collars and cuffs instead of starched ruffs and falls of lace and lawn. Their clothing was sober hued and plain of cut, their hose black. Ben Jonson speaks of them as having

"Religion in their garments and their hair
Cut shorter than their eyebrows,"

and of the Cavalier love-locks the savage Prynne spoke as "that bush of vanity whereby the devil leads and holds men captive."

sidering the reform of the church; the bishops had joined the king, and affairs ecclesiastical were in utter confusion. To Scotland Pym turned for example and aid. In return for military assistance against the king, Parliament promised to take the Covenant by which the Scots had established their own kirk. On September 25, 1643, 25 peers and 288 of the commons signed the "Solemn League and Covenant," binding the government to make the religion of the three kingdoms uniform in faith and worship. Two thousand Church of England clergymen left their pulpits rather than accept the Covenant which was now offered everywhere as a test of loyalty to the Parliament. An executive committee of Scottish and English was charged with the conduct of the war. This union drove the king to an alliance with the red-handed Irish rebels.

Alliance with Scotland.

The death of Pym in December saddened but could

Death of Pym.

not dismay his party. In January Leslie, with the Scots army, forded the Tweed. Fairfax and Waller scattered the Irish contingent before it could succor the king. Toward night-fall on the 2d of July, 1644, Prince Rupert, whose brilliant and rapid movements had thus far made him the most notable Royalist figure in the war, attacked the allies on Marston Moor, in Yorkshire. The Scotch quailed before the fury of his charge, but Cromwell's steadfast Ironsides outmarched the Cavaliers and chased them from the field. "God made them as stubble to our swords," said their commander, whom this victory placed in the front rank of the parliamentary forces. The north of England, with York and Newcastle, surrendered to the parliamentary leaders. In the South, however, the Royalists still had the best of the struggle.

<small>Marston Moor, 1644.</small>

In the fall and winter the Royalists of the Scottish Highlands, led by the Marquis of Montrose and aided by a contingent from Ireland, harried, burned, and slaughtered in the Lowlands, in the vain hope of recalling Leslie's army from England. In October Charles again marched on London, but was repulsed at Newbury. Cromwell thought that mere repulse was not enough; such an army as he would construct would have made short work of the king. He justly complained to Parliament that the generals were "afraid to conquer." The majority of Parliament wished to force Charles to resume the throne and govern as a Presbyterian sovereign, under proper checks and limitations. They did not wish to kill him, or "to beat him too badly." For these half-way measures Cromwell had no use. He proposed a sweeping military reform, a new-modeling of the whole army on the Ironside plan.

<small>Rising of Montrose.</small>

The withdrawal of the Royalists and the acceptance

of the Covenant had left Parliament almost unanimously Presbyterian. Archbishop Laud had been executed for treason (January, 1645), and the Church of England liturgy had been replaced by a simpler service like that of the Scottish Kirk. The Westminster Assembly of Divines was drawing up a creed, a liturgy, and a system of church government for English Presbyterians. In April, 1645, Presbyterianism was by law established, and it was the purpose of Parliament to enforce conformity by measures as stringent as those of Laud himself. *Presbyterianism established.*

Cromwell's plans of military reform were adopted in April, 1645. By a "self-denying ordinance" all members of Parliament—except Cromwell, who was now deemed indispensable—were removed from military command. Sir Thomas Fairfax succeeded Essex as captain-general, with Colonel Cromwell next in command.[1] The entire force was reorganized on the plans of the famous regiment of horse. "Honest men of religion, whose heart was in the cause," were its commissioned officers, whether they were draymen, butchers, or gentlemen of family and fortune. So far as possible the same principles were carried into the rank and file, and when the "New Model," as the force was called, took the field, the king's gay Cavaliers faced the most remarkable military body that had ever *Cromwell reforms the army.* *The New Model.*

[1] "The parliamentary forces had been made up of (1) volunteer regiments raised by popular leaders, (2) the train-bands of London, (3) the militia of the county associations, (4) the local militia raised at time of need, (5) irregular bands recruited by zealous individuals by authority of Parliament. The New Model introduced permanence and regularity by disbanding the volunteers and county levies and reorganizing them into new regiments, newly officered and paid by Parliament. The officers, chiefly earnest men of religion, soon impressed their own spirit upon the men. They preached and prayed to their troops and even went up into church pulpits and preached to the people. The fine for swearing amounted to nearly half a day's pay. A drunken soldier forfeited a week's wages. The orders of at least one colonel punished severely any one found idly standing or walking in the street in sermon time, or playing at any games upon the Sabbath or fast day." (Condensed from C. Oman.)

been mustered in England. Prayer-meetings, psalm-singings, sermons, and exhortations were the avocations of these warriors.

While the New Model was mustering and drilling, and the Parliament wavered between war and peace, the Royalists caught glimpses of success. They saw their enemies divided and considered the army a rabble of raw recruits under inexperienced officers. Montrose wrote from Scotland that he should soon be able to send reënforcements. In February, 1645, the king had obstinately refused to come to terms with Parliament; in June he took the offensive and attacked the New Model at Naseby. Cromwell commanded the cavalry. Officers and soldiers no longer feared to conquer. The raw troops routed the king's men, captured camp, royal papers, artillery, and two thirds of the army.

Naseby, June 14, 1645.

The civil war was over. The defeat of Montrose at Philiphaugh, September 13, destroyed the Royalist party in Scotland, and on March 26, 1646, the soldiers of Parliament won the last battle at Stow.[1]

Philiphaugh.

End of the war.

The defeat of the Royalists left two parties in the kingdom—Parliament and the New Model—*i. e.*, the extraordinary body of earnest men who made up the army. The former was bent upon forcing Presbyterianism upon the nation. The latter, in which the Independents were influential, demanded that the toleration of all Protestant sects should form part of any settlement which should be made with the king. In May, 1646, Charles gave himself up to the Scottish army, which was still encamped in the North. He did not realize that he was conquered, but believed that the

Parliament vs. New Model.

The king in the Scots camp.

---

[1] Sir Jacob Astley, who commanded the Royalists at Stow, sat on a drumhead after the battle and grimly said to his captors, "Gentlemen, you may now sit down and play, for you have done all your work, if you fall not out among yourselves."

dissensions of his enemies would yet make his triumph possible. The agreement which Parliament asked him to sign restored him to the throne, but placed the militia under the command of Parliament for twenty years and sanctioned Presbyterianism. This suited neither the king nor the various sects in the army, who desired toleration for creeds outside the Established Church. For the sum of £400,000 the Scots surrendered Charles to Parliament and marched home (February, 1647). *The Scots deliver Charles to Parliament.*

Feeling between the New Model and the Presbyterians grew more intense. The party of the Independents in Parliament had gained strength by new elections to fill the seats of absent Royalists. The army, which was determined to secure the religious liberties for which it had fought, defied the order of Parliament to disband. Cromwell, accused of inciting mutiny, fled from the wrath of the Commons to the camp. Cornet Joyce, with a detachment of the New Model, seized the ill-guarded king at Holmby House (June, 1647). *The army seizes the king.* All parties were now negotiating with Charles, and his sense of his own importance was inordinately increased. He heard them all, pretended to favor each, but was sincere with none. On November 11, 1647, he escaped to the Isle of Wight, where he signed a secret treaty with Scotland. *Escape of Charles.* The Scots were rabidly Presbyterian, and resolute to force the same system upon England, in spite of the liberal ideas of the New Model. Charles promised to aid them in return for armed assistance. In May, 1648, the kingdom was again at war. The Royalists rose in half the counties; the Presbyterians in Parliament vehemently opposed the Cromwellian army,[1] and a Scottish force prepared *Renewal of war.*

[1] The army, democratic to the core, held a mass-meeting and resolved "to go out and fight against those potent enemies, . . . and then to call Charles Stuart—that man of blood—to account for the blood he had shed."

to invade England. Cromwell put down the Royalist revolt, and Parliament, having declared the Independents of the army heretical and blasphemous, reopened its treaties with Charles. The Scotch invasion under the Duke of Hamilton was met and hurled back by Cromwell in a three days' fight at Preston Pans, August 17–19, 1648. Fairfax reduced the South to submission. The army again seized the king, and giving up all idea of compromise marched upon London.

Preston Pans, 1648.

Having determined with prayerful deliberation what course to pursue, Cromwell, now supreme in the New Model, stopped at nothing. On the sixth and seventh days of December, 1648, the Commons, on entering their hall, had to pass by Colonel Pride, whose soldiers arrested those members whom he pointed out. "Pride's Purge" cost Parliament its Presbyterian majority. The remnant—"the Rump" its enemies called it—some sixty Independent members, continued to act as Parliament, executing the will of the council of officers which Cromwell directed. A special tribunal of one hundred and thirty-five persons—the High Court of Justice—was set up to try the charges brought against the king. The Lords declining to participate, the Commons declared themselves the sole legislature of the realm. Men shrank from the impending act. Barely half the commissioners attended the trial. Charles made no defense beyond denying the court's jurisdiction. But the court was satisfied of its authority. Sentence of death was passed upon him January 27, as "tyrant, traitor, murderer, and public enemy," and on the 30th Charles Stuart was beheaded at Whitehall. Upon the Commons' order it was proclaimed in every English town "that whosoever shall proclaim a new king, Charles Second or any other, without authority of

Cromwell supreme.

"Pride's Purge," 1648.

Execution of Charles I., 1649.

Parliament, in this nation of England, shall be a traitor and suffer death."

TOPICS FOR READING AND SPECIAL STUDY WITH LIBRARY NOTES.

1. THE GUNPOWDER PLOT.
   What Was Gunpowder Plot? S. R. Gardiner.
2. ARCHBISHOP LAUD AND THE SCOTTISH CHURCH.
   History of Scotland. J. H. Burton.
   History of England, 1603-1642. S. R. Gardiner.
   Sketches of Scottish Church History. T. McCrie.
   William Laud. W. H. Hutton.
3. THE PURITAN EXODUS TO AMERICA.
   The Beginnings of New England. J. Fiske.
   The Genesis of the United States. A. Brown.
4. THE STUARTS' STRUGGLE FOR PREROGATIVE.
   History of the Great Civil War. S. R. Gardiner.
   Letters and Speeches of Oliver Cromwell. Edited by Carlyle.

FICTION, ETC.

John Inglesant. J. H. Shorthouse.

The Fortunes of Nigel. Scott.

The Maiden and Married Life of Mary Powell. Anne Manning.

King and Commons. (Cavalier and Puritan Song.) Edited by J. H. Friswell.

CHAPTER XIII.

THE COMMONWEALTH AND THE RESTORATION, 1649 A. D.–1685 A. D.—FROM THE EXECUTION OF CHARLES I. TO THE DEATH OF CHARLES II.

The Commonwealth, 1649–1660.

THE Commons House of the Long Parliament, bereft of its Royalist members, purged of its Presbyterians, and by its own act freed from the House of Lords, remained at the death of Charles I. (January, 1649) the poor representative of constitutional government. This "Rump" established a Council of State. England was proclaimed a Commonwealth and Free State, and monarchy and the House of Lords were abolished—forever, as it was supposed.

Prince Charles in Holland.

The new government was beset with dangers, and forced to depend upon Cromwell for protection against its enemies at home and abroad. Charles Stuart, the son of the late king, had found a refuge at The Hague, where his sister was the wife of the reigning stadtholder. In the eyes of many Englishmen he was their rightful and defrauded sovereign. The Marquis of Ormond invited him to Ireland, and in August, 1649,

Cromwell in Ireland, 1649.

Cromwell was sent thither to punish the Royalists and restore order. He stormed Drogheda and Wexford and put their garrisons to the sword. "I am persuaded," so he reported these massacres to Parliament, "that this is a righteous judgment of God upon these barbarous wretches . . . and that it will tend to prevent the effusion of blood for the future." "Order was insured by planting colonies of Scotch and English upon the confiscated lands of the Royalists.'

Cromwell's next service was in Scotland, where Charles Stuart had landed and taken the Covenant to rule as Presbyterian king. The army of Parliament was outmaneuvered, and might have been lost had not the over-confidence of the Scots thrown away their advantage. At dawn of September 3, 1650, as the enemy descended from the heights of Dunbar the Puritan army, chanting a psalm of David, fell upon them and smote them hip and thigh. Edinburgh and Glasgow surrendered; but while Cromwell was busy settling the North Charles II. dashed over the border into England, with the parliamentary forces in hot pursuit. On the anniversary of Dunbar the king's army was routed at Worcester and the fugitive Stuart

The Cromwellian settlements.

Cromwell in Scotland, 1650.

Dunbar, 1650.

OLIVER CROMWELL.

Worcester, 1651.

[1] Three provinces, Ulster, Leinster, and Munster, were swept clean of their landed proprietors, who were ordered to settle upon waste lands beyond the Shannon. Their estates were bestowed upon Cromwell's soldiers and upon the corporations and capitalists who had advanced the money for the expedition. The "plantations" were accompanied by great hardship. Some resisted eviction and were either slain or retired to the mountains, where they lived as outlaws and brigands. Widows and orphans were sold into slavery in the West Indies. The Irish Royalist army took refuge on the Continent, where the "Irish exiles" did valiant service in the armies of Catholic kings.

barely escaped with his life.[1] "It is for aught I know a crowning mercy," wrote Cromwell to Parliament concerning the Worcester fight, and its anniversary, September 3, he fondly called his "fortunate day."

Rump and army at odds.

The great soldier and popular hero had now become an object of dread to the Parliament. The army demanded the election of a Parliament which should represent the people, and when the Rump would have passed a bill intended to perpetuate its own control, Cromwell entered the hall with a file of soldiers (April 20, 1653) and drove the members from their chamber. The Council of State fell by the same blow.

First dissolution of the Long Parliament, 1653.

Barebone's Parliament.

A plan for a Parliament was devised by Cromwell and the army. Some one hundred and sixty Puritan gentlemen conspicuous for the godliness of their walk and conversation were summoned by name to this "Little Parliament," better known as "Barebone's Parliament," from the odd name of one Praise-God Barebone[2] who sat in it. These men of religion turned out to be whimsical and incapable of government. "Overturn, overturn," was their whole policy, Cromwell complained. This short-lived assembly named a commission which drew up a written constitution or "Instrument of Government." Cromwell was to be chief magistrate with the title of "Lord Protector," and the power of legislation and taxation was vested in a parliament of one House, to be chosen triennially. The Lord Protector brought to a happy end the naval

Oliver, Lord Protector.

---

[1] Though Parliament offered a reward of £1,000 for the apprehension of "Charles Stuart, son of the late tyrant," the money was never claimed. Such was the loyalty of the Royalists to their hereditary sovereign that though six weeks passed before he could escape from the island, and his secret became known to fifty persons of all ranks in society, no one betrayed him.

[2] The Bible was the only household book of the Puritans. Their conversation was larded with Scripture phrases, and the Old Testament was ransacked to supply names for their sons and daughters. The emigrants carried the same spirit and practice to New England. See "Curiosities of Puritan Nomenclature," Bardsley.

war¹ which the Rump had begun with Holland,² but the parliamentary apparatus failed to work and after five months of turbulence Oliver dissolved it in disgust.

Unconstitutional as it was, the strong and just rule of Cromwell brought glory to England. The great days of Elizabeth seemed to return. Scotland became orderly and at rest. Ireland, scourged into submission, received thousands of thrifty colonists. The exploits of Blake and his fellow-admirals recalled the deeds of Drake and Howard. The hero of the Dutch wars chastised the Barbary pirates; Venables and Penn captured Jamaica from the Spaniards; the persecuted Vaudois Protestants found safety in the protection of England.³ England ranged herself with France for war with Spain (1656–1659). The battle of the Dunes,⁴ in June, 1658, gave the town of Dunkirk in the Spanish Netherlands to England—some recompense for Mary Tudor's loss of Calais.

<small>Brilliant foreign policy.</small>

To govern restive England was a more exacting

¹ From the beginning of the century the English and Dutch East India Companies had been hot rivals for the spice trade, frequently coming to blows in the East Indies. The English Navigation Act practically excluded the Dutch from trading with England or the English colonies in America. Further disputes concerned fishing rights in the Channel and finally the refusal of Dutch admirals to salute the English men-of-war in the English seas resulted in war.

² For want of trustworthy admirals Parliament assigned the command of the fleet to Robert Blake and two other military officers as "Admirals and Generals-at-Sea." This Dutch war is notable in British naval history (1) for the first employment of a "marine" corps of landsmen on board ship; (2) for the first distribution of medals to naval officers; (3) for the use of the type of vessel afterward famous as the "frigate"; and (4) for the introduction of the maneuver of breaking through a hostile line and engaging it from windward.—*Clowes*. By the terms of peace the Dutch agreed that their ships, merchantmen, and men-of-war alike "meeting any of the ships of war of the English commonwealth In the British seas, shall strike their flags and lower their topsails" according to ancient right and custom.

³ The Duke of Savoy was harrying the Vaudois with fire and sword. Cromwell made it a condition of his alliance with France that this religious massacre should be stopped. And it was stopped. The Protector himself subscribed £2,000 for the relief of the sufferers. It was on this occasion that Milton, the Latin secretary of the Commonwealth, wrote the impassioned sonnet beginning
"Avenge, O Lord, thy slaughtered saints."

⁴ In the battle of the Dunes the allied French and English fought the Spaniards, among whom were many English Royalists, including the Dukes of York and Gloucester, the younger sons of Charles I.

business than to defeat the Dutch in the Channel or the Spanish on the high seas. Royalist risings were frequent and only the overpowering might of that splendidly disciplined army kept the peace. After Penruddock's rising, in March, 1655, the Protector divided the island into ten military districts, each commanded by a major-general at the head of an armed force supported by tithes upon the property of Royalists. In November, 1655, the Protector was obliged to modify his policy of toleration.[1] The friends of the king were commonly the friends of the old church. Accordingly Cromwell forbade public services of the Anglican Church and the use of the prayer-book. Priests were banished from the island. Quakers, Anabaptists, and other new sects were put under restraint—not because of their intolerable religious opinions, but because men of those opinions were for royalism, or against the established order of the Commonwealth.

The ten major-generals.

In September, 1656, the Protector summoned a second Parliament, still indulging the hope that a stable constitutional government might be established. Papists and Royalist "malignants" were ineligible for membership, and nearly one fourth of the successful candidates were rejected by the Protector's council because of their violent opinions. The House, even after these purgings, could not let the constitution alone. Its "Petition and Advice" recommended the adoption of certain of the ancient forms of government—a parliament of two houses and the title of king. Cromwell rejected the title but accepted the principal recommendations, though

"Petition and Advice."

---

[1] One of its features had been the return of the Jews, 365 years after their expulsion. The "Judaic Spirit" of the Puritans is supposed to have led to their recall. Cromwell himself said, "Great is my sympathy with this poor people whom God chose, and to whom he gave the law." The Spanish and Portuguese Hebrews who seized the opportunity to settle in London did much to further the commercial interests of the city, which was the rising rival of the Dutch markets.

some of the stanch republicans were shocked by the royal pomp with which he renewed his oath as Protector in Westminster Hall (June 26, 1657)—the purple robe, the gilded Bible, and the scepter of gold.

The Parliament of 1658 met with a house of peers, sixty-three members, of whom only six had sat in the House of Lords. The wranglings of the session exhausted Oliver's patience within a fortnight. "I can say in the presence of God," he declared before them, "I would have been glad to have lived under my woodside, to have kept a flock of sheep, rather than under-

Disputes in Parliament.

ST. PAUL'S CATHEDRAL.

taken such a government. But, undertaking it, I did look that you, who offered it to me, should make it good." After charging them with postponing the settlement he so desired he concluded, "If this be the end of your sitting, I *do dissolve this Parliament*, and let God be judge between you and me!"

The Protector dissolves Parliament, February, 1658.

This was his last recorded speech. The cares of state and the death of a dearly beloved daughter had shattered his sturdy constitution, and in the end of August, 1658, it became apparent that his end was nigh. On his "fortunate day," the anniversary of his victories at Dunbar and Worcester, the Puritan hero was dead.[1]

Death of Cromwell, September 3, 1658.

Oliver's son, Richard, was peaceably inaugurated as Protector, but his weak hand could not govern the storm-tossed ship of state. Powerless to control the headstrong leaders of the army he retired from office in April, 1659. The constitution was overturned and the Rump of the Long Parliament reinstated at Westminster.

Richard Cromwell, 1658-1659.

While confusion reigned at London the military leaders in the North were taking measures to bring back the Stuart king. General Monk supported by many Scots marched on London. The Rump received again (February 26, 1660) the Presbyterian members, of whom Colonel Pride had purged it, and on March 16 decreed its own dissolution.

General Monk.

End of Long Parliament.

On the 14th of April, 1660, Charles Stuart, who was in correspondence with Monk, issued the Declaration of Breda, offering pardon to his English enemies, security of property, and toleration of peaceable religious sects. The newly elected "Convention Parliament," which met on April 25, enthusiastically voted to restore the ancient constitution and urged Charles to resume his father's crown. In May the royal exile landed at Dover, and the Londoners welcomed him

Return of Charles Stuart.

---

[1] "The devil is fetching home the soul of the tyrant," the Royalists whispered when the September gale roared about the palace, but the Protector's dying prayer breathed no bitterness: "Lord, thou hast made me, though very unworthy, a mean instrument to do them some good, and thee service; and many of them have set too high a value upon me, though others wish and would be glad of my death. Lord, however thou do dispose of me, continue to go on to do good to them. . . . Teach those who look too much on thy instruments, to depend more upon thyself. Pardon such as desire to trample upon the dust of a poor worm, for they are thy people too. And pardon the folly of this short prayer, even for Christ's sake. And give us a good night if it be thy pleasure. Amen."

with glad acclaims.¹ The Commonwealth, which had cost so much to establish, fell without a blow.

Charles II. was a Stuart of a new type, witty—"He never said a foolish thing," said Rochester—and profligate—"and never did a wise one," ran the equivocal quip.² He was handsome, gay, pleasure-loving, and his court became a nest of intrigue and vice. To rebuke the so-called "hypocrisy" of the strait-laced Puritan *régime* society flaunted its immorality. Of real religion the king had none, but his mother was a Catholic, as was his brother James, Duke of York. Thus it was a cynic, a libertine, and a skeptic, who succeeded the God-fearing Oliver. For the theory of government for which his grandfather argued and his father lost his head Charles II. cared little. He had experienced enough hardship already to curb his greed for absolute power. Whatever might happen, to use his own careless phrase, he was "resolved to go no more on his travels."

Charles II., 1660-1685.

In the first enthusiasm of the Restoration the Convention Parliament was as subservient as Stuart heart could wish. The judges who had condemned Charles I. to the block were excepted from the general amnesty and were cruelly hunted as far as the arm of the law could reach.³ The bodies of Cromwell and others were dug up and gibbeted at Tyburn. A fixed

The Royalist reaction.

---
¹ Charles was delighted with his reception but perhaps not entirely deceived by the flattery. He said, "I doubt not it has been my own fault I was absent so long, for I see no one who does not protest he has ever wished for my return."

² The witty monarch lightly parried the thrust by the explanation that "his discourse was his own, but his actions were his ministers'."

³ Of these "regicides" were Cromwell's cousin, Lieutenant-General Edward Whalley, and Major-General William Goffe, who were hunted like wild beasts through the forests of Massachusetts and Connecticut by the king's detectives. Pastor Davenport of New Haven defied the king in exhorting his flock to protect these fugitives, "Christ's witnesses," and the king took vengeance by taking away the colony charter. Hawthorne's story of "The Grey Champion" makes effective use of the tradition which connects the regicides with the Connecticut valley.

annual revenue of £1,200,000 was assigned to the king.

Clarendon.
The Earl of Clarendon, who was for seven years the chief adviser of the young king, as he had been of his unfortunate father, labored to undo the work of the Commonwealth. The Irish and Scottish members no longer sat in Parliament at Westminster. The Scottish Church was humbled by the reëstablishment of episcopacy. For reliance against such an emergency as that which had found his father so ill prepared, the king maintained in his own pay a few regiments of picked troops as the nucleus of a standing army.

The Cavalier Parliament.
The "Cavalier" Parliament of 1661 was strong for church and king. By its order the Solemn League and Covenant, the pledge of Presbyterian rule, was burned by the common hangman, and a series of enactments were aimed at the Presbyterian interest, still powerful in the large towns. The Corporation Act restricted town offices to persons who should take the Anglican communion, renounce the Covenant, and admit the wickedness of resisting the monarch. The Act of Uniformity forced all churches to use the prayer-book, required all teachers to assent to its doctrines, and reserved to the bishops the right to ordain ministers. The enforcement of this law (on St. Bartholomew's Day, 1662) drove two thousand non-conformist preachers from their pulpits. Two years later these dissenters were followed up by the Conventicle Act, forbidding religious gatherings at which the prayer-book was not used. In 1665 the Five Mile Act excluded from their former parishes those non-conforming preachers who refused the oath that they would "endeavor no alteration of church or state." It was in these years of persecution that John Bunyan, Baptist exhorter, wrote in jail his immortal allegory, and John

Legislation against non-conformity.

Bunyan and Milton.

Milton, the blind scholar, composed the great Puritan epic.

Clarendon carried these harsh measures in the face of two elements of opposition, the Catholics, who enjoyed the thinly veiled favor of the king, and the Presbyterians. The championship of the Catholic religion and of absolute authority had passed from Spain to France. Under Richelieu and Mazarin the French monarchy had acquired unprecedented power, and the ambition of the young king, Louis XIV., was boundless. His cousin, the king of England, fell easily under Louis's influence. It was agreed that Charles should have the support of France in restoring England to the bosom of the Church of Rome. *France and Louis XIV.*

JOHN MILTON.

The first step was the marriage of Charles to a Catholic princess of Portugal,[1] and the sale of Cromwell's trophy Dunkirk[2] to France for £400,000. An outburst of popular indignation checked further progress for the time.

From 1665 to 1667 England and Holland, the commercial rivals, were again at war. The inefficiency of the government reduced the navy to such a condition that the Dutch fleet dashed up the Thames unopposed *War with Holland, 1665-1667.*

---

[1] The city of Bombay, the first acquisition of England in India, was a part of the rich dowry of this princess.

[2] Dunkirk was a fortress of the first importance, the Gibraltar of that age. It was popularly believed that the king's adviser Clarendon had been bribed to consent to the transfer, and his new mansion was significantly nicknamed "Dunkirk House."

and destroyed docks and shipping. Men sighed for the good old times when Oliver had made England the terror of her foes. In the midst of the Dutch war London met with twin disasters. In April, 1665, the populous city of 350,000 souls was swept of one third of its population by a plague. Close upon its heels came the Great Fire[1] which broke out on Sunday morning, September 2, 1666, and burned unchecked for three days, destroying property valued at £50,000,000.

The fire and plague.

The reverses of the Dutch war and the harsh ecclesiastical laws made Clarendon unpopular. In 1667 Charles was glad to rid himself of the great minister. The cabinet which succeeded him is known as the "Cabal" from the initials of its members.

The "Cabal": Clifford, Arlington, Buckingham, Ashley, Lauderdale.

Their envoy, Sir William Temple, touched a popular chord by negotiating with Holland and Sweden the "Triple Alliance" (January, 1668), a Protestant check to the designs of Louis. Meanwhile the perfidious Charles was secretly bargaining with Louis for an annual subsidy, pledging the support of England to the Catholic cause. When in 1672 the king involved England in Louis's war with Holland the eyes of the nation were unsealed. The outcry against popery took form in the Test Act, which drove the Duke of York and other Catholics from their military and civil offices.[2] The Cabal fell to pieces, but Ashley, now Earl of Shaftesbury, continued to fight in the House of Lords for a Protestant succession to the throne. Danby, the

Secret treaty of Dover, 1670.

The Test Act.

---

[1] An area of 436 acres was burned over, including 13,200 dwellings, the cathedral, and eighty-nine parish churches, and many famous mansions, schools, and hospitals. The burnt district was half a mile wide and a mile and a half long, in the most densely populated region of the metropolis. Sir Christopher Wren and John Evelyn proposed plans for systematic and regular rebuilding of the city, but the ancient lanes and streets were not disturbed. Brick and stone took the place of the ancient timbered houses.

[2] The disabilities of Catholics were not removed until 1829, when the efforts of Daniel O'Connell, the Irish "Liberator," secured the passage of the Catholic Relief Bill, admitting Roman Catholics to seats in Parliament.

next minister (1673-1679), strove vainly to maintain an alliance with Holland, but the king remained faithful to his paymaster, Louis. In September, 1678, a "Popish Plot" to kill the king and massacre the Protestants came to light. The informer was one Titus Oates, a wretched renegade on whose perjured testimony many innocent persons were condemned. The very existence of the conspiracy has been doubted, but Shaftesbury utilized the popular frenzy to advance his policy. Catholics were disqualified for membership in Parliament. Danby fell under suspicion of connection with the king's French negotiations and Shaftesbury again came into power. The question of the succession would not down. Charles and his court rallied about the claims of the Catholic Duke of York, brother of the king. Shaftesbury put forward the Duke of Monmouth, the eldest of the king's natural sons. The terms "Tory" and "Whig" originated in the bitter partisan strife of this time.[1] Thrice the king dissolved Parliament to frustrate its designs against his brother. Shaftesbury was disgraced and died a fugitive, without seeing the accomplishment of his ends. In 1683 the discovery of the "Rye House Plot," against Charles and James, brought some of the leading Whigs to the block, though Monmouth himself escaped to Holland. To cripple his enemies the king annulled the ancient charters of the towns—the Whig strongholds—assuring the return of members of Parliament devoted to the crown. Death intervened in his preparations for despotism (February 6, 1685). To the courtiers at his bedside the flippant Stuart made his playful apology for

[1] The rough-riding Scottish peasants who had opposed the king's High Church policy in Scotland were first called "Whigamores," or "Whigs," and in return they gave to the partisans of the crown the derisive epithet of "Tory," a name originally applied to Irish outlaws, too handy with the shillelah against the Protestant colonists.

being so long time a-dying, and his last breath was a plea for the pretty actress who had enjoyed his favor, "Do not let poor Nelly starve!"

Death of Charles II., 1685.

TOPICS FOR READING AND SPECIAL STUDY, WITH LIBRARY NOTES.

1. OLIVER CROMWELL.
    Oliver Cromwell. S. H. Church.
    Letters and Speeches of Oliver Cromwell. Carlyle.
    Oliver Cromwell. F. Harrison. (English Statesmen Series.)
    The Chief Actors in the Puritan Revolution. P. Bayne.

2. MANNERS AND MORALS UNDER THE RESTORATION.
    Samuel Pepys and the World He Lived In. Wheatley.
    The Court of Charles II. J. J. Jusserand.
    The Diary and Correspondence of John Evelyn.
    The Diary and Correspondence of Samuel Pepys.

3. THE PROTESTANT PLANTATIONS IN IRELAND.
    The Story of Ireland. Emily Lawless.
    History of Ireland. Joyce.
    The Cromwellian Settlement in Ireland. Prendergast.

4. SCOTLAND UNDER CROMWELL AND CHARLES II.
    History of Scotland. J. H. Burton.
    History of the Commonwealth and the Protectorate. Gardiner.
    Montrose. M. Morris.

FICTION, ETC.

Woodstock, Old Mortality, and Peveril of the Peak. Scott.
St. George and St. Michael. George Macdonald.
The History of the Plague in London. Defoe.
Dryden's Poems. (The Hind and the Panther, Absalom and Achitophel, Annus Mirabilis.)
Deborah's Diary. Miss Manning.
Cherry and Violet. A Tale of the Great Plague. Miss Manning.

CHAPTER XIV.

THE ERA OF THE PROTESTANT REVOLUTION, 1685 A. D.–1714 A. D.—FROM THE ACCESSION OF JAMES II. TO THE DEATH OF ANNE.

JAMES II. was past fifty when he succeeded to the throne of his brother. Though a Catholic himself, his daughters had been reared in the Protestant faith. The gentle Mary was the wife of the prudent ruler of Holland, William of Orange, and her sister Anne had married a Danish prince. The king's second marriage with the Catholic Mary of Modena was thus far childless.

James II., 1685-1688.

The apprehension which pervaded the nation upon the accession of a Catholic sovereign was soothed by several circumstances.[1] James swore to maintain the Church of England unchanged, and it was believed that he would keep his oath, remembering the loyalty of the church to his father. Should he prove faithless the patient nation looked to his Protestant daughters to set all things right after a few years at the most. The harrying of the Presbyterians was bitterly pressed. The Scottish Parliament of 1685 made it a treasonable offense to take the oath of the Covenant, and death and forfeiture were made the penalty of preaching in a private room, or attending an open-air meeting or

English patience.

Persecutions of the Covenanters.

---

[1] The Society of Friends, commonly called Quakers, who, like the Catholics, had suffered for their faith under the Commonwealth and the Restoration, took heart at the accession of James. Their address to him said: "We are told that thou art not of the persuasion of the Church of England no more than we; wherefore we hope thou wilt grant us the same liberty which thou allowest thyself. Which doing, we wish thee all manner of happiness."

conventicle. The zealous dragoon officer John Graham of Claverhouse was the detested instrument of the persecution.

Claverhouse.

Parliament, thanks to the precautions of the late king, was strongly Tory, and registered James's will in everything. But the Whig exiles at The Hague plotted incessantly.

Execution of Argyle, June 30, 1685.

JAMES II.

The Duke of Argyle crossed over to Scotland and called his countrymen to overthrow the persecuting Parliament and the bishops. But the country failed to rise and Argyle was taken and executed. At the same time Monmouth, the hope of the Protestants in the previous reign, landed in the west of England with eighty followers and asserted his claim to the throne. The powerful Whigs kept aloof and Monmouth's army of rustics was dispersed by the royal troops at Sedgemoor, July 6, 1685, the last battle fought in England. The Protestant duke perished on the scaffold.[1] Colonel

Monmouth's rebellion.

[1] On the scaffold Monmouth, who had lost heart since his capture, played the man. He exhorted the headsman, Jack Ketch, to use his best skill, giving him gold with the promise of more if he should do his work well. Then having doubtfully tried the edge of the axe he laid his head on the block. The executioner was unnerved and missed his first stroke; the duke raised his head and cast a reproachful look upon him. The axe fell again and again without mortal effect and the throng of witnesses were frantic with horror and sympathy when the end came. Many of them rushed forward and dipped their handkerchiefs in the blood of the Protestant champion.

Kirke's wanton and bloodthirsty dragoons, "Kirke's Lambs," had granted no quarter to the fugitives, but the king's vengeance was not appeased. He sent Jeffreys, the most brutal of judges, to try the rebels in the West.¹ In this "Bloody Assize" three hundred persons were condemned to execution and many more sold into slavery.

<small>Jeffreys. The Bloody Assize.</small>

Such cruelty cooled the ardor of Parliament. Furthermore the king's relations with the Jesuits exposed him to suspicion. Louis XIV., his friend and mentor, by revoking the Edict of Nantes had exposed the French Protestants to persecution.² Thus warned, the English Parliament resisted James's demand for the repeal of the Test Act (which excluded Catholics from office). Supported by troops in his own pay and by servile judges, the king undertook to govern without recourse to Parliament. The new despotism made rapid strides. The king claimed the right to dispense with obnoxious laws, and the courts approved his action in disregard of the Test Act. The church took alarm and the king provided a new Court of Ecclesiastical Commission to enforce the silence and submission of the clergy.³

<small>The second Stuart tyranny</small>

In April, 1687, the king issued a "Declaration of

---

¹ One of Jeffreys's victims was Mrs. Gaunt, who had piously harbored a fugitive. To save his own neck he basely informed against his benefactress, whom Jeffreys sent to be burned at the stake. Lady Lisle, the widow of one of the murdered regicides, was put on trial for sheltering two fugitives from Sedgemoor. Her plea that she did not know of their guilt, and that so far from sympathizing with Monmouth she had sent her own son to fight against him, could not save her. Jeffreys compelled the reluctant jury to condemn her, and constrained the king to deny all prayers for her pardon.

² The severity of the Catholic monarch against the Huguenots drove tens of thousands of sober, hard-working artisans into Holland, England, and America. Probably 60,000 came to England, where they established their home industries, especially the weaving of brocades and figured silks, velvets, etc.

³ Hall, the king's printer, was licensed to issue Catholic missals and tracts, contrary to an act of Parliament. Compton, bishop of London, was called before the commission and suspended for refusing to discipline one of his clergy who had been so bold as to preach on the difference between the Roman and Anglican Churches.

Declaration of Indulgence, 1687-88.

Liberty of Conscience," granting toleration to all religions in England and Scotland, with a view to removing the disabilities of the Catholics. The next year the declaration was repeated. The clergy generally disregarded the royal command to read it from their pulpits and the seven bishops who presented their solemn protest against it were sent to the Tower on charge of uttering a "false, malicious, and seditious libel."

The Seven Bishops.

The patient nation was startled by the report that the queen had borne a son (June 10, 1688), thus endangering the succession of the Protestant Princess Mary. The Whigs declared that the nation was being tricked and that the babe, James Francis Edward Stuart, as he was christened, was a spurious child. In the midst of the popular excitement the acquittal of the seven bishops was hailed with transports of delight. The cheers from the royal camps at Hounslow smote the ear of the king.[1]

The bishops' acquittal.

All parties were deserting the despot. On the day of the bishops' discharge Admiral Herbert bore to William of Orange,[2] the husband of the Princess Mary, a secret invitation to come over and deliver England from her king. Among the seven patriots who signed the note all parties were represented.[3]

The Seven Patriots.

---

[1] Even the guards of the bishops had openly expressed their sympathy for their prisoners. James had been reviewing his troops on Hounslow heath when he heard the uproar in the camps. "It is nothing," said the commanding officer, "nothing but the rejoicing of the soldiers over the acquittal of the bishops." "Do you call that nothing?" replied the thwarted monarch.

[2] Orange (the name a corruption of the Latin Arausio) is a principality in southeastern France. From 1530 to 1713 it was ruled by princes of the House of Nassau, the greatest of whom, William the Silent, became a Protestant, achieved the independence of the Dutch from Spain, and (1581) was chosen hereditary stadtholder of Holland. His grandson William II., also stadtholder, married Mary Stuart, daughter of Charles I. of England. The William who now came upon the stage of English affairs was thus both nephew and son-in-law of King James II.

[3] The seven signers were "The Whig Earl of Devonshire, the Tory Earl of Danby, the Earl of Shrewsbury, Bishop Compton, of London, the republican Henry Sidney, Lord Lumley, of the army, and Edward Russell, of the navy."

William was thirty-eight years of age. His government of Holland had proved his energy and prudence, while his resistance to the rapacious designs of Louis XIV. displayed the vigor and breadth of his statesmanship. In October he issued a declaration to the English nation setting forth their grievances and announcing his decision to accept the invitation to come over with an army to secure the assembling of a free Parlia-

William of Orange.

BUCKINGHAM PALACE.

ment. On November 5, 1688—the anniversary of the Gunpowder Plot—William landed at Torbay with 14,000 men.[1]

Too late James changed his tone and began bidding for the support of the church and Tories. But the current could not be stemmed. The gentry of the North and West flocked to William's camp. John Churchill and his fellow-generals, who had sworn fidelity to James, deserted to his enemy, and even Kirke led his "lambs" to the Dutch shepherd. Under

James makes concessions.

[1] William's flag bore the arms of Nassau quartered with those of England, and to his family motto, "I will maintain," he added the words "the liberties of England and the Protestant religion." The "Protestant Wind" held the royal fleet in the Thames while the Dutch swept past and through the straits of Dover in full view of the throngs on the cliffs of Kent.

the influence of Churchill's wife, Sarah Jennings, the Princess Anne abandoned her father's waning cause. "God help me," he said, "my own children forsake me." Having sent the queen and her babe to France the king himself eluded his willing captors and rejoined them (December, 1688). Louis received him as a brother-king and granted him the royal residence of St. Germain with revenues suitable to his rank.

Flight of the king.

The Parliament of England declared "that it hath been found inconsistent with the safety and welfare of this Protestant kingdom to be governed by a popish prince." The crown was offered to William and Mary jointly (February 13, 1689) and accepted. A Declaration of Rights[1] was voted, setting forth the limitations upon the power of the sovereign. That the Stuart dynasty retained a stronghold in some hearts appears from the fact that six bishops and several hundred rectors were deprived of their livings for refusing to take the oath of allegiance to the new sovereigns.

William and Mary, 1689-1694.

William, sole king, 1694-1702.

Non-jurors.

The first work of the revolution was to reform the administration. The ministry was required to lay before Parliament annually an estimate of necessary expenses, as a basis for specific appropriations. Thus the control of expenditure came into the hands of the House of Commons. A Mutiny Act settled the vexed question of the control of the armed forces. The officers of

Annual budgets.

---

[1] This document declared: (1) That it is illegal for the king to make laws or suspend their action without consent of Parliament. (2) That the king may not grant dispensations from the laws. (3) That the Court of Ecclesiastical Commission and others like it are unlawful. (4) That the king may not raise money without the consent of Parliament. (5) That it is lawful to petition the sovereign. (6) That no standing army may be maintained without the consent of Parliament. (7) That private persons may keep arms. (8) That parliamentary elections must be free. (9) That parliamentary debate must be free. (10) That excessive bail shall never be demanded from an accused person. (11) That every trial shall be by jury. (12) That grants of estates as forfeited before the conviction of the offender are illegal. (13) That Parliament shall be held frequently.

the crown were empowered for one year to enforce discipline. To secure the annual renewal of this authority and the annual appropriation for the payment of the forces it became necessary for the sovereign to summon Parliament each year. The declaration was enacted as the Bill of Rights, which further confirmed the title of William and Mary and forever barred Roman Catholics from the English throne.

<small>Bill of Rights.</small>

In April, 1689, William and Mary were proclaimed at Edinburgh joint sovereigns of the kingdom of Scotland. The Presbyterian government of the Scottish Church was revived. Claverhouse, now known as Vis-

WINDSOR CASTLE, EAST FRONT.

count Dundee, rallied the Highland clansmen in the name of King James. But he fell in the pass of Killiecrankie[1] in the moment of victory, and his following was dispersed. The pacification of the northern

<small>Dundee at Killiecrankie.</small>

[1] Wordsworth made this victory of the clansmen over veteran forces the text of one of his most spirited appeals against Napoleon. See his sonnet, "In the Pass of Killiecrankie." Dundee, whom the harassed Covenanters abhorred as a fiend, was revered as a martyr by the Jacobites. For a spirited ballad on this romantic character, "the last of the Scots," see Aytoun's "Burial March of Dundee."

kingdom was stained by the massacre of Glencoe.¹

James in Ireland. In March, 1689, King James passed over from France to Ireland, where the Earl of Tyrconnel had drilled an army devoted to the Catholic cause. The panic-stricken Protestants crowded into the poorly defended towns of Londonderry and Enniskillen, and though beset by overwhelming numbers held out for more than one hundred days, until the relief came. In 1690 William invaded Ireland and routed the Jacobite forces in the

The Boyne. battle of the Boyne (July 1). James fled to France, leaving the brave Patrick Sarsfield to prolong the contest.² The next year he, too, had to yield, though he gained the privilege for his soldiers to enter the French

The Irish exiles. service. Ten thousand Irish exiles passed into the armies of Catholic Europe.

The Grand Alliance. William's diplomacy had united the emperor, Spain, Sweden, Savoy, with Holland and England in a "Grand Alliance" against the great king of France (1689). After two years of indecisive fighting Louis gathered all his strength to crush his foes. One army was to invade England while a host of 100,000 men threatened Holland. But the invaders never crossed the straits.

Battle of the Hogue. On the sea and at the Hogue, sixteen hundred ninety-two, Did the English fight the French—woe to France,³

---

[1] The Highlanders were given until the end of December, 1691, to take the oaths of allegiance to William and Mary. Maclan, chief of the clan Macdonald of Glencoe, waited until the last day to give in his submission. By a misunderstanding and the difficulty of reaching the proper magistrate on account of the snow on the mountains he was unable to obtain his certificate until January 6. Dalrymple, William's representative in Scotland, harbored a grudge against the unfortunate clan and suppressed the fact of their yielding. The king, probably innocent of the contemplated perfidy, approved measures for extirpating "that sept of thieves." Dalrymple's soldiers were sent to the glen and hospitably entertained for twelve days in the homes of the Macdonalds. On the thirteenth they fell upon their hosts and slaughtered nearly forty in cold blood. Of those who escaped the sword many died in the snow on the mountain side. See Aytoun's ballad, " The Widow of Glencoe."

[2] "Change kings with us and we will fight you again," said an Irish officer when taunted by an Englishman with the result of the Boyne. The anniversary of the victory is observed as a holiday by the Protestant Irish. In 1795 a secret society of "Orangemen" was formed among them to defend the Protestant ascendancy in the island.

[3] See Browning's "Hervé Riel."

and Tourville's shattered fleet relinquished its aim. The campaign against Holland was indecisive.

The Tories controlled the second Parliament of William (1690-95). Their leanings were still strongly toward the Jacobites. The king's allowances were cut down, and Jacobite offenders were amnestied. William's first plan of taking his ministers from the two parties had created discord, and in 1693 he made up an all-Whig cabinet. This "Junto" included Montague, the financier, who met the war deficit by a plan, new to English finance, of borrowing money on interest. A loan of £1,000,000 contracted at ten per cent became the nucleus of the funded national debt.[1] The deficit of the following year (1693-94) was met by a loan from a syndicate of London merchants who were rewarded by certain banking privileges, which their successors still hold as the "Governor and Company of the Bank of England."[2]

THE BANK OF ENGLAND.

National debt, 1693.

Bank of England, 1694.

The death of the queen (December 28, 1694) left her husband sole monarch of the three kingdoms. The

William III., 1694-1702.

[1] Instead of issuing bonds the government obtained the money by selling annuities. The funds for payment were derived from an increased excise tax on beer.

[2] The Triennial Act of 1694 made it obligatory for the king to order a general election for members of Parliament at least once in three years. This period was later extended to seven years by a law still in force. The Long Parliament of Charles I. had gagged the press by an act requiring all prints to be licensed. Milton's free spirit had protested against this restriction upon writing, but the law was enforced with some degree of strictness until 1695, when it lapsed, and Parliament declined to renew it. Newspapers sprang up as soon as the old law perished.

continental war dragged heavily and in 1697 Louis agreed to the peace of Ryswick, recognizing William's sovereignty and the right of the Princess Anne to succeed him.

Peace abroad renewed William's difficulties in England. The English jealousy of his Dutch favorites took shape in petty annoyances and protests. He was accused of wasting the resources of the island to advance his plans on the Continent. But the event soon vindicated his sagacity.

Spanish succession. The question of the succession to the Spanish crown had long concerned the diplomacy of Europe. The German emperor claimed the kingdom for his son, the Archduke Charles, while Louis of France put forward the claims of his own grandson, Philip of Anjou. While the courts were devising means to preserve the balance of power the Spanish king died (November, 1700), naming Philip as his successor. Louis XIV. saw the realization of his dreams of empire. "The Pyrenees exist no longer," he exclaimed to his grandson, departing to claim his inheritance.

The close union of the Spanish monarchy with France imperiled all that William had given his best energies to secure, and the steadfast Hollander resolved to prevent its consummation. The reckless haste of Louis in breaking his treaty obligations with England and reaffirming his support of the Jacobite cause made it easier to arouse England at this crisis. Parliament rallied to William's support, and the Grand *The Grand Alliance revived.* Alliance of England and Holland with the emperor was revived in September, 1701, in order to place the Archduke Charles on the Spanish throne, expel the French from Holland and her colonies, and prevent the union of the French and Spanish crowns. William died March 8, 1701, before hostilities broke out.[1]

Anne Stuart, daughter of James II. and sister of the late queen, was immediately proclaimed queen, her insignificant husband, Prince George of Denmark, being admitted to no share in her authority. She was a good-natured, dull, matronly Englishwoman, who had early fallen under the masterful influence of Sarah Jennings, the ambitious wife of the aspiring young military genius, John Churchill.

Death of William III., 1701.

Queen Anne, 1701-1714.

Though Churchill had been false to his first master James II. and had since been disgraced for correspondence with the Jacobites, William had advised his successor to give him the command of the English forces in the impending war. Within a week after Anne's accession he was made commander-in-chief, and at once dealt France a stinging blow on the Netherlands frontier. For his successes in the first campaign Churchill was created Duke of Marlborough. His friend Godolphin as prime minister supplied him with men and money. The Dutch entrusted their army to the English general, who was united in a generous friendship with Prince Eugene of Savoy, the dashing commander of the imperial forces. In 1704 they achieved their first great triumph, intercepting the French army of invasion at Blenheim.[2] The duke's charge at the head of the cavalry won the day. There had not been such a harvest of French lilies in the sixty years of Louis's reign. Two thirds of the French troops were slain or

The Churchills.

Marlborough.

Blenheim, August 13, 1704.

---

[1] William's last illness began with an accident. His horse stumbled at a mole-hill and threw him heavily, breaking his collar-bone. It is said that the Jacobite revelers used to toast William's horse and drink to the health of "the little gentleman in velvet"—the mole whose mine unhorsed the king.

[2] See Addison's poem, "The Campaign," also Southey's "Battle of Blenheim." The manor of Woodstock was twelve miles in circuit and Parliament expended a quarter of a million pounds upon the palatial mansion. The architect was Sir John Vanbrugh, the subject of the celebrated epitaph :

"Lie heavy on him, earth—for he
Laid many a heavy load on thee."

taken, and their commander was among the 11,000 prisoners. The nation rewarded Marlborough with the royal manor of Woodstock and built the palace of Blenheim for his residence.

Gibraltar taken.

The allies pressed France hard. The fortress of Gibraltar surrendered to an English fleet.[1] Peter-

BLENHEIM CASTLE.

borough, scarcely less fortunate than Marlborough, captured Barcelona, while Churchill and Eugene won Ramillies (1706) and Oudenarde (1708) in the North. Louis sued for peace, but could not accept it upon terms that required him to withdraw his grandson Philip from Spain by force. "I will fight my enemies rather than my own children," he said; and his troops reflected his desperate spirit on the next field, Malplaquet (1709).

Malplaquet.

[1] Though the English were fighting in behalf of the Archduke Charles of Austria they raised their own flag over the famous rock and have held it to this day against all comers. For its subsequent history and sieges see "The History of Gibraltar," by J. H. Mann.

Marlborough bought this victory so dearly that a French marshal reported, "God grant such another defeat and your majesty could count your enemies destroyed."

On the first of May, 1707, the two kingdoms of England and Scotland, which for a century had accepted the same sovereigns, became the united kingdom of Great Britain,[1] approving the Protestant succession as laid down in the Act of Settlement,[2] a common Parliament, and a common coinage. Scottish law and the Scottish Church were to remain unchanged. James II.'s son, the Pretender, appeared in Scotland in 1708 to profit by Scottish dissatisfaction with the union, but the Jacobites failed to respond and he retired to France. *Union with Scotland, 1707.*

The cost of the protracted war had begun to overbalance the popularity of its victories. The Whigs had been its main support, and Lady Churchill had secured the queen's favor. But Anne's Tory sympathies were strong, and the Tory leaders, Robert Harley and Henry St. John (afterward Viscount Bolingbroke), were consummate politicians. Harley supplanted the imperious Sarah's influence at the palace by the insinuating arts of her cousin Abigail Hill. Godolphin was dismissed (1710) and Harley became the chief minister, as Earl of Oxford and Mortimer. *The war unpopular.* *Abigail Hill.*

Marlborough returned to London to arrest the storm. But he who had never lost a battle was no match for the Tory politicians.[3] He was met by accusations of mis- *Marlborough's fall.*

[1] The cross of St. Andrew of Scotland was combined with that of St. George in the flag of Great Britain.

[2] By his act to settle the succession, passed in William's lifetime (1701), it was provided that in the event of William and Anne dying without surviving issue the crown should go to the only Protestant line of Stuarts, represented by Sophia, Electress of Hanover in Germany, granddaughter of James I. by his daughter, Elizabeth of Bohemia.

[3] The horde of scurrilous pamphleteers was turned loose against him. The street rabble hooted him and called him "thief!" Though he returned to England after Anne's death he never regained his influence. His health was broken and in 1722 he died. Lady Marlborough survived him until 1744, and employed her enormous wealth in vindicating his memory and taking vengeance on her enemies and her husband's.

use of government funds, and was dismissed from all his offices. The House of Lords was "packed" by the creation of twelve new Tory peers, and the negotiations with Louis were concluded at Utrecht (1713). His grandson Philip was confirmed as king of Spain. France renounced its support of the Stuart claims, approved the Protestant settlement of the English succession, and permitted England to retain her conquests in Nova Scotia, Newfoundland, Gibraltar, and elsewhere.

Peace of Utrecht, 1713.

As Anne approached her death, widowed and childless, the much-confirmed succession was once more in danger. The heir-at-law by the Act of Settlement was the Electress Sophia's son George, a German prince of no distinction, a stranger to England and its language. Many Englishmen were reluctant to receive another foreign lord, and the Jacobites, ever plotting, saw an opportunity of pressing the Stuart pretender's claim. Perhaps Bolingbroke in the cabinet was in their plots. He quarreled with Harley in the royal presence, which resulted in Harley's dismissal from office. The queen broke down under the excitement, and while Whig and Tory were contending, she gave the badge of the prime minister's office to the Duke of Shrewsbury, one of "the seven patriots" of 1688. His selection assured the succession of the Protestant line. Queen Anne expired on August 1, 1714, and her distant cousin George I. was quietly proclaimed in her stead.

Struggle over the succession.

Shrewsbury.

TOPICS FOR READING AND SPECIAL STUDY.
WITH LIBRARY NOTES.

1. THE REBELLION OF MONMOUTH.
   History of England. Macaulay.
2. THE LIFE AND DEATH OF DUNDEE.
   Claverhouse. Mowbray Morris.

3. MARLBOROUGH AND HIS CAMPAIGNS.
    The Life of John Churchill. General Wolseley.
    Marlborough. George Saintsbury.
    History of the Reign of Queen Anne. J. H. Burton.
    The Age of Anne. E. E. Morris.
4. RESULTS OF THE REVOLUTION OF 1688.
    History of England. Macaulay.
    Essay on Mackintosh's Causes of the Revolution. Macaulay.
    Constitutional History of England. Hallam.
    Life of William III. H. D. Traill.

FICTION, ETC.

Lorna Doone. R. D. Blackmore.
Micah Clarke. A. Conan Doyle.
Lochinvar, and Men of the Moss Hags. S. R. Crockett.
Henry Esmond. Thackeray.
Lays of the Scottish Cavaliers. W. E. Aytoun.
Jacobite Songs and Ballads. G. S. Macquoid, Ed.
A Lady of Quality. F. H. Burnett.
Social Life in the Reign of Queen Anne. J. Ashton.

CHAPTER XV.

THE HANOVERIAN SOVEREIGNS, 1714 A. D.–1837 A. D.—FROM THE ACCESSION OF GEORGE I. TO THE DEATH OF WILLIAM IV.

George I., 1714-1727.

GEORGE I. had never been in England until he came thither to be crowned September 18, 1714. From his father he had inherited the duchy of Brunswick-Lüneburg and the electorate of Hanover, and to the Protestantism of his mother Sophia, granddaughter of James I., he owed his claim to the United Kingdom under the Act of Settlement.

A constitutional sovereign.

In his own little German state Duke George had been very much his own master, but the Revolution of 1688 had raised such barriers against despotism in England that neither this sovereign nor his son cared to risk getting through or over them. He prudently declined to interfere with the determination of the nation to govern itself by means of Parliament and ministers. He meekly entrusted the government to a cabinet of Whigs (the party who had supported his claim) and was content to draw his allowances from the treasury and take his pleasure with his German cronies, while he presided over the affairs of his duchy to the best of his moderate ability.

The Riot Act.

The Whigs were in for a long lease. They impeached Anne's Tory ministers and quelled the Jacobite tumults by passing the Riot Act.[1] The Earl of Mar in

---

[1] Unlawful assemblies must disperse on the "reading of the Riot Act" by a magistrate, on pain of being adjudged guilty of felony.

Scotland roused the Highlanders to arms in behalf of the Pretender, "James VIII. and III." Twelve thousand men took the White Cockade, but were beaten at Sheriffmuir, before the Stuart claimant could reach the scene of action. A few north of England Catholics were captured in arms and severely punished. The death of Louis XIV. (1715) was a blow to Stuart hopes for a generation. Having struck down their leading opponents the Whigs entrenched themselves in Parliament by the Septennial Act—still in force- extending the duration of Parliament from three years to seven. The Tory legislation which was aimed to exclude dissenters from the universities and the public service was swept away.

Jacobite rising of 1715.

GEORGE I.

Septennial Parliaments.

The realm seemed to be entering upon a period of peace and commercial expansion when in 1720 it was convulsed by the bursting of the "South Sea Bubble." In 1713, shortly before the peace of Utrecht, a joint-stock concern, styled "The South Sea Company," had been chartered. It was to have a monopoly of the trade with Spanish South American ports, fondly believed to be a mine of wealth. A speculative craze forced the price of shares to ten times their par value, and scores of rival stock companies shared in the infla-

South Sea Bubble, 1720.

tion. The bursting of the bubble ruined hundreds of families. The outcry against the government for its complicity in the speculation brought Robert Walpole[1] to the front as prime minister. For twenty-one years this sagacious statesman kept England at peace while Europe was broiling in war, fostering English manufactures, extending English commerce, and directing the finances with consummate ability.[2] Parliament was a facile instrument in his hands, which were stained with bribes, and the Tory opposition was too feeble to make head against the masterful premier.

Robert Walpole, premier, 1721-1742.

The death of the king in June, 1727, brought his son George II. to the throne. The Whig supremacy continued, though Walpole encountered growing opposition from the ambitious spirits in his own party, whose factious demands were supported by the Tories. In 1739 their clamor forced him into a war with Spain, and its ill success broke his popularity. In 1742 he resigned his office and retired to the House of Lords.

George II., 1727-1760.

The era of peace gave place to many years of war. King George's support of Maria Theresa in her struggle for the imperial throne of Germany involved England in the conflicts which were raging in Western Europe. The wars with Spain and France were closed in 1748 by the treaty of Aix-la-Chapelle. England gained little or nothing except the expulsion of the Stuarts from France. Charles Edward, called the Young Pretender, in distinction from his father, James Edward, the "Old Pretender," had taken advantage of the party strife

The Young Pretender.

---

[1] When other means of control failed, Walpole made unblushing use of bribery among the members of the House of Commons. The saying that "every man has his price," which has been attributed to him, is not fully authenticated, but it suits with his methods.

[2] Trade with the American colonies, which was fostered by Walpole (who removed many restrictive duties), increased enormously in volume and value. Manchester and Birmingham gained their importance by manufacturing goods for the markets of the New World and Liverpool rapidly became the great seaport of the same traffic.

and foreign entanglements of England to renew the Stuart claims. Landing in Scotland in July, 1745, he rallied the ever-faithful Highland chieftains to his father's banner, swept aside the government forces at Preston Pans (September), and advanced into the heart of England. Then, alarmed at the popular apathy toward his cause and the approach of a formidable force, he retreated to Scotland, where in April, 1746, his troops were beaten and then butchered at Culloden by the Duke of Cumberland. The noble prisoners who were sent to the block on Tower Hill were the last victims of the English headsman's axe. The Pretender himself escaped to France after wanderings as romantic as those of Charles II. after the Worcester fight.[1] On his expulsion from France he lived in Italy, where he died, childless, in 1788. *Battle of Preston Pans, 1745. Battle of Culloden, 1746.*

The unopposed march of the Jacobite bands into the heart of the island revealed the weakness of the government. France, strong in its alliance with Spain, was everywhere on the aggressive, stirring up the native princes of India against the British trading company, and in America claiming the Ohio Valley and dotting with forts the country west of the Alleghanies. The defeat of Braddock's expedition against Fort Duquesne (1755), barely saved from destruction by the skill of a Virginian militia officer named George Washington, was *Braddock's defeat, 1755.*

---

[1] The fidelity of the Highlanders to "bonny Prince Charlie" was proved by the fact that though a reward of £30,000 was offered for his capture and the secret of his identity was entrusted to more than one hundred individuals, none betrayed him. The heroine of the escape was Flora Macdonald, who conducted him, disguised as a maid-servant, through the midst of his foes. See Boswell's "Journey of a Tour to the Hebrides," also for a further account of the Pretender's vicissitudes, "Pickle, the Spy," by Andrew Lang.

Of the many songs of the Highland Jacobites none breathes more sincere devotion than this:

"I ance had sons, but now hae nane,
I bred them toiling sairly;
And I wad bear them a' again,
And lose them a' for Charlie."

followed by the "Seven Years' War" (1756-1763).

Seven Years' War, 1756-1763.

England seemed compassed with disaster. Her generals were incompetent, her only ally, Frederick the Great of Prussia, was beset by three powerful empires, her king was foreign by birth and sympathy, and his advisers lacked the confidence of the nation. At this juncture (1757) William Pitt, the great commoner, became the leading spirit in the government.[1] The generals of his choice turned the tide of war. Fort Duquesne fell, and Fort Pitt (Pittsburg) rose upon its site. Amherst took Ticonderoga, and James Wolfe's victory on the Plains of Abraham won not only Quebec but all Canada. News came from the far East that with the loss of twenty-two soldiers killed and fifty wounded Robert Clive had won the battle of Plassy (June, 1757) and by the conquest of Bengal inaugurated the British Empire in India. Despondent England was surfeited with victories and Pitt was the hero

William Pitt.

Wolfe wins Canada.

Clive in India.

WILLIAM PITT.

[1] Pitt's clear vision saw how the native strength of the nation and the vast resources of the empire were being wasted by dulness and incompetence and he was supremely convinced of his ability to conserve and direct them. He said to the Duke of Devonshire, "My lord, I am sure that I can save this country, and nobody else can."

of the hour,[1] when the death of the king, October 25, 1760, brought his headstrong grandson to the throne.

George III. was the first Hanoverian sovereign who was born in England. His mother's precept had been "Be king, George, be king," and he was not content like his predecessors to leave government to his ministers. Little sympathy could exist between Pitt's royal nature and the dull perversity of the crowned head. Upon the failure of his proposal for a war with Spain he resigned, and Lord Bute, a mere court favorite, became prime minister. The peace which was concluded with France and Spain (1763) left Canada and the Ohio Valley in English hands.

George III., 1760-1820.

Lord Bute.

LORD CLIVE.

The House of Commons had sunk to a state of disgraceful corruption. Less than 160,000 votes were cast at elections. The ancient basis of representation which was still preserved was productive of scandalous injustice. While populous cities of recent growth went unrepresented, the decayed boroughs still chose their two members as in ancient times. The great land-

Need of parliamentary reform.

---

[1] Anecdotes abound which prove the spirit displayed by the British commanders in this war. Admiral Hawke overhauled the French fleet on a dark night in a Biscay gale, off a rocky coast. The pilot advised against hazarding an engagement. "You have done your duty in remonstrating," said Hawke, "I will answer for everything. I command you to lay me alongside the French admiral." The battle resulted in an English victory.

holders and the king, the greatest and wealthiest landholder of all, were able by bribery, more or less open, to control the choice of members and influence their action in the house.[1] Subjected to savage criticisms, Parliament undertook to curb the plain-speaking of the newspaper press. John Wilkes, a member, was repeatedly expelled for printing harsh criticisms of the king's speech and other matters in his journal, the *North Briton*. From 1769 to 1772 the letters signed "Junius" appeared in the *Daily Advertiser*, attacking the government with the sharpest pen ever used in political controversy. In 1771 Parliament undertook to prohibit the publication of its debates, but yielded the point to public opinion.

John Wilkes.

Junius Letters.

America was oftenest the theme of parliamentary debate. The English colonies, having no voice in Parliament, denied the right and resisted the efforts of that body to levy taxes on the people of America to defray the expense of the late war.

Quarrel with America.

The self-confident Lord Grenville, Bute's successor, obtained the "Stamp Act" (1765) as a means of raising the obnoxious revenue. The colonists gathered in congress to make their protest effective. Rockingham succeeded Grenville, and Pitt, from his place in the Lords, and Edmund Burke, the Whig orator in the Commons, pleaded for generous treatment. Parliament repealed the Stamp Act but reasserted its right to tax. The king's obstinacy was thoroughly aroused against his American subjects and for twelve years (1770–82) he used the ministry of Lord North to force them to submit. They were better Englishmen than the king, and his repressive measures drove them to a

The Stamp Act.

Lord North, premier.

---

[1] By scandalous use of patronage the crown built up a faction in Parliament known as the "King's Friends," who always voted together in the interest of the royal policy.

revolt which became a successful War of Independence (1775-1783). England's continental foes, France and Spain, recognized the independence of the American colonies and lent substantial aid. The surrender of Lord Cornwallis to the French and Americans (1780) practically closed the war in America, and left one great section of the Anglo-Saxon race to develop along lines of its own.

<small>Independence of the United States of America.</small>

The tidings from Yorktown struck Lord North like a bullet in the breast. Seven costly campaigns had failed to reduce the revolted states. England faced a hostile Europe. Ireland clamored for "home rule."

THE THRONE ROOM, WINDSOR CASTLE.

Even the long-suffering Parliament reflected the nation's disgust with the ministerial policy. North gave up the struggle. His successors granted Ireland a Parliament, and recognized the independence of the United States of America (1783).[1]

<small>Failure of Lord North's policy.</small>

[1] One incident of these years was the anti-Catholic outbreak in June, 1780. The government's intention to remove some of the civil disabilities of Catholics, Lord George Gordon aroused the London populace with the cry of "No popery" and terrorized the city for five days. See Dickens's "Barnaby Rudge."

Captain Cook's voyages.

The rays of light in these gloomy years came from the far East, where in India Warren Hastings was consolidating an imperial domain, and in Australasia, where the discoveries of the navigator Captain James Cook opened new realms for Anglo-Saxon expansion.

The younger Pitt.

Under the wise leadership of the younger Pitt (1783-1801), son of the great Lord Chatham,[1] Great Britain rallied from the loss of America, consolidated her foreign possessions, and as "a nation of shopkeepers" amassed such wealth that she became the last prop of Europe against the ambition of Napoleon. The last half of the eighteenth century was marked by a series of inventions which revolutionized the mining and manufacturing industries of the island. These were the objects of Pitt's fostering care, while his diplomacy opened the world's markets to English trade.

Industry and commerce.

Charles James Fox, the eloquent leader of the Whig opposition, was the boon companion of the Prince of Wales, and when in 1788 the king's mind became clouded Fox demanded a regency as Prince George's right. The prime minister succeeded in postponing the appointment, and meanwhile the king's health improved.

The French Revolution.

From 1789 to 1815 affairs in France held the attention of the world. After centuries of Bourbon despotism the nation had risen in revolution, abolished all privilege, and framed a constitution after the British model. Many Englishmen gloried in the principles of the French Revolution with the threefold watchword, "Liberty, equality, brotherhood." Wordsworth gives voice to the feeling of ardent youth:

Sympathy in England.

---

[1] Pitt had gone from the university to Parliament, and before his twenty-fifth birthday was virtual ruler of Great Britain.

" A sight to make surrounding nations stare,
A kingdom trusted to a schoolboy's care!"

Bliss was it in that dawn to be alive
But to be young was very heaven!

Fox hailed it with delight. Pitt sympathized with the French in their struggle for liberty, though Burke warned his former associates that disaster would follow the overthrow of government.[1] His prophecy was quickly verified. The French Republicans beheaded King Louis and Queen Marie Antoinette, and, offering its aid to all "the oppressed peoples" of Europe, was soon involved in war with Holland, Spain, Germany, and England (1793-1802).

Reaction

England's navies swept the sea, and her subsidies kept ill-generaled armies of Austria and Prussia in the field, but the enthusiasm of the French and the genius of their leaders were irresistible on the land. Napoleon Bonaparte, a young Corsican officer of artillery, compelled Austria to sign a humiliating peace (1797). Pitt's heart was not in the campaign and he too would have made terms. The "United Irishmen" rose (1798), expecting aid from France to establish their independence, but the power of England in the Channel was too formidable. The insurrection was drowned in blood, and the French turned their victorious arms to the East. Admiral Nelson followed them to Egypt and destroyed their fleet at Aboukir (August, 1799). General Bonaparte returned to France (October, 1799) to make himself its master. Pitt had formed a Second Coalition of the powers, Russia, Austria, Portugal, Naples, and Turkey, against the French, but Napoleon, now First Consul, shattered it at Hohenlinden (1801).

Napoleon Bonaparte.

Irish insurrection of 1798.

Nelson and the Nile.

Second Coalition, 1799-1801.

[1] See his "Reflections on the Revolution in France, etc." (1790), which ran through twelve editions in one year and brought expressions of approval from the crowned heads of Europe. In May, 1791, in the House of Commons Fox indulged in a sneer at certain passages in his friend's book. Burke replied with emphatic warnings, and formally broke the friendship which had bound him and Fox together for twenty years.

The great minister had lost the favor of the king. Throughout the wars with France Ireland had been a thorn in England's side. The measure of home rule granted in 1782 had failed miserably, and the Irish Parliament was a scandal. On January 1, 1801, the legislative union of Ireland with Great Britain was inaugurated, and Irish members were received into the Parliament at Westminster. Among the inducements by which the consent of the Irish Catholics had been gained for the measure was the pledge of liberal concessions to men of their religion.[1] These pledges Parliament refused to redeem, and all the stubborn spirit of the king was provoked by Pitt's proposals. The project was

NELSON COLUMN, TRAFALGAR SQUARE.

---

[1] The execrable penal code against the Catholics of Ireland not only excluded them from all public office, but attacked them at every relation of life. Their children must be educated as Protestants or grow up in ignorance, they could not buy land from Protestants, marriages between Catholics and Protestants were void, and the officiating priest might be hung. To convert a Protestant to Catholicism was a capital offense. Its multifarious and intolerable details Burke characterized as "a machine of wise and elaborate contrivance, and as well fitted for the oppression, impoverishment, and degradation of a people and the debasement in them of human nature itself, as ever proceeded from the perverted ingenuity of man."

defeated, and the majority of the Irish nation have ever since pointed to the union as a monument of bribery and fraud. Pitt resigned his post in dismay. *Pitt's resignation.* The new cabinet, of which Lord Addington was premier, broke up the league which the Baltic states had formed against England, and concluded a treaty of peace with France. *Peace of Amiens, 1802.* Napoleon utilized the fourteen months of peace in making stupendous preparations for the invasion of the British Isles. Hostilities were renewed in May, 1803, and the voice of the nation again called Pitt to the post of responsibility. He prepared men and ships for the defense of England [1] and inspired a Third Coalition, consisting of Austria, Sweden, and Russia, to attack Napoleon, who had assumed the title of emperor. *The Third Coalition.* "Give us the Channel for six hours and England is ours," Napoleon had said, scanning the opposite coast from his camps at Boulogne. But the Channel was Nelson's. By a rapid change of front Napoleon turned and struck Austria at Ulm, even as Nelson was crushing the combined French and Spanish fleets at Trafalgar. *Trafalgar, 1804.* England was saved, but the battle of Austerlitz (1805) detached Austria from the coalition and left England again almost alone. "Roll up that map," Pitt said, pointing to the map of Europe, when the news of Austerlitz reached London, "there will be no use for it these ten years." A month later he was laid by the side of his honored father in Westminster Abbey. *Death of Pitt, January 23, 1806.* The triumph of Napoleon had been his death-stroke.

Napoleon next attacked British commerce by his "Berlin Decree," which closed the ports of Europe to British trade and declared the British Isles in a state of *Berlin Decrees and Orders in Council.*

[1] See Wordsworth's sonnets, "To the Men of Kent," "In the Pass of Killicrankie," "October, 1803," "Calais, August, 1802," "September, 1802," "London, 1802," and "November, 1806."

blockade. England retaliated by issuing her "Orders in Council," declaring France to be in a state of blockade. Prussia and Russia joined the emperor in the enforcement of his "Continental System" against England, and only the prompt action of the English government in seizing the neutral Danish fleet kept the gateway of the Baltic open to British commerce. To perfect his system the conqueror occupied Portugal and Spain (1807). England supplied men and money for the Peninsular War which ensued. Sir Arthur Wellesley drove the French from Portugal, and for his subsequent successes in Spain he was rewarded with the title of Viscount Wellington.[1]

Continental System.
The Peninsular War.

It was Wellington who on the 14th of June, 1815, at Waterloo in Belgium put an end to Napoleon's career. The disturber of Europe was caged on the British islet of St. Helena and the Congress of Vienna, in which the nations stripped France of her conquests, added still further to the colonial empire of Britain.

Wellington
Waterloo, 1815.

The enforcement of the commercial regulation, which grew out of the Napoleonic wars, together with the British practice of searching neutral vessels and impressing alleged English subjects for her naval service, brought about a second war with the United States (1812–1815), in which the successes of English arms on land were balanced by their failure on the sea.

Second war with the United States, 1812–1815.

During the closing decade of the reign, the Prince of Wales, a frivolous man of fashion, was regent in the stead of his blind and demented father. The government faced perplexing problems. The laboring classes were distressed and clamorous, and riotous bands broke the power looms and spinning frames which were

The Regency, 1811–1820.

[1] In the winter of 1808–9 the English commander, Sir John Moore, conducted the famous retreat to the Spanish port of Corunna in the face of Napoleon and Marshal Soult. See Wolfe's verses "Death of Sir John Moore."

accused of being "labor-saving" at the expense of the laborer. Loud calls were heard for reform in the system of representation in Parliament, and for the removal of the disabilities of Catholics. One great reform was accomplished when in 1807 the abolition of the slave trade crowned the labors of Pitt, Clarkson, and Wilberforce. On January 20, 1820, the broken-down king breathed his last.

ARTHUR WELLESLEY, DUKE OF WELLINGTON.

Slave trade abolished, 1807.

George IV., 1820–1830.

George IV. gave his ministers free scope. Their repression of radical agitators[1] led to a plot, "The Cato Street Conspiracy," for which one Thistlewood with several of his accomplices was hanged. Canning, the leading spirit of the cabinet, placed England on the side of the "Liberal" party in Europe, as opposed to the "Holy Alliance," by which the monarchical powers were repressing the sentiments of the French Revolution. He recognized the independence of the rebellious Spanish-American states, aided Portugal against Spain,

The Cato Street Conspiracy.

Canning.

[1] On August 16, 1819, an assemblage of upwards of 60,000 men, women, and children who had met in St. Peter's Fields, Manchester, to listen to speeches in the interest of parliamentary reform, was charged by cavalry and eleven persons were killed. This was the "Manchester Massacre," or, as the opponents of reform called it, "The Battle of Peterloo."

Groves against the Turk. Such was the tide in favor of true Liberal ideas that even the Tory ministry of Wellington and Peel could not withstand the measure for Catholic emancipation (1829), successfully championed by Daniel O'Connell, "the Liberator." By the death of his elder brother (June 26, 1830) the sailor prince came to the throne as William IV. The

DANIEL O'CONNELL.

reform of the parliamentary system overshadowed all other questions. The inborn opposition to constitutional change had been confirmed by the crimes which had been committed in the name of liberty in France. But the writings of Cobbett and others, demanding the admission of the people to a larger share in the government, became irresistible. Wellington's military fame did not secure him from obloquy for his opposition, and the king was hooted in public. The Tory ministry yielded and the Whigs, headed by Earl Grey and Lord John Russell, came into power. The oligarchy fought hard but in vain,[1] and on June 7, 1832, the Reform Bill became a law. It is hard at this day to understand how such a measure, providing for a reapportionment of members of the House of Commons in accordance with changes in population and some extensions of the electoral franchise, could have been the cause of such real alarm. Wellington expressed the forebodings of his party—the Conservatives—when he said of the first reformed Parliament: "We can only hope for the best; we cannot foresee what will happen; but few people will be sanguine enough to imagine that we shall ever again be as prosperous as we have been." Yet the new House of Commons did not subvert the government. It abolished slavery in every land under the British flag; modified and ameliorated the poor-laws which had fostered pauperism for two centuries; cleared the town and city governments of their chartered corruption; broke up the trade monopoly of the East India Company, and showed energy, prudence, and wisdom. The king once tried to rid himself of his "Liberal" ministers, but the country rallied to their support. In June, 1837, the death of the king prepared the way for the long and eventful reign of his brother's child, Victoria.

Passage of the Reform Bill, 1832.

The first reformed Parliament, 1833.

TOPICS FOR READING AND SPECIAL STUDY, WITH LIBRARY NOTES.

1. THE REVOLT OF THE AMERICAN COLONIES.
    The American Revolution. John Fiske.
    History of England from the Peace of Utrecht. Stanhope.

The Liberal newspapers came out in mourning rules. The public was wildly excited against the peers. The king lent his aid to the ministry with such effect as to change the mind of the Lords, and on June 4, 1832, the bill was finally enacted into law.

2. THE FOUNDING OF THE BRITISH POWER IN INDIA.
   Rise of British Dominion in India. A. Lyall.
   Macaulay's Essays on "Clive" and "Warren Hastings."

3. ENGLAND IN THE NAPOLEONIC WARS.
   The Life of Nelson. Mahan.
   History of the Peninsular War. Napier.

4. THE PASSAGE OF THE REFORM BILL.
   Constitutional History of England. May.
   History of England from 1815. Walpole.
   Fifty Years of the English Constitution. Amos.

FICTION, ETC.

The Four Georges. Thackeray.
Two Chiefs of Dunboy. Froude.
Kidnapped and David Balfour. R. L. Stevenson.
Waverley. Scott.
John Halifax, Gentleman. Craik.
The Shadow of the Sword. Buchanan.

CHAPTER XVI.

THE VICTORIAN ERA, 1837, A. D.—1897.—FROM THE ACCESSION OF QUEEN VICTORIA TO THE "DIAMOND JUBILEE" OF HER REIGN.

THE Princess Victoria Alexandrina, whose father, the Duke of Kent, was the fourth son of George III., came to the throne upon the death of her uncle. She was a gentle and serious maiden of eighteen, and showed a deep sense of the responsibilities which were laid upon her. Her accession terminated the connection between the crowns of England and Hanover, for her sex excluded her from the sovereignty of the German state, which passed to her father's brother, the Duke of Cumberland. The queen's marriage in 1840 with her kinsman Albert, a German prince of high character and cultivation, marked the founding of a family whose home life was to exhibit a simplicity and purity rare in any station.[1]

Victoria, 1837-.

Albert, Prince Consort without sovereign authority, died 1861.

"Chartism" and "free trade" were the absorbing public questions of Victoria's earlier years. The reforms of 1832, which had horrified the aristocracy and pleased the middle class, were denounced as inadequate and partial by the leaders of the workingmen. The latter, perceiving the strength which lay in numbers, asked for a

[1] The surviving children of this union (1898) are: (1) Princess Victoria (Empress Frederick), widow of Frederick I., Emperor of Germany; (2) Albert Edward, Prince of Wales, married Alexandria, daughter of King Christian IX., of Denmark; (3) Prince Alfred, Duke of Edinburgh, married Marie, daughter of Emperor Alexander II., of Russia; (4) Princess Helena, married Prince Christian of Schleswig-Holstein; (5) Princess Louise, married John, Marquis of Lorne, son of Duke of Argyll; (6) Prince Arthur, Duke of Connaught, married Princess Louise of Prussia; (7) Princess Beatrice, married Prince Henry, son of Prince Alexander of Hesse.

new parliamentary reform which should admit them to a share in the government. Their demands, set forth in a petition to which the Irish orator, O'Connell, gave the name of "the People's Charter," were as follows: (1) Parliaments to be elected annually; (2) manhood suffrage; (3) vote by ballot; (4) abolition of property qualification for membership in the House of Commons; (5) salaries for members of Parliament, and (6) equal electoral districts. Sixty years ago these moderate demands were considered preposterous and revolutionary.[1] Riots followed the rejection of the petition. In 1848 the "Chartists" again brought forward their grievances, and London was in such terror that its citizens enrolled themselves for its defense under the hero of Waterloo. The petition, with nearly two million signatures, was duly presented, but

QUEEN VICTORIA IN HER CORONATION ROBES.
From the painting by Sir George Hayter, R. A., in Windsor Castle.

[1] Several of these "points" have since become parts of the English constitution. The second was practically accomplished by the later reform bills. The third is now a fact, and the lack of property no longer bars a man from membership in the House of Commons.

there was no turbulence. The cloud blew over, and Chartism, despite the frantic appeals of its leaders, was laughed out of existence. Its chief demands have gradually been granted.

The free trade agitation was better managed. For the "protection" of the landowners of Great Britain, *i. e.*, the aristocrats, the raising of grain was fostered by a set of enactments known as "corn-laws." Their object was to support the price of domestic cereals by collecting heavy duties upon imported breadstuffs.

Free trade.

The corn-laws.

JOHN STUART MILL.

A group of thoughtful and able men, among whom Richard Cobden and John Bright were foremost, protested that such legislation was to the advantage of the few producers and to the immense disadvantage of the more numerous consumers. By pamphlet and newspaper, at the hustings and in Parliament, these men, who in 1838 formed at Manchester the "Anti-Corn-Law League," labored early and late for the removal of these restrictions upon trade.[1] The law-making

Richard Cobden and John Bright.

---

[1] Ebenezer Elliott, the "corn-law rhymer," helped to arouse public sentiment by his popular poetry, in which he depicted with great originality and power the sufferings of the working people. See "Corn-Law Rhymes."

class was also the landowning class, and it was no easy matter to extort from them the repeal legislation for which the people at last became clamorous. The Cobdenites found chief support among the Liberals; and it was to some extent the fear that this party would bring in free trade that led to its overthrow in 1841 and the second elevation of Sir Robert Peel to the head of the Conservative ministry, among whose younger members was William E. Gladstone. In 1842 this new cabinet revised the tariff, reducing the duties upon many articles.

Irish famine. Famine in Ireland won free trade for Great Britain. The failure of the potato crop of 1845 convinced the prime minister that the duties upon imported food supplies must be repealed. Lord Russell, the Liberal leader, declared his conversion to Mr. Cobden's principle, "buy in the cheapest market and sell in the dearest." Thereupon Sir Robert went over to the free traders, and, though many of his own party deserted him, he carried, with Liberal assistance, a measure which not only repealed the corn-laws by gradual reduction of duties, but utterly abandoned the protectionist theory.[1] Disraeli, just springing into prominence in the Conservative party, wittily said of Peel's sudden adoption of the Whig free trade ideas, "Peel caught the Whigs in bathing and ran off with their clothes." In June, 1846, the bill became

Repeal. a law. From the repeal of the corn-laws dates the supremacy of free trade in Great Britain.

After the battle of Waterloo England remained at peace with European nations for nearly forty years. But the restlessness of the Irish and the constant broils

---

[1] "The monopolist might execrate me," said Peel, "but it may be that I shall be remembered with good-will in the abodes of men whose lot it is to labor and to earn their daily bread by the sweat of their brow—a name to be remembered with expressions of good-will when they shall recreate their exhausted strength with abundant and untaxed food, the sweeter because it is no longer leavened with a sense of injustice."

on the distant frontiers of the empire furnished the army with almost incessant employment. Insurrections in Canada led to reforms (1840-47, 1867) which united the Dominion and endowed it with substantial home rule. From 1839 to 1842 the royal arms were directed against China, a nation which was resolutely opposed to European trade. This "opium war" opened the Chinese market to the British East India traders. The conquerors seized Hong Kong, and have since held it as a commercial and naval station. Other Chinese wars sprang from the bad blood then engendered.

JOHN TYNDALL.

The wars of the century.

Opium war.

Jealousy of Russia inspired a new and lasting dread in the British mind. The immense domain of the czar in Asia, and his persistent efforts to extend his boundaries toward the south, alarmed the government for the safety of British India. In 1838 England undertook to expel Dost Mohammed, the Afghan prince or ameer, from his country (Afghanistan) and to replace him with a friendly sovereign. The plan of invasion was at first successful, and Cabul, the capital, was taken, but fortune soon changed and the invaders were repeatedly beaten, until

Russia.

Afghan troubles.

The retreat from Cabul.

they were compelled to reinstate the dethroned sovereign and leave the country. The Afghans promised safe conduct, and in the winter of 1841-42 the retreat toward India began. A prey to cold and treachery, the army was massacred in the mountain passes. Only one man, Dr. Brydon, out of the sixteen thousand who began the march, lived to reach the British camps at Jellalabad. England abandoned her attempt to force the obnoxious sovereign upon an unwilling people. By a second war (1877-81) Great Britain reasserted her influence among the Afghans.

The Eastern Question early thrust itself upon the attention of Europe. The strategic importance of Constantinople, the rapid decay of the Ottoman Empire, and the ambition of Russia were the elements of the problem. The czar Nicholas remarked of Turkey in 1853: "We have on our hands a sick man — a very sick man; it will be a great misfortune if one of these days he should slip away from us before the necessary arrangements have been made." For nearly forty years the European nations have been quarreling over the necessary arrangements. England believes that the Russian possession of Constantinople would imperil her own possessions in India. Russia is unwilling to allow the Bosphorus — the outlet of Russian Black Sea commerce — to pass into English or Austrian hands. So the "sick man" is maintained alive. In 1853 war broke out between Russia and Turkey, the ostensible ground being the sultan's refusal to recognize the czar's claims as protector of the Greek Christians in the Ottoman Empire. Western Europe interfered in time to save the sick man's inheritance. France, where the nephew of Bonaparte had recently made himself Emperor Napoleon III., and England formed an alliance to aid the

Turks. War was declared in 1854, and Lord Raglan, a pupil of Wellington, was sent to the Black Sea with a British army, to coöperate with the French in an attack upon the Russians in the Crimea. They landed in that peninsula in September, 1854, defeated the Russians in the battle of the Alma, and laid siege for 349 days to the fortress of Sebastopol. The Russians made desperate efforts to beat them off, failing at Balaklava,[1] October 25, and again at Inkerman, November 5. In the autumn of 1855, when the siege had lasted nearly a year, the Russians evacuated the town. The Crimean War was terminated by the peace of Paris in March, 1856, in which Russia renounced her claims and Turkey took out a new lease of life.

Siege of Sebastopol.

Balaklava.

Peace of Paris, 1856.

In the summer of 1857 England stood aghast at the tidings from India. That immense and populous empire was governed by the British East India Company,

CHARLES DARWIN.

---

[1] At Balaklava occurred "the charge of the heavy brigade," in which Scarlett with 500 horse broke up the enemy's 3,000 cavalry. Lord Raglan sent an order to the Light Brigade to try to prevent the enemy carrying away certain guns. The blundering bearer of the message indicated the wrong battery and the cavalry, 678 strong, rode into the valley of death and were mowed down by the cannon. See Tennyson's two poems, "The Charge of the Heavy Brigade at Balaklava," and "The Charge of the Light Brigade."

The Sepoy Rebellion, 1857.
whose force consisted almost entirely of native troops, or "sepoys," officered by Englishmen. On Sunday, May 10, 1857, the sepoys at Meerut mutinied, and killed their officers. The rumor had spread among them that the British had designs on their religion; that the greasy cartridges of their new Enfield rifles were smeared with a mixture of cow's fat and hog's lard—the cow being the sacred animal of the Hindu and the hog the unclean beast of the Mohammedan. The mutineers proclaimed the native king of Delhi emperor of India, and called upon their countrymen to exterminate the impious English. General dissatisfaction with the company's rule fed the revolt, which rapidly grew to a fanatical rebellion. Before troops could arrive from England the worst had been done.

THOMAS H. HUXLEY.

Massacre at Cawnpore.
At Cawnpore a thousand English of both sexes and all ages, who surrendered themselves to Nana Sahib, were mercilessly butchered. In September the English took Delhi by storm and deposed the Mogul emperor. In September General Havelock cut his way through the ring of the besiegers about Lucknow

and brought timely relief to the garrison.[1] But the ring closed up behind him, and his little army was saved from massacre two months later by the arrival of Sir Colin Campbell with troops fresh from England. The taking of Lucknow in March, 1858, snuffed out the mutiny. Parliament relieved the East India Company of all its share in the government of the Indian Empire, and on September 1, 1858, the sovereignty of the queen was proclaimed throughout the peninsula. Twenty

Relief of Lucknow.

RUINS OF RESIDENCY, LUCKNOW.

years later (January 1, 1877) the title "Empress of India" was added to the queen's dignities.

"Empress of India."

The acute disorder in India was easier to cure than

[1] Havelock's fame and knighthood rests on this one march to the relief of Lucknow. He left Allahabad July 7, with but 1,000 men; on the 12th, having been somewhat reënforced, he put to flight an army of double his numbers. On the 16th he defeated Nana Sahib before Cawnpore. In September the arrival of Outram raised his forces to 2,500, and with them he defeated 10,000 and brought succor to the blockaded city September 25. See Tennyson's "Defence of Lucknow." Havelock, worn out by his exertions, died two months later, saying to a friend, "I have for forty years so ruled my life that when death came I might face it without fear." Before the sad tidings reached London the queen had made him a baronet.

the chronic discontent in Ireland. O'Connell promised his countrymen that the early years of Victoria should witness the "repeal of the union"—meaning the repeal of the act of 1800, which united Ireland with Great Britain under the control of Parliament. The Roman Catholics—five sixths of the Irish nation—had never become reconciled to the union, and the priests and bishops of that church became O'Connell's most active lieutenants. His magic eloquence stirred Irish patriotism to its depths. In 1843 the British government broke up his meetings, and when the Irish people found that their leader would not take arms for Ireland's liberties, they deserted him.

Irish discontent.

O'Connell's failure.

The failure of the island's single crop (potatoes) brought famine in its train (1846-57), and, as the promises of O'Connell faded, the Irish felt their miseries increase. The spirit of the times—the year 1848 was marked by "liberal" uprisings in half the kingdoms of Europe—taught the more ardent Irishmen to win by force the independence which O'Connell's eloquence had failed to secure. "Young Ireland" was organized in the name of liberty by Smith O'Brien, Mitchell, Meagher, and other hot-headed Celts, fresh from college or active in journalism. Their reckless newspaper attacks upon the British government compelled the authorities to suppress them. The leaders of this "Rebellion of '48" were condemned for treason and transported to Australia. Secret brotherhoods sprang up in the wake of the Young Ireland agitation, the most formidable of all being the Fenian Association.[1] In 1867 an attempt to raise Ireland in a general insurrection failed utterly; the execution of a few pris-

1848, the year of revolutions.

"Young Ireland."

[1] The Fenians, so called after the name (Fianna) of the military force of ancient free Ireland, consisted largely of Irish veterans of the American Civil War.

WILLIAM EWART GLADSTONE.

306 *Twenty Centuries of English History.*

oners and the temporary suspension of the Habeas Corpus Act restored the appearance of peace in the Emerald Isle.

Gladstone's policy.

Mr. William Ewart Gladstone became prime minister in 1868, and inaugurated a new method of dealing with Ireland. His policy was not to allow Ireland to rule herself, but to rule her in accordance with Irish ideas. In 1869, the state church of Ireland, which had been forced upon an unwilling nation at the time of the English Reformation, was disestablished. Its govern-

Disestablishment.

ment support was removed, and it sank to the condition of the Roman Catholic, Presbyterian, and Wesleyan denominations, as simply a free and independent organization. This measure provoked the bitterest denunciations from the Irish Protestants. The next year Mr. Gladstone attacked the Irish land tenure system. His land law of 1870 recognized that the tenant had some right to his holding, and must be compensated for any improvements which he might make. Yet Ireland was not satisfied with these concessions; the cry of "Home Rule"—the restoration of the Irish Parliament—once raised by O'Connell, was repeated in the British Parlia-

HENRY M. STANLEY.

ment by Mr. Butt (1870), and afterward (1880) by
Mr. Parnell. In 1886 Mr. Gladstone became a convert *Home rule fails.*
to home rule, and resigned his office in consequence of
his defeat on the question in Parliament. Coupled with
the home rule
agitation was a
plea for further
reforms in the
land tenure sys-
tem, but no
satisfactory re-
sult has been
attained, and
the Irish ques-
tion, despite the
Liberal phy-
sicians and the
Conservative
surgeons, re-
mains an open
sore.

The legis-
lation of the
reign covers a
wide field.
Cheap postage
and postal tele-

WHIFFINGHAM CHURCH, ISLE OF WIGHT.
Queen Victoria's church.

graphy, the extension of inland and foreign commerce
by means of railroads and fast steamships, the great *Legislation.*
advance in all departments of manufacture have given
the government a new set of problems to deal with.
Peel's Reform Bill of 1832 has been twice extended.
In 1867 the Conservative ministry, in which Lord Derby
was chief, with Mr. Disraeli as leader in the Commons,

Democratic government.

carried a reform bill which was characterized as "a leap in the dark." It greatly lowered the property qualification for voters, franchising in boroughs all householders who paid poor tax, and lodgers paying at least £10 yearly rent. County voters must hold property worth £5 a year, or occupy lands or tenements of at least £12 yearly rental. This act admitted workingmen to full political rights. "Now we must educate the men whom we have made our masters," said a member of Parliament. In 1870 the Gladstone government established a national public school system throughout England and Wales, in 1871 the same administration abolished the purchase of commissions in the army, and in 1872 substituted secret ballot for the open method of voting for members of Parliament. In Mr. Gladstone's second ministry (1880–85) a new reform bill made the elective franchise equal throughout England, Wales, Scotland, and Ireland; adding two millions to the number of voters, and bringing the whole number up to five millions, and making the government of Great Britain more than ever "a government of the people, by the people, and for the people."

Public schools.

Foreign wars.

Since the suppression of the Indian mutiny no serious rebellion has vexed the peace of the empire. The forces in India and Burmah have found constant occupation in preserving the boundaries from marauding tribes, while the defense of Egypt from the Arab fanatics, and the forcible extension of the area of British trade and dominion in South Africa have led to bloody campaigns.

E. Mahdi.

Boer wars.

The isle of the Angles has become the head of a world-empire of 10,000,000 square miles of territory inhabited by 350,000,000 of people. This Greater Britain, upon whose flag the sun never sets and whose morning drum-beat follows the sun around the globe, is policed and defended at enormous cost by a fleet of war-ships which is maintained at a strength superior to that of any other two nations. A chain of fortresses and coaling stations, Gibraltar, Malta, Cyprus, Alexandria, Aden, with the Suez Canal, insure communication with the vast possessions in the East, while the Bermudas, Halifax, the Canadian Pacific Railway, Vancouver, and Hong Kong link London with the ultimate West. The problem of the government of these dependencies is pressing for solution. The narrow colonial policy which led to the successful revolt of the North American colonies in 1776 has given place to a generous pride in the Greater Britain in which London and Bombay, Liverpool and Auckland, Vancouver and Cape Town are sister cities. It will be the duty of the historian of the next century to record whether the political genius of the Anglo-Saxon was equal to the task of devising institutions under which these trophies of discovery and conquest may become a federated empire greater in wealth, population, and power—and

Greater Britain.

Military highways.

QUEEN VICTORIA.

Imperial federation.

in freedom and civilization far greater—than Augustan Rome.

The multitudes that gathered in London from all parts of the empire in 1887 to celebrate the fiftieth anniversary of the queen's coronation, and the still more impressive festivities of the Diamond Jubilee of 1897, when soldiers of many subject lands escorted Victoria to St. Paul's Cathedral in commemoration of the completion of her sixty years of sovereignty, afforded impressive evidence of the greatness of her realm. The attitude of modern England toward her colonial empire has been declared by the poet laureate in the spirited lines :

> Britain fought her sons of yore—
> Britain failed ; and never more,
> Careless of our growing kin,
> Shall we sin our father's sin,
> Men that in a narrower day—
> Unprophetic rulers they—
> Drove from out the eagle's nest
> That young eagle of the West
> To forage for herself alone ;
>   Britons, hold your own !
>
> Sharers of our glorious past,
> Brothers, must we part at last ?
> Shall we not thro' good and ill
> Cleave to one another still ?
> Britain's myriad voices call,
> " Sons, be welded each and all
> Into one imperial whole,
> One with Britain, heart and soul !
> One life, one flag, one fleet, one throne ! "
>   Britons, hold your own !

TOPICS FOR READING AND SPECIAL STUDY, WITH LIBRARY NOTES.

1. THE INDIAN MUTINY.
    History of the Indian Mutiny. Kaye and Malleson.
    Sir Henry Havelock. W. Brock.
    Life of Lord Lawrence. R. B. Smith.
2. THE TRIUMPH OF FREE TRADE.
    The Epoch of Reform. J. McCarthy.
    Life of Cobden. J. Morley.
    History of the Anti-Corn-Law League. A. Prentice.
    Life and Times of John Bright. W. Robertson.
    History of England During the Peace. H. Martineau.
3. THE CRIMEAN WAR.
    The Invasion of the Crimea. Kinglake.
    History of Our Own Times. J. McCarthy.
4. GREATER BRITAIN.
    Oceana. Froude.
    English Colonization and Empire. Caldecott.
    A Scheme for Imperial Federation. Cuningham.
    The Imperial and Colonial Constitutions of the Britannic Empire. Creasy.

FICTION, ETC.

Coningsby and Lothair. Disraeli.
Alton Locke. Kingsley.
On the Face of the Waters. Flora Annie Steele.
Marcella. Mrs. Humphry Ward.

INDEX.

Afghanistan, 299.
Agincourt, battle of, 142.
Aix-la-Chapelle, treaty of, 280.
Albert, Prince Consort, 295.
Alfred the Great, 55.
American War, 284, 285.
Angles, 38.
Anglo-Saxons, 39; language, 132.
Anne of Cleves, 179.
Anne, Queen, 263, 272-6.
Anselm, 79, 82.
Argyle's rebellion, 264.
Armada, Spanish, 209-11.
Arthur, King, 40.
Arthur, Prince, 101.
Aryans, 28, 38.
Ashdune, battle of, 55.
Askew, Anne, 182.
Assize of Arms, 93; of Northampton, 93; Bloody, 265.
Athelstan, 59.
Attainder, Bills of, 180.
Augustine in Kent, 46.
Bacon, Francis, 222.
Balaklava, 301.
Ball, John, 137, 138.
Bank of England, 271.
Bannockburn, battle of, 121.
Barebone's Parliament, 252.
Barnet, battle of, 156.
Barons' War, 109-10.
Bayeux tapestry, 69.
Beaufort, Cardinal, 145.
Becket, Thomas à, 90-2.
Bede, the Venerable, 50.
Bedford, Duke of, 145, 146.
Benedictines, 60.
Benevolences, 165, 170.
Bertha, Queen, 46.
Bible, the English, 177, 181; King James's, 218.
Bill of Rights, 269.
Bishops excluded from Parliament, 240.
Bishops' Wars, 235, 236.

Black Death, 131.
Blenheim, battle of, 273.
Blondel, 98.
Boadicea, 34.
Boleyn, Anne, 165, 178.
Book of Common Prayer, 197.
Boroughs, 72.
Bosworth, battle of, 159.
Bothwell, Earl of, 202.
Boyne, battle of the, 270.
Breda, Declaration of, 256.
Bretwalda, 41.
British Isles, location, 12.
Britons, 28; described, 31, 32, 42.
Bruce, Robert, 119.
Brunanburgh, battle of, 58.
Buccaneers, 206.
Budget, annual, 268.
Bunyan, John, 258.
Burleigh, Lord, 199.
Bute, Lord, 283.
Cabal ministry, 260.
Cædmon, 50.
Cæsar in Britain, 29.
Canada, taken, 282; government settled, 299.
Canning, George, 291.
Canterbury, 22; Augustine at, 46; burned by Danes, 55; shrine of St. Thomas, 92.
Canute, 62.
Caractacus, 34.
Carr, Robert, 221.
Cassivelaunus, 31.
Castles, 80, 165.
Catharine of Aragon, 166, 171.
Cathedral towns, 18.
Cato Street Conspiracy, 291.
Cavalier Parliament, 258.
Caxton, William, 154.
Cecil, Robert, 221.
Celts, 28.
Cerdic, 40.
Channel Islands, 13.
Charles I., 222, 223, 225-48.

314 *Index.*

Charles II., 256-62.
Charles Edward Stuart, 280, 281.
Charter of Henry I., 82, 103.
Chartism, 295-7.
Chaucer, 133.
Church of England, missionaries from Ireland, 45; conversion of England, 46-8; Synod of Whitby, 49; under Lanfranc, 75; under Anselm, 79; right of investiture, 83; delivers England from anarchy, 88; under Henry II., 91; Becket, 91-2; under John, 101-2; Wyclif, 134-7; Lollardry, 135; the king's supremacy established, 172-4; monasteries dissolved, 174-6, 180; first influence of Reformation, 176, 177; "Six Articles," 178, 182, 185, 186; Council of Trent, 181; changes under Edward VI., 185, 186; Catholic reaction under Mary, 189-94; Elizabeth's policy toward, 197, 199, 201, 205; the Thirty-nine Articles, 201; Test Act, 201; rise of Puritans, 204; persecution of Jesuits, 205; the Millenary Petition, 216; Hampton Court Conference, 218; King James's Bible, 218; Laud's persecution of Puritans, 232; Presbyterianism established, 243, 245; Anglican service forbidden, 254; Anglican service restored, 255; legislation against non-conformists, 258; Declaration of Indulgence, 266; the Seven Bishops, 266.
Churchill (Marlborough), 267, 273-6.
Churls, 43.
Cinque Ports, 22.
Civil War, 241-9.
Clarence, Duke of, 155.
Claverhouse (Dundee), 264, 269.
Climate, 15.
Clive, Robert Lord, 282.
Cobden, Richard, 298.
Commonwealth, 250-7.
Constitutions of Clarendon, 91.
Continental System, 290.
Contract, the Great, 220.
Conventicle Act, 258.
Conversion of English, 46.
Cook, Captain James, 280.

Corn-law repeal, 297-8.
Coronation chair, 115.
Corporation Act, 258.
Covenant, 234, 243, 258, 263.
Cranmer, Archbishop, 172-7.
Crecy, battle of, 127.
Crimean War, 300.
Cromwell, Oliver, 232, 237, 242-57.
Cromwell, Richard, 256.
Cromwell, Thomas, 172-9.
Crusades, 80, 97, 98.
Culloden, battle of, 281.
Curia regis, 74.
Cymri, 29.
Danegelt, 61.
Danelaw, 55.
Danes, 53; in Ireland, 54; burn London, 55; masters of half Britain, 56; massacre of, 61; conquer England 62, 63.
Darnley, Henry Lord, 201, 202.
Debt, national, 271.
Defender of the Faith, 176.
Despenser, Hugh le, 122.
Disraeli, Benjamin, 298.
Divine right of kings, 219.
Domesday Book, 76, 77.
Douay, 205.
Drake, Sir Francis, 206, 210.
Druids, 32.
Dudley, Earl of Leicester, 208.
Dunbar, battle of, 257.
Dunes, battle of, 253.
Ealdorman, 43.
Earls, 43.
East Anglia, 41.
East India Company, 213.
Edgar, 59.
Edgar the Atheling, 64, 70.
Edgehill, battle of, 242.
Edinburgh, 47.
Edmund Ironside, 62, 67.
Edward I., 112-9.
Edward II., 114, 120-3.
Edward III., 124-32.
Edward IV., 153-6.
Edward V., 156, 157.
Edward VI., 184-8.
Edward, the Black Prince, 127-32.
Edward the Confessor, 63, 64.
Edward the Elder, 57, 58.

Index. 315

Edward the Martyr, 61 (note).
Edwin of Northumbria, 46.
Egbert, 51.
Eliot, Sir John, 220, 226, 228, 229.
Elizabeth, Queen, 172, 195-215.
Ely, defense of, 70.
Ethelbert, 46.
Ethelred the Unready, 61.
Evesham, battle of, 110.
Exchequer, 93.
Falkirk, battle of, 117.
Famine in Ireland, 304.
Fenian Association, 304.
Feudal system, 72.
Field of Cloth of Gold, 169.
Fisher, Bishop, 173.
Five Mile Act, 258.
Flodden, battle of, 168.
Forests, royal, 81.
Fox, Charles James, 286.
France, Normans in, 68; at war with Richard I., 100; Hundred Years' War, 124-30, 142-9; Edward III. renounces his claim, 129; Henry V. claims crown, 142; Henry VI. proclaimed king, 143; Bedford's campaigns in, 146; Joan of Arc, 146-9.
Friars, 110.
Gaels, 29.
Gardiner, Bishop, 184-9.
Gaunt, John of, 130, 151.
Gaveston, Piers, 120.
Geddes, Jenny, 234.
Genealogical tables: The Conqueror's Children, 86; Edward III.'s Claim to the French Crown, 126; Descent of Henry IV., 139; Lancaster and York (descendants of Edward III.), 151.
Geoffrey of Anjou, 84.
Geoffrey of Brittany, 95.
George I., 276-80.
George II., 280-3.
George III., 283-91.
George IV., regent, 290; king, 291-2.
Glencoe, massacre of, 270 (note).
Glendower, revolt of, 140.
Gibraltar, 274.
Gladstone, W. E., 298, 306.
Godiva, 63.
Godolphin, 273, 275.

Godwin, 63.
Grand Alliance, 270, 272.
Grand Remonstrance, 240.
Gregory VII., 75.
Grenville, Lord, 284.
Grey, Lady Jane, 166, 189, 192.
Gunpowder Plot, 219.
Hampden, John, 227, 228, 231, 237.
Hampton Court Conference, 218.
Hanover, 278, 295.
Harley, Robert (Oxford), 275, 276.
Harold, 64-6.
Harold Hardrada, 65.
Hastings, battle of, 66.
Hawkins, Sir John, 207, 210.
Hengesterdun, battle of, 54.
Hengist and Horsa, 39.
Henry I., 81-4.
Henry II., 84, 89-96.
Henry III., 106-10.
Henry IV., 139-41.
Henry V., 141-3.
Henry VI., 145-56.
Henry VII., 158, 161-6.
Henry VIII., 166-83.
Henry, "the Young King," 94-6.
Heptarchy, the Saxon, 41.
Heresy, Statute of, 141.
Hereward, 70.
Hexham, battle of, 155.
High Commission, court of, 232, 239.
Hogue, battle of, 270.
Home rule, 306.
Howard, Admiral, 210, 211.
Hundred Years' War, the, 125, 142-9.
Hyde, Edward (Clarendon), 237.
Impositions, 220.
Independents, 204, 218.
India, Trading Company chartered, 214; first foothold, 259 (note); Clive in, 246; mutiny in, 301; empress of, 303.
Innocent III., 102.
Investiture, 83.
Iona, 45.
Ireland, early Christianity, 45; overrun by Danes, 54; Strongbow in, 94; Tyrone's revolt, 212; plantation of Ulster, 221; Wentworth in 235; Ulster massacres, 239; battle of the Boyne in, 270; legislative

union with Great Britain, 288; O'Connell's agitation for repeal, 304; Gladstone's policy toward, 306, 307.
Ironsides, Cromwell's, 242.
Jacobites, in Ireland, 270; in Scotland, 275, 276, 279, 280, 281.
James I., 202, 216-25.
James II., 257, 263-8, 270.
James Edward Stuart, 266, 275, 279, 280.
Jeffreys, Judge, 265.
Jesuits, 198, 205.
Jews, persecuted, 96; expelled, 120; restored, 254.
Joan of Arc, 146-9.
John, King, 95, 96, 98, 99, 101-5.
Jubilee, Victorian, 310.
Junius, Letters of, 284.
Junto, the Whig, 271.
Jutes, 38.
Killiecrankie, battle of, 269.
Knox, John, 203.
Lanfranc, 75.
Langland, William, 133.
Langton, Stephen, 103.
Language, 132, 133.
Latimer, Bishop, 182, 189, 194.
Laud, Archbishop, 230, 245.
Lewes, battle of, 110.
Llewellyn, Prince of Wales, 114.
Lollards, 135, 141.
London, 21; (Londinium) burned, 34; burned by Danes, 55; Tower of, 80; plague and fire, 260.
Londonderry, siege of, 270.
Longchamp, William, 98.
Magna Charta, 103.
Malplaquet, battle of, 274.
Marston Moor, battle of, 244.
Martyrs, the first English, 141; Marian, 193.
Mary I. (Tudor), 172, 189-95.
Mary II., 268-72.
Mary Queen of Scots, 183, 200, 209.
Massachusetts, 230.
Matilda, "Empress," 83, 84, 86, 87.
Mercia, 41, 51.
Middlesex, 41.
Millenary Petition, 216.
Milton, John, 259.

Monasteries, 60; dissolution of, 174.
Monk, General, 250.
Monmouth, Duke of, 201, 264.
Montfort, Simon de, 108, 110.
Montrose, Marquis of, 244.
More, Sir Thomas, 173.
Mortimer, Roger, 122, 124.
Morton's Fork, 165.
Mutiny Act, 268.
Mythology, northern, 42.
Napoleonic Wars, 287-90.
Naseby, battle of, 246.
Nelson's victories, 287.
Neville's Cross, battle of, 128.
New England, 230.
New Model, 245.
Normandy, 68; joined to England, 80, 83; lost, 101.
Normans, 68.
Northampton, battle of, 152; treaty of, 124.
Northmen, 53.
Northumbria, 50.
Oates, Titus, 261.
O'Connell, Daniel, 292, 304.
Oldcastle, Lord Cobham, 141, 142.
Opium war, the, 299.
Ordainers, 129.
Ordeals, 71.
Oswald, 48.
Oudenarde, battle of, 274.
Oxford, Provisions of, 109.
Parliament, 108; Simon de Montfort's, 110; the "perfect" Parliament, 117; separate houses, 130; under Henry VII., 164; under Henry VIII., 169, 170, 180; under Elizabeth, 213; under James I., 219; the Addled Parliament, 220; protests to the king, 224; first two Parliaments of Charles I., 225, 226; third, 228; the Short Parliament, 236; the Long Parliament, 237, 256; attempt to arrest the five members, 240; takes arms against the king, 241; takes the Covenant, 243; quarrels with the army, 246-8; purged of its Presbyterians, 248; the Rump, 248, 250; Barebone's Parliament, 252; Cromwell's second Parliament, 254. Cromwell dissolves Parliament, 255. recall of the Rump,

256; convention Parliament, 256; Cavalier Parliament, 258; obtains control of expenditure, 268; controls army, 269; passes Septennial Act, 279; the Reform Bill, 293; the Chartists' demands, 296.
Peasants' Revolt, 137.
Peel, Sir Robert, 298.
Pembroke, Earl of, 106.
Penda, 47.
Petition and Advice, 254.
Petition of Right, 224.
Philip II. of Spain, 191, 209, 210.
Philiphaugh, battle of, 246.
Pilgrimage of Grace, 174.
Pinkie, battle of, 185.
Pitt (Wm.), Lord Chatham, 282.
Pitt, Wm. (the younger), 286-9.
Plague in London, 266.
Plantagenet, 84.
Plassy, battle of, 282.
Poitiers, battle of, 129.
Pole, Cardinal, 192, 195.
Popish Plot, 261.
Præmunire, 140.
Presbyterians, 218, 245.
Preston Pans, battle of, 248.
Pretenders, the Stuart, 279.
Pride's Purge, 248, 256.
Protestantism of Wyclif, 134-7; and Henry VIII., 176-82; under Edward VI., 185; betrayed by James II., 264-6; legal religion of the monarch, 276.
Protestation, the, 224.
Prynne, William, 232.
Puritans, 204, 216-8.
Pym, John, 237, 239, 243.
Quebec taken, 282.
Raleigh, Sir Walter, 212.
Ramillies, battle of, 274.
Reform Bill, 282.
Reformation in England, 176.
Religion of early Britons, 32, 33.
Restoration, the, 256.
Revolution, the, 266-9.
Richard I., 96-100.
Richard II., 135-9.
Richard III., 151, 152, 156-9.
Riot Act, 278.
Romans in Britain, 29-38.

Roses, Wars of the, 149-59.
" Rump," 250, 256.
Runnymede, 103.
Rupert, Prince, 241.
Rye House Plot, 261.
Ryswick, peace of, 272.
St. Albans, battle of, 152.
St. Brice's Day, 61.
St. Chad, 48.
St. Columba, 45.
St. Cuthbert, 48.
St. Dunstan, 59.
St. Edmund, 55.
St. John (Bolingbroke), 275, 276.
St. Patrick, 45.
St. Thomas, 92.
Saladin, 98.
Salisbury Oath, 76.
Saxons, 38.
Scone, Stone of, 115, 116.
Scotland, 13; subject to William I., 70; submits to Henry II., 95; purchases liberty, 97; Edward I. in, 114, 115, 119; Wallace, 116; Bruce, 119, 121; independence acknowledged, 124; opposes Henry VIII., 182, 183; relations with France, 185, 199; Mary Queen of Scots, 200-2; personal union under James VI. and I., 216; church affairs under Charles I., 233; the Covenant, 234; the Bishops' Wars, 236; alliance with English Parliament, 243; persecution of covenanters, 263; Argyle's rebellion, 264; accepts William and Mary, 269; Dundee's rebellion, 269; legislative union with England, 275; Jacobite rising of 1715, 279; Jacobite rising of 1745, 281.
Sebastopol, siege of, 301.
Senlac, battle of, 66.
Sepoy Rebellion, 301-3.
Septennial Act, 279.
Settlement, Act of, 276.
Seven Bishops, trial of, 266.
Seven Years' War, 282.
Seymour, Edward (Somerset), 184, 188.
Sheriffmuir, battle of, 289.
Ship money, 231.
Sidney, Sir Philip, 208.

Simnel, Lambert, 163.
Slave trade abolished, 291.
Sluys, battle of, 126.
South Sea Bubble, 279.
Spanish succession, 272.
Spurs, battle of the, 168.
Stamford Bridge, battle of, 65.
Stamp Act, 284.
Standard, battle of the, 87.
Star Chamber, court of, 165, 231, 239.
Stephen, 86, 87.
Stirling, battle of, 116.
Stonehenge, 33.
Strongbow, 94.
Supremacy, Act of, 172.
Sussex, 40.
Sweyn, 61.
Test Act, the, 265.
Tewkesbury, battle of, 156.
Thames, 20.
Thanes, 43.
Theodore of Tarsus, 49.
Thirty-nine Articles, 201.
Toleration, 246, 254, 266.
Tonnage and poundage, 164.
Tory, 261.
Towton, battle of, 153.
Trent, council of, 181.
Triennial Act, 238.
Triple Alliance, the, 260.
Troyes, treaty of, 143.
Tudor, Owen, 158.
Tyler, Wat, 137.
Ulster, plantations in, 221; massacres in, 239.
Uniformity, Act of, 258.
Union of Scotland and England, 275; of Great Britain and Ireland, 288.
Universities, rise of, 111.
Utrecht, treaty of, 276.
Verneuil, battle of, 146.
Victoria, 295-307.

Vikings, 53.
Village community, the, 42.
Villiers, George (Buckingham), 221-9.
Vortigern, 39.
Wakefield, battle of, 153.
Wales, 13; origin of name, 40; conquered by Edward I., 112, 113; statute of, 114; Glendower's revolt, 140.
Wall, Roman, 39.
Wallace, William, 116.
Wallingford, treaty of, 88.
Walpole, Robert, 280.
Walter, Hubert, 99, 101.
Warbeck, Perkin, 163.
Warwick, the "king-maker," 152, 155.
Wedmore, peace of, 56.
Wellington, Duke of, 290, 292.
Wentworth, Thomas (Strafford), 221, 228, 230, 238.
Wessex, 40, 51.
Westminster Abbey, 64, 66.
Westminster Assembly, 245.
Whig, 261.
Whip of Six Strings, 177.
Whitby, Synod of, 49.
William I., the Conqueror, 58, 64-77.
William II., Rufus, 78-81.
William III., of Orange, 263, 266-73.
William IV., 292.
Winchelsey, Bishop, 118.
Witenagemot, 43.
Wolfe, James, 282.
Wolsey, Thomas, 168, 171.
Wool-growing, 187.
Worcester, battle of, 251.
Wyatt's Rebellion, 191.
Wyclif, 134, 135, 137.
Wykeham, William of, 131.
"Young Ireland," 304.
Zutphen, battle of, 208.

www.ingramcontent.com/pod-product-compliance
Lightning Source LLC
Chambersburg PA
CBHW030809230426
43667CB00008B/1130